*Politics in Newfoundland and Labrador
and the Road to the 2015 Election*

TURMOIL

AS USUAL

James McLeod

Canada Council   Conseil des Arts
for the Arts   du Canada

Canada

Newfoundland
Labrador

We gratefully acknowledge the financial support of the Canada Council for the Arts,
the Government of Canada through the Canada Book Fund (CBF),
and the Government of Newfoundland and Labrador through the Department
of Tourism, Culture and Recreation for our publishing program.

Cover Design by Todd Manning • Layout by Joanne Snook-Hann
Printed on acid-free paper

Published by
CREATIVE PUBLISHERS
an imprint of CREATIVE BOOK PUBLISHING
a Transcontinental Inc. associated company
P.O. Box 8660, Stn. A
St. John's, Newfoundland and Labrador A1B 3T7

Printed in Canada

Library and Archives Canada Cataloguing in Publication

McLeod, James, 1985-, author
    Turmoil, as usual : politics in Newfoundland and Labrador
and the road to the 2015 election / James McLeod.

MIX
Paper from
responsible sources
FSC   FSC® C011825
www.fsc.org

ISBN 978-1-77103-081-6 (paperback)

    1. Newfoundland and Labrador. House of Assembly--
Elections, 2015. 2. Newfoundland and Labrador--Politics and
government--2003-. 3. Elections--Newfoundland and Labrador.
I. Title.

JL209.A5M5 2016   324.9718'05   C2015-908398-2

Politics in Newfoundland and Labrador
and the Road to the 2015 Election

TURMOIL
AS USUAL

James McLeod

St. John's, Newfoundland and Labrador, 2015

To Mom, who argued with me about writing,
and Dad, who argued with me about politics,
(and vice versa.)

TABLE OF CONTENTS

Introduction

Paul Lane, the Honourable Member for Mount Pearl South, was on stage doing an absolutely amazing rendition of "Rebel Yell" by Billy Idol.

Twenty minutes earlier, Lane and I were huddled over the songbook at Karaoke Kops, a dingy George Street bar where all the staff dressed in cheesy police uniforms, and according to the bar's slogan, "Fun is the law." It was cramped in there, and the bar was very dark, with a smoke machine running flat-out. Green lasers and strobe lights framed the stage. A sign on the wall said, "MOTHERS DAY SPECIALS: WHITE RUSSIANS $5.50 — ALL LABATT BEER $3.95 — HAPPY MOTHERS DAY" — in October. When I first walked in, a tough-looking guy with a heavily scarred face was belting out "Brown Eyed Girl" on stage. Hey, I wasn't going to be the one to tell him he didn't have the pipes to sing Van Morrison; he looked like he could kick my ass.

Lane and I were at Karaoke Kops for a mutual friend's birthday, and we both looked pretty out of place.

It was past midnight and I was stone cold sober. Lane was nursing a beer, trying to look relaxed, without much success. He was clearly not there to cut loose. The fact that he was about 6'6" with a rumpled brown suit jacket draping over his hulking frame made him stick out a little bit.

I had no intention of getting up on that stage — I don't have the voice to do Van Morrison either — so I spent my time hanging out with Lane and goading him into singing something.

"Hey! They have 'Do Re Mi' from The Sound of Music. I think I could really nail that," I said.

"I would've thought you're more of a 'The Hills are Alive With the Sound of Music' kind of guy," Lane replied.

I was joking when I suggested that Paul do "Rebel Yell."

He looked at me with a totally straight face and said, "I can do that one."

I thought I was calling his bluff when I said I'd go up to the manager's booth at the front and put in the request, but Lane just said again, "Yeah, I can do that one."

The joke's on me, I guess. When he got up on the stage, Paul Lane sang "Rebel Yell" better than Billy would've.

•••

This book isn't a tell-all about Newfoundland and Labrador politics. I'm not spilling secrets here. I don't know everything that happened in the last couple of years, and I still don't understand why a few things happened the way they did.

But as the political reporter for *The Telegram*, Newfoundland and Labrador's largest daily newspaper, I followed the tumultuous politics of the province in recent years just about as closely as anybody could. Most of what I saw and heard has appeared in the newspaper in some form or another. If you're a faithful daily reader, this book likely won't offer any shocking revelations, but I hope you'll find it worthwhile all the same. For one thing, there are some episodes — like the encounter with Paul Lane at Karaoke Kops — that just don't end up in print. Moreover, daily news coverage can be frantic and hard-boiled, and it can obscure the larger narrative arc of events that play out across weeks or months. Above all, that narrative is what I'm trying to convey here.

I'm sure some of the players who are mentioned in these pages will say that I missed the real story. They may even be right. This is only what I saw, what I was told, and what I believed to be true at the time when I wrote it.

My fervent hope is that whether you're a diehard political junkie, or a casual citizen interested in learning more about the people who run our government, within these pages you'll learn one or two new things about Newfoundland and Labrador.

And I hope you'll laugh. Politics can be weighty business, but it's also often farce. None of this should be taken too seriously.

It was the absurdity of it all that first caused me to start writing things down. This book began as a lengthy email I sent to my friend Bekah following the September 2013 Progressive Conservative Party convention. "This is my second year covering this event, and it's *unbelievably bloody weird*," I wrote to Bekah.

In the newspaper story I wrote about the convention, I focused largely on then-premier Kathy Dunderdale's comments in a series of speeches she gave over the course of the weekend. I also wrote a separate blog post for the newspaper's website about the Tories' farcical policy "debates" at the convention. Absent from my reporting, though, was anything about an old lady threatening to kill me for my political coverage, or Dunderdale trying to pull me out onto the dance floor as party members cut loose on a Saturday evening.

These little bits — the bloody weird bits — tend to fall by the wayside because they're not consequential in the truest sense of the word, and therefore they're not deemed to have much place in serious news reporting. In the space of a 500-word newspaper article, the priority is on the hard facts of what a politician said, what it means for public policy and how it will impact the ups and downs of political strategy. The colour and flavour of politics, the human dynamics, and the absurdity of it all frequently gets lost in the grind of daily news coverage.

So that's what I wrote in my email to Bekah, and that's what I kept writing for another two years afterwards.

The rest of this book should be read as such — as a long email to a friend. After emailing Bekah, any semblance of stability within the N.L. political world went all to hell. There were three and a half premiers in the space of one year. The New Democrats imploded in spectacular fashion. The Liberals … well … the Liberals were there for it all, too.

But I'm getting ahead of myself.

The title of this book is cribbed from N.L. political giant John Crosbie, who has a much, much longer memory for politics in this province than I do. If Crosbie says that Newfoundland and Labrador is usually in turmoil, I won't presume to argue. All the same, I do think you can make a case that the two years leading up to the 2015 election were among the most turbulent in the province's history.

This is the story I wrote, as it happened.

CHAPTER 1
PARTISANSHIP
SEPTEMBER 20, 2013

Premier Kathy Dunderdale was in high dudgeon, and the crowd was eating it up.

Right from the very first words of Dunderdale's speech, it was clear that she knew her situation was grim, and somehow, the crowd was eating that up too.

"I want to start this evening off with a few facts that people are not likely to hear on Open Line shows, read in *The Telegram* editorials or get from our political opponents," Dunderdale said. "Whenever someone tells you how bleak things are in Newfoundland and Labrador, set the record straight."

Dunderdale was under siege. Politically, she only had four months left to live.

The Open Line shows hadn't been kind to her in the preceding year, especially since a series of newspaper stories detailed a systematic effort by the PC Party to game the system, manipulate online news sites' public opinion polls, and stack the call-in radio shows in their favour. When Dunderdale sacked close to a thousand public servants as part of massive government cost-cutting effort, the chatter on Open Line got even worse. *The Telegram* commentary section hadn't been great either; less than two weeks before Dunderdale's big speech at the PC Party convention in Gander, the paper ran a front page column headlined, "Dunderdale, it's time to go." As for the opposition parties, well, they were never likely to say anything flattering about Dunderdale's government. Their job was to do pretty much the exact opposite. But polling published in September 2013 showed the PC Party was dead last in the eyes of voters, which seemed to indicate that a lot of people were more inclined to believe the opposition parties' version of things instead of what the Tories were saying.

But *this* crowd, in the ballroom of the Hotel Gander, was more likely to give Dunderdale a sympathetic hearing than pretty much any other collection of Newfoundlanders and Labradorians. These were the diehards, the party faithful, the hardcore partisans.

As she spoke, the emotion intensified. She wasn't happy; she was defiant. The contempt dripped from her voice as she spoke about the disastrous policy ideas that the opposition parties were "threatening to inflict on us" — everything from new social programs to reckless government transparency and accountability. Dunderdale practically shuddered at the very thought of it.

From the podium, she said people should be suspicious when the other political parties demanded better services from government, or made expensive promises: "Every new demand they make, every new dollar they promise to spend is a dollar they would tear from the hands of hard-working Newfoundlanders and Labradorians. ... They must realize that there is no such thing as the government's money; it is the people's money."

Less than a minute later in her speech, without a hint of irony, Dunderdale listed off the "investments" her government was making. "This year alone, we have been able to invest $2.9 billion in health care, $1.3 billion in education, $185 million to support children and families ... $230 million for sustainable communities, $140 million for poverty reduction and $100 million in incentives to grow businesses ... These are solid investments in the people of Newfoundland and Labrador."

It all went over well, of course. Any other audience might have been tempted to notice the inherent hypocrisy of boasting about spending billions of government dollars right after lamenting the taxes torn viciously from the wallets of honest folks. But here at the PC Party annual convention, people nodded sincerely, applauded spontaneously, and interrupted Dunderdale five times with standing ovations.

Immediately following the speech, there was the ceremonial "Thank You." This was the first in a gruelling parade of speeches for Dunderdale[1], and it was also the first in a parade of sycophantic gestures by party members. In this case, the "Thank You" was delivered by an earnest woman named Chantalle Bath who was head of the PC Women's Association and also happened to be an administrative assistant in the premier's office.

"I'm delighted to be here this evening to thank the premier for that wonderful, uplifting speech tonight. Every time I hear the premier speak, she reignites my passion for this family we know as the Progressive Conservative Party," Bath began, before she was drowned out by cheers. She continued: "I am very lucky and fortunate; I work with Premier Dunderdale so I get to hear her speak very often. I only wish that everybody in this province could hear her as often as I do, so they could hear the passion that she has for this province and its people."

Bath thanked the premier for being an inspiration, thanked her for being a great leader, thanked the her for being a woman, thanked the premier for giving such a great speech, and just generally thanked the premier for anything else she could think of.

In front of pretty much any other audience in the province, this sort of thing would come off as unctuous, bordering on cultish. But here, people murmured approvingly and felt a warm sense of camaraderie. If you're the sort of person who ends up at a political party's convention, you're a member of a very specific tribe. And when the tribe all gathers together, it's a chance to be comfortable, to be yourself. For one weekend of the year, you're surrounded by people who talk the same language as you, care about the same

---

[1] She'd give four different speeches in less than 24 hours.

3

things you care about and hate the same people you hate. Nobody here was going to judge you for getting really worked up about something that 99 per cent of the population doesn't give a crap about. More likely, they'd respond with nods and encouraging noises.

Partisans are just a different breed.

• • •

When the hardcore partisans of the province descend on Gander for a weekend, it's a mix of drunken revelry, shared political enthusiasm and serious business — in that order. It's a chance to do a bit of political organizing and a lot of catching up with friends. In this case, we're examining the Tories, but in most ways, a Liberal confab is really no different.[2]

The convention starts on Friday night with a banquet and the "keynote" speech from Dunderdale. Tories have trekked in from far and wide, and registered at a table in the lobby of the Hotel Gander. Volunteers have been hard at work in that lobby, taping up Dunderdale campaign posters leftover from the 2011 election — I count at least 35 or 40 posters that have either Dunderdale's name or her big smiling face on them. The place is also adorned with plenty of blue and white balloons and a three-metre long banner that says "DUNDERDALE" in chunky blue letters.

After everybody has dropped off their luggage in their rooms and they've gotten changed, they migrate back down to the mezzanine of the Hotel Gander. The banquet hall is locked and all the doors are guarded by members of the organizing committee, so everybody ends up milling about in the foyer. An enterprising reporter can sneak into the banquet hall through the kitchen, to put their camera bag down by the audio tech guys at the back of the room or set up a tripod if you're working for TV, but all the delegates are forced to wait outside.

Everybody is done up in their best Tory blue attire and they're getting hungry. While waiting for things to start, there's a cash bar

---

[2] The conventions don't always happen in Gander, but it makes for a frequent venue because it's central, and because of the plethora of hotels in town.

in the lobby, so people get a drink or two. The mood is cheerful and familiar; longtime volunteers are renewing old acquaintances, and making connections with like-minded comrades from around the province. The booze is flowing. Most of the Tories' 34 elected MHAs and cabinet ministers are mingling with the delegates, and pretty quickly it gets so crowded that you can barely move without weaving and squeezing between people.

The doors to the banquet hall remain locked for a good reason, though. Once they open up, there's a frenzied and pitiful power dynamic that plays out. Each of the elected politicians is the Big Man (or Woman) in their own district, but now they're at the province-wide convention and they've got half a dozen or more members of their local PC district association in tow. They each want to lay claim to one or two tables close together for their people, and hopefully close to the podium and whatnot. They all jockey for position and get really territorial; sometimes you'll see a first-term MHA even try (and fail) to talk his way past the volunteers to stake out a couple tables before the doors open.

These sorts of games may seem petty and inconsequential, but they're a part of the partisan DNA. The us-versus-them competitive mentality doesn't get acrimonious when it's a bunch of MHAs duking it out for a prized location in the banquet hall, but the same drive to beat the other guy and get the prize is what wins elections and scores cabinet posts.[3]

As people get settled at their tables, an emcee steps up on stage and greets everybody, trying to get the crowd fired up. High-energy music starts playing, and the emcee calls up MHAs one at a time, by name and electoral district, like he's an announcer for the NHL All-Star game. "From the great district of Bonavista North! Eli Cross!" and Cross, a hulking middle-aged guy with grey curly hair and a moustache, gets up to amble and squeeze his way between tables up to the stage at the front of the room. "From the beautiful and diverse district of Port au Port! Tony Cornect!" And then it's

---

[3] In the ballroom at the Hotel Gander, Finance Minister Jerome Kennedy and his people are consigned to the hinterland, a table in the dark way at one end of the room. Clearly, he just didn't have the fire in his belly. As coincidence would have it, less than two weeks following the Gander convention, Kennedy would announce his resignation from politics.

Cornect's turn; he's more wiry and athletic, and he bounds up after Cross, going for an awkward high five with a random delegate along the way. One by one, more than 30 of them make their way up on stage, fuelled by the steady cheering of the party faithful. Then the room goes quiet before the whole affair climaxes with the lady of the hour, the leader, the big kahuna, Kathy Dunderdale. She gets her own music — "Get the Party Started" by Pink — and a standing ovation from delegates as she waves, weaves, and occasionally stops to hug somebody before ending up at the reserved table closest to the stage.

Once the premier gets to her spot, the rest of the MHAs disperse back to their tables, and the emcee immediately sucks all the life out of the room by going through a long list of thank-yous that nobody really listens to — the organizing committee, the hotel staff, the premier's office, the local MHA, the local district association, and on and on and on. One MHA's daughter sings "O Canada," and a reverend says grace. Then everybody tucks into the basket of bread in the centre of their table and waits for the serving staff to bring out the plates of stuffed chicken breast and mashed potatoes.

After supper, Dunderdale gives her speech, and Bath gives her thank you.

There are other short speeches and housekeeping announcements, and then everybody retires back to the lobby to get more booze. The tables are cleared from the banquet hall, and a DJ plays country music and the sort of recognizable pop hits that get people dancing. I wish I could stick around; when the serious drinking starts, people ease up and let their guard down enough to talk to a journalist. Instead, I go back to my hotel room to furiously write up a story that captures none of the events I've just told you about, and instead focuses just on Dunderdale's speech. The big headline is when Dunderdale dismisses the party's abysmal public opinion polling by saying bad numbers just "keep us on our toes." It's too late to make the print deadline but it'll be posted on the web first thing in the morning.

• • •

On Saturday morning, I missed Dunderdale's 8 a.m. breakfast speech to the PC Women's Association, but I managed to catch her 45 minute "Leader's Report" at 9 a.m. If you're keeping track, that's three speeches in less than 24 hours to basically the same group of people. For the Leader's Report, Dunderdale wandered back and forth talking in front of probably 150 or so PC delegates.[4]

During the speech, Dunderdale went straight into the lion's den and tackled the most controversial decisions she'd made as premier: Muskrat Falls and Bill 29.

On Muskrat Falls, she made essentially the same argument that she'd been making for three years; the $7.7 billion[5] hydroelectric project was the cheapest source of electricity for the province, and the fringe benefits were nearly endless. On Bill 29, Dunderdale argued that despite the sweeping, restrictive legislative amendments to the province's access to information law, her government was not trying to keep things secret. Despite amending the law to allow the government to deny access to reams of information, Dunderdale said the government was actually making more documents accessible to the public than ever before. I won't get bogged down in the detail on it, except to say that probably 20 per cent of the speech was absolutely true, another 40 per cent of the speech was arguably true, and the remaining 40 per cent was straight-up misrepresentation and spin. But never mind the facts. Dunderdale was relaxed, confident and appeared to have a humble and sincere conviction about her. She spoke without notes and rattled off facts and details in a way that was very impressive to watch.

The partisans ate it up. It was comforting to feel her unwavering confidence in the face of so much public skepticism and anger. It was inspiring to watch your leader juggle facts and explain complex policy issues in down-to-earth ways.

Kathy Dunderdale excels most as a politician in low-key meetings and unscripted situations, although it doesn't do her a whole

---

[4] That's less than half the total number of people who were packed into the same room last night, but a lot of folks are still sleeping off their hangovers, and 9 a.m. is feeling awfully early.
[5] Well, that was the price tag back in 2013, anyway.

lot of good. Politics, when you rise to the very top, is about surviving the crucible. Whether it's question period in the House of Assembly, or the Big Speech delivered during an election campaign, or a frenzied press conference with reporters shouting questions, some people thrive in those high-pressure moments. Some people just don't. In those critical situations, Dunderdale was always just a bit off-key; she often came across as arrogant or stammering or angry.

But when she was just chatting with her people in a ballroom in Gander, she was at her best. Ministers privately tell me that it was the same way in small meetings, and around the cabinet table. She did well behind the scenes. Unfortunately, as she got more unpopular, she hired more communications staff, and they only made things worse. It's awfully hard to come up with a messaging strategy when your greatest communication skill is speaking off-the-cuff unscripted.

In casual conversations over the whole weekend, I kept hearing the same thing over and over again from Tories: "If only they could get to know her like we know her, then everything would be different." It doesn't really matter, but they're right. If most people got the chance to sit down and listen to Dunderdale just shoot the breeze about government policy for an hour or so, they'd probably be a lot more inclined to cut her some slack.

Too bad that's not how politics works.

At the end of Dunderdale's sprawling 45-minute convention speech, Agnes Richard had heard enough. Under party rules, Dunderdale knew she was safe from a leadership review 30 days before the convention; anybody wanting to challenge her job at the helm needed to give advance notice in writing to the party office. But Richard charged up to a microphone, and said she didn't care what the rules said. She wanted to speak up anyway. "I move that we endorse the leadership of Kathy Dunderdale," Richard said, before she was drowned out in cheers, applause and shouts of "hear, hear" from the other delegates.

The PCs were in third place in the polls, and nearly four out of five Newfoundlanders and Labradorians responded to one poll saying Dunderdale was not the best choice for premier of the province, but at the PC Party annual convention, there was no hint of wavering support. That's partisanship.

After Dunderdale's speech, the party president gave a quick update and so did the treasurer. They both praised Dunderdale's speech, and her leadership in general — another one of those sycophantic gestures — before getting down to brass tacks. The organization of the party was strong and the Tories had more than $700,000 in the bank — which is A LOT for a province the size of Newfoundland and Labrador, two years out from an election. By comparison, the Liberals were around $800,000 in debt, which lead to chortling and jokes about how the Tories almost had enough money to pay off the Liberals' debt.

●●●

A little later in the morning, I had my first run-in with Marjorie.

She's small, with short white hair, probably in her late sixties. She's got a raspy voice and a thick Southern Shore accent. She started in on me by saying I had "some nerve" showing up at the convention at all, and that was probably the kindest thing she said to me all weekend. Mostly, she said things like "I'll kill ya" and "I'll rip your guts out."

Among the Tories, Marjorie is kind of like a mascot, and a beloved old unflinching member of the faithful. She worshipped the ground that Danny Williams walked on, and she'd very sincerely tell you that Natural Resources Minister Tom Marshall was the smartest man in Newfoundland and Labrador. Period. The people she likes, she loves with as much force as a human being can muster. And the people she hates, she despises just as enthusiastically. Marjorie is a fixture of Open Line radio; she calls in at least once or twice per week to perform a Gatling gun tirade about how the PC Party is making Newfoundland a better place, and how anybody who disagrees is the scum of the earth.

A few months before the convention, I wrote some stories about the Tories failing to keep their election promises, which led to a little public tussle with Finance Minister Jerome Kennedy. In an interview, Kennedy said that the "commitments" in the party's election platform weren't really promises. He said the platform was just a blueprint, not a hard and fast promise. After the story went to print, Kennedy called in to Open Line on VOCM radio to say that I quoted him unfairly, and my story was misleading. We went back and forth on it all week: he claimed I quoted him out of context; I posted the full transcript of the interview; he issued a lengthy news release detailing all the election promises the government had kept; I wrote a story for the paper pointing out that the release didn't mention the promises they'd broken.

Then Marjorie called in to VOCM.

"If the crowd in government listened to me, they wouldn't talk to *The Telegram*," she said. "I met McLeod, by the way, out at the PC convention in Gander last year, and I was mad at him then."

"Why?" Host Bill Rowe asked.

"Because he's an ignorant pig," Marjorie explained.

Things sort of went off the rails from there. She called me a "monster" and declared that the PCs are "the best government we ever had."

At the 2013 convention — a year after my first encounter with her — Marjorie charged up to me and started taking me to task for all the "lies" and "twisted" quotes that I print in my stories, making good Tory cabinet ministers look bad. I should be ashamed of myself, she said. But really, she added, she'd murder me if I wrote a bad story about this weekend's convention. As though murder wasn't bad enough, she threatened to "crucify" me by calling in to Open Line on Monday to take me to task. This went on for five or ten minutes. At first it was hilarious, and I laughed and tried to keep things jovial.

After a while, it just got weird.

I asked her to do an interview. She briefly considered it, but then refused, saying that no matter what she said, I'd print nothing but lies. She said she'd save her words for VOCM Open Line radio where there's no way to twist it around.

I gave up, and went on my way.

Marjorie is the perfect archetype of a certain sort of partisan. I secretly suspect that if we actually sat down for a calm conversation, she wouldn't be able to explain a single PC Party policy position. She knows the slogans — "Fiscal responsibility!" "No more giveaways!" — but I don't think she'd be able talk in any detail about topping up the public sector pension liability or access-to-information policy principles. Her calls to VOCM are mostly about praising a cabinet minister or vilifying a government critic.[6] For her, it's all about the people, not the ideas. People like Marjorie gravitate to partisanship for the same reason that other people gravitate to sports. By calling in to Open Line once a week, she gets to wear a blue jersey, play a position and feel like she's on the team with Jerome Kennedy and Tom Marshall and Kathy Dunderdale and Danny Williams. It's not about the government policy; it's about the camaraderie.

My first run-in with Marjorie was funny, but as the day wore on and I kept seeing her, it got harder and harder to keep laughing. I don't know if she took my upbeat tone as encouragement to continue the lighthearted death threats, or if this little old lady was really trying to intimidate me. At times, she'd talk to me quite sincerely about her love for the Tories, and for Dunderdale, and for certain favourite cabinet ministers. The sincerity was the most unnerving part, because when she talked earnestly about how much she loves the premier, and people should stop saying nasty things about her, it's a little bit scary that she intersperses her speech with little phrases like "I'll rip your guts out," and, "They'll never find your body."

● ● ●

In the afternoon, the Tories turned the sycophantic up to 11 for the policy session. It was 90 minutes on the schedule, but there were way too many resolutions for them to get through. That might have been a problem, except that none of the "policies" mattered even slightly. Each policy resolution was a fawning endorsement of current government policy.

For the most part, the local district association for a minister put forward a resolution endorsing some aspect of the portfolio that their guy manages. Here's a sample policy resolution on "Business Growth," from the Ferryland PC District Association — the district that elected Keith Hutchings.

[6] I expect when this book comes out, I'll catch hell from her on the radio at some point.

"WHEREAS the Progressive Conservative government of Newfoundland and Labrador has significantly lowered the tax burden on all businesses in the province over the past several years, resulting in Newfoundland and Labrador currently having the lowest small business tax rate of all the provinces but one east of Manitoba; and

WHEREAS since 2005 the Department of Innovation, Business and Rural Development has invested in excess of $135 million in economic and business development initiatives, 70 per cent of which has been invested in rural communities;

THEREFORE BE IT RESOLVED that the Progressive Conservative Party of Newfoundland and Labrador expresses its support for the provincial government's investment to grow businesses small and large throughout Newfoundland and Labrador."

Hutchings was the minister responsible for — you guessed it! — Innovation, Business and Rural Development.

In total, party members "debated" eight such resolutions, with speaker after speaker stepping up to the microphone to talk about what a good job the government was doing. It was self-congratulatory to the point of being almost unseemly to watch. Ambitious backbench MHAs and cabinet ministers stepped up to talk about what good work their government departments were doing. Hutchings spoke about the resolution being put forward by his own people, patting himself on the back for a job well done.

Each resolution was passed unanimously. None of the partisans seemed to think that this was a moribund practice, symptomatic of a party devoid of exciting new ideas that require real debate and honest discussion. To everyone in the room, it seems, this was just what party unity looks like.

Older and wiser people with longer memories tell me that this was the influence that Danny Williams had on the PC Party. When he was in charge, it was a one man show — not so much a political party as a cult of personality. The rank and file of the party didn't debate policy; the organizing structure was 100 per cent top-down. Ideas came from Danny and his palace guard, and disagreeing with Danny was a recipe for trouble. During the early years of Tory government, Danny ran all of the potential dissenting voices out of the party. By the time Danny left politics and Dunderdale took over, the PC Party was a well-oiled machine. Party workers, MHAs, and rank-and-file members were experts at voting "yes" on whatever was put in front of them.

• • •

After the policy session, they whisked the reporters out of the room for the "election planning" session, so I went back to my hotel room for a nap. I got back at about 7:30 p.m. and the mezzanine was once again jammed with people. On Saturday night, the party arranged for a variety show with a comedian, and a band of sassy ladies doing covers of songs by Tom Jones and Elvis and The Monkees. Once the variety show wrapped up, there was more drinking and more dancing.

I stuffed my notepad in my pocket, and I just tried to talk casually with people and develop relationships. It's tricky, developing sources while at the same time maintaining professional distance. It helps to just sip on a Coke and chat with people, as a way to remind them that you're a real human being, and not just a bastard and a byline. Dunderdale tried to drag me out onto the dance floor two or three times — not for herself, she said, although she definitely likes to dance, but for some of the other girls in there. I resisted, and stuck to making small talk in the mezzanine.

Around 11 p.m. I found myself chatting with Joe the cop. Joe was a plainclothes police officer with the Royal Newfoundland Constabulary who specialized in criminal intelligence. He was part of the premier's protection detail. Dunderdale had cops protecting her since 2011 when she first took the job. I never knew what the specific threat(s) were, but the times I chatted with Joe, he always led me to believe that there are legit security concerns that nobody ever hears about.

We were sort of kindred spirits at this thing: outsiders and observers in the middle of a sea of partisans. We were also both technically on the clock, while everybody around us was kicking back and getting drunk. We swapped a couple stories about this and that – it turns out that he worked a robbery case a few years back, and I ended up interviewing the criminal in jail after she was convicted. Small world.

So there we were, hanging out, when Justice Minister Darin King showed up. King definitely had had a few drinks, and cheerfully greeted me as "TelegramJames!" — my Twitter username.

And then, out of nowhere: Marjorie.

She was looking to talk to me about a couple things. Firstly, she wanted to threaten me some more, but at the same time, she was trying to pump me for information. And she seemed to have no idea that the unremarkable looking guy to my right was a plainclothes RNC officer.

Right off the bat, Marjorie made it clear that she still didn't like me, but at the moment, the person she really wanted to murder was David Zelcer, a CBC reporter who'd been writing a bunch of not-nice stories about Tory cabinet minister Kevin O'Brien. Marjorie wanted to go tear his arms off, and she wanted to know if I knew where he is.

Oh and by the way, she said in passing, if you print a nasty story in Monday's paper about the convention, she'd kill me too. Joe was just sort of standing there nervously, because this sort of thing could graduate from "just talking" to "uttering death threats" in a real hurry. He was sort of chuckling, but also looking at me, as if to decide whether I was laughing or whether I was worried for my own safety.

Meanwhile, I was buckled over laughing so hard I could barely answer Marjorie's questions to tell her that Zelcer wasn't at the convention that night. King was tipsy and laughing too, but he was also gingerly trying to cut in and tell Marjorie that she probably shouldn't be joking about death threats with a cop standing right there. But of course, she was undeterred, and King trying to diffuse the situation only added fuel to the fire. When King mentioned that Joe was a cop, Marjorie belligerently declared, "If I wants to kill ya, even the Pope couldn't stop me."

This was about all I could handle, so I wandered off looking for a different crowd to talk to.

●●●

Sunday morning was pretty low-key.

There's a tradition that MHAs and cabinet ministers serve breakfast for convention delegates in the morning before everybody heads home. I popped in to get a photo of Jerome Kennedy wearing a white paper hat and serving eggs and bacon from a buffet line.

Since Friday night, there was a running joke going around the convention about Kevin O'Brien — the minister Zelcer had been going after. In the weeks leading up to the convention, O'Brien had been raked over the coals by the CBC for allegedly threatening the Gander Chamber of Commerce to get two NDP politicians uninvited from a charity pancake breakfast. O'Brien, so the story goes, claimed he wanted to keep the event non-political, so he used his clout to make sure that *he* was the only politician who'd be there slinging pancakes. At the banquet Friday night, Tories joked that O'Brien should have made a peace offering to the New Democrats by by letting the NDP caucus serve the Tories dinner.

On Sunday morning, everyone was in high spirits and once again joking about the New Democrats. A couple of MHAs were lamenting the fact that they didn't have the time to print cardboard cutouts of New Democrat MHA George Murphy's face. It would have been the height of hilarity, they all agreed, if they'd been wearing George Murphy masks to serve breakfast in the morning.

A couple months later, I got to chatting with then-Tory backbencher Paul Lane about the whole affair. Personally, I just didn't get it. I mean, getting the New Democrats uninvited from the event seemed like such a petty political win. Any halfway sensible political strategist looking at that situation would have seen that the upside to edging out the New Democrats was tiny, but the downside when the story hit the media was huge. What's the point in playing for a small win when you're risking a huge embarrassment to get it?

Lane saw things differently. He said that in his district, he makes sure he's at as many community functions as possible. He shows up to everything, listens to everyone and tries to keep everybody happy. He's the representative of Mount Pearl South in the House of Assembly. It's not a partisan thing; showing up to all those community functions is just part of the MHA's job.

In Lane's mind, if he showed up and participated in some community charity fundraiser in George Murphy's district, *that* would be political. Similarly, Lane said if he arrived at a pancake breakfast in his district and found George Murphy serving food — "By God, by the time I was done, he'd be wearing those pancakes. That would be my first reaction." But Lane didn't think that O'Brien was blameless in the whole mess. He said it's important to swallow that first reaction — to keep those partisan urges in check. And anyway, Lane said, he would never be "betrayed" by any of the community groups in his district. None of those groups would ever invite a Liberal or a New Democrat to a function and make things political, because Lane had good relationships with all of them. He told me his first reaction when the pancake scandal happened was that it looked like O'Brien had some problems in his district, and wasn't well liked.

Personally, I thought it was petty politics. Partisans just see the world differently.

CHAPTER 2
MELTDOWN
12:30 A.M. SUNDAY, OCTOBER 20, 2013

"Tomorrow morning, a letter will go to Lorraine, signed by the four MHAs, demanding a leadership convention."

This was the start of a really, really awful week for the NDP.

"She doesn't have it yet, but tomorrow morning she's getting a letter," my source told me. "You didn't hear it from me, but I just came from a party, where a very drunk MHA told me."

Publicly, Lorraine Michael was one of the most popular politicians in the province. In polling back in 2013, she scored as the most popular opposition party leader in Canada — the seasoned face of the NDP, and the steady hand that guided the party to heights it had never achieved before. She's a former nun and teacher, with a long history in social justice activism. Her New Democrat bona fides are rock solid, and her political instincts are tempered from five long years playing 47-against-one as the lone New Democrat politician elected to the House of Assembly.

But in the week of October 20, 2013, Michael was to be the person who tore it all to pieces, and would guide her party back towards the political hinterland.

• • •

Despite my best efforts, I was unable to independently confirm anything about the emailed letter. But people I spoke to on Sunday said that the party was coming apart at the seams, and there was widespread brewing discontent with Lorraine's leadership. In October 2011, the party elected four more MHAs to sit alongside Michael in the House, but by all reports, she still ran things as a caucus of one — with four new employees. The word I kept hearing thrown around was "imperious" and sometimes in interviews, I'd catch hints of the old nun and school teacher coming out.

The closest I came to getting independent confirmation on Sunday was a terse email from MHA Dale Kirby, saying, "Sorry buddy I can't talk."

Meanwhile, my original source sent me a private message on Twitter, "Ok, now I have been informed that 'the die has been cast' that's all I got."

I replied: "That's ... dramatic. Hopefully whatever happens goes more smoothly than it did when Julius Caesar said that."

A few moments later, I get another message: "No joke ... it was sent to me in Latin."

• • •

CBC reporter David Cochrane broke the caucus revolt story Monday night on the supper-hour news. His sources are better than mine. He also got an interview with Michael, who gave a master class in political tactics. She'd just returned from a lengthy vacation in India, but she hit the ground running.

"I was really quite shocked," Michael opened by saying. "And the shock turned into disbelief."

When she got the letter, she didn't start by calling up Kirby, or any of the other MHAs who signed it. First, she talked to her chief of staff, and then she talked to the party president.

18

"They were just as shocked as I was, because they had no idea either. It blindsided all of us," Michael told Cochrane.

I don't know what to make of that, because it certainly didn't blindside me. And it didn't blindside any of the New Democrats I spoke to on Sunday. They claimed they didn't know about the letter specifically, but the average response was basically, "Yeah, this sort of thing has definitely been brewing for a while."

Michael framed it differently in the CBC interview: "I think that there is a small, dissenting group within the party," she said.

And then, Michael delivered the quote which would come to define the whole mess.

"It must have been very tough to get that letter, and read it," Cochrane asked. "How did it affect you personally, when you saw that?"

"I felt betrayed by the letter," Michael said. "I thought, what's this all about? You know, I'd just come back. I wasn't even home seven hours from my holiday. And I said, why didn't they wait, and sit down and talk?"

Lorraine Michael knew that she, personally, was one of the most popular politicians in Newfoundland and Labrador. She's also one of the most wily politicians in the House of Assembly. All of a sudden, it wasn't about stagnating NDP poll numbers, it wasn't about her leadership style, it wasn't about her age, or the fact that even many of her ardent supporters didn't believe she had what it takes to win the 2015 general election. All of a sudden, it was about Lorraine Michael being betrayed by her fellow New Democrats, and they didn't even have the decency to say it to her face.

Within hours, one of my politically engaged friends — not a New Democrat — posted on Facebook, "NDP essentially support breaking up with their girlfriend via text message. Unreal."

● ● ●

By the time she went to bed Monday night, everything was firmly back under control for Lorraine Michael. She'd talked to caucus members Gerry Rogers and George Murphy, and flipped them. "I think they certainly are indicating that they're open to sit down and talk. Anybody who knows me, I think, knows that I'm always ready to discuss," Michael told Cochrane. "They certainly have indicated to me that yes, they're open to sit down and talk about the issues."

By talking to party president Kathleen Connors — an ally of Michael's — she'd also successfully thwarted the most obvious threat to her leadership. If the party executive voted two-thirds for a leadership convention, then Michael could be pushed out. But as long as she had the party brass on her side, the only way Michael could be forced out was with hundreds of party members signing a petition — and that wasn't likely to happen. Monday night, after the CBC interview aired, the party executive spoke on a conference call, and made it clear that they weren't going to force Michael out.

The NDP caucus revolt lasted one day for Lorraine Michael. She was presented with a problem on Sunday, and by Monday evening it was all back under control.

By the time I got in touch with Dale Kirby late Monday evening, he was already sounding a bit like a man who'd been left twisting in the wind. He picked his words carefully, and his tone was defensive.

"There's no intent here to be confrontational or call for Ms. Michael's resignation, or to be critical in any way."[1]

But at the same time, Kirby was already criticizing Michael for making an ugly situation even worse for the NDP.

"It's unfortunate. We did not intend for this to be a public document, and it was read out on the air on CBC tonight. But as far as I know from talking to my colleagues, none of us provided that to anyone in the media."

Later in the week, Cochrane would confirm that while he had solid information, he didn't actually have a copy of the letter Monday evening when he broke the story. Cochrane had excerpts of the letter, though, because Michael's chief of staff read it out to him over the phone before she came over to the TV studio to do an interview. It wasn't any of the caucus members who wanted it out in the media at first; it was Lorraine Michael herself. If it was all out in the open, she'd be able to win.

---

[1] This was an odd thing for him to say, given that the letter plainly did confront Michael, and call for her resignation. Politics is like that sometimes, I guess.

The political naïveté on display from Kirby and the three other MHAs who signed the letter was nothing short of breathtaking. Kirby definitely knew he was trying force her to resign as leader, even if he got mealy-mouthed about it once the whole thing went public. But it seems like it never even occurred to him that she might fight back. From what I can tell, Christopher Mitchelmore wanted her gone too.

As for the other two, Gerry Rogers and George Murphy seemed to think that they were just asking for "renewal" in the party. They said they wanted to *discuss* leadership without actually ditching Michael. My working theory at the time was that they were looking over at the Liberals — who at this point were enjoying a 10 point bump in the polls because they were in the midst of a leadership race — and wanted to benefit from the same sort of thing. I think on some level, Rogers and Murphy thought that if they went through the motions of a leadership process, they could trick the voters into thinking the party was renewed, refreshed and re-energized going into the 2015 election — without actually switching leaders.

Breathtaking naïveté.

• • •

Tuesday afternoon, I arrived at the NDP caucus office to do an interview with Lorraine Michael. The mood was very different from what I'm used to. The NDP's offices are tucked up directly behind the House of Assembly in the Confederation Building, and conveniently located roughly ten steps away from the press gallery. When I'm covering the House, I spend a lot of time in the NDP caucus office, because they've got the best coffee — fair trade, organic, locally roasted, and it doesn't taste half-bad either. They've got irreverent posters on the wall, and the staffers are happy to shoot the shit. One of the researchers always bellows "FIRE IN THE HOLE!" when he sees me, alerting everybody within earshot that there's a journalist around, and all of the Top Secret Socialist Revolutionary Plans should be hidden. The Liberals are right across the hall, and they've usually got a pot of coffee on too, but it's not as good, and the office is a lot less friendly. The Liberals' caucus space feels like a government office; the NDP feels more like a university student union.

But on Tuesday, when I walked in, the vibe was different. Normally, Mark at the reception desk would say "hello" and walk me around to the coffee machine, and I'd help myself to milk from the carton in the fridge. Today, he insisted that I needed to stay right at the front door until somebody was ready to escort me into Michael's office for the interview. As if to maintain some semblance of normalcy, he went and got a cup of coffee while I waited by the door. He handed it to me black, and then sheepishly remembered that I take milk, and so he went back to get the milk carton out of the fridge.

I tried to make small talk with Mark while I was waiting. "How's it going?" and as the words came out of my mouth, I realized it was a pretty shitty week for everyone in the NDP, whether they were ready to admit it out loud or not. We tried to chat, without much success. After an uncomfortable 10 minutes waiting, I was ushered in to interview Lorraine.

Michael was relaxed, and not too cheerful, but clearly she was feeling just fine. She delivered the "betrayed" line again, and offered up pretty much the exact same interview she gave Cochrane the night before. When I asked her if she thought she had any responsibility for the situation, she flatly said no. There was no failure on her part; it was everyone else's fault. "I do not feel failure. I feel sadness over this, because I'm not sure where it's all coming from. ... No, I don't feel a failure. Far from it. ... I can't see what I could have done to stop the letter from happening, because it's not dealing with anything concrete. Like, it's not telling me anything to do with our ongoing work here."

In fact, the letter dealt with a few concrete things. For one thing, the four MHAs said they sent it "out of genuine concern for our Party's ability to attract quality candidates and build on our level of public support in advance of the 2015 election." Her political lieutenants just didn't believe that Michael could win the 2015 election, and it's important to remember that back in 2013, a lot of new Democrats saw winning as a real possibility for the first time in their party's history. Sure, they'd been polling ahead of both the

Liberals and the Tories, after all. That changed as soon as the letter went public, though.

I wasn't able to get a decent photo of Michael during the interview. She kept smiling whenever I went to take a picture, and a photo of a grinning, chipper leader doesn't really fit under a headline like "NDP in crisis; Michael under fire." But even though Michael was smiling, down the hall, George Murphy wasn't having such a good day. I ended up running his photo in the paper instead, looking morose, with his head in his hands, his eyes on the verge of tears. "I'm feeling like I betrayed Lorraine," he told me. "It was a mistake, and that's all I can say about it."

Murphy used to be a bouncer on George Street in another life; I heard that he was big and intimidating, but whenever there was a fight that needed breaking up, George would run the other way. He's just too nice.

He's also loyal to a fault. Before the 2011 general election, Murphy was a cab driver, best known for being the "Gas Man" who ran the numbers through the Public Utilities Board's arcane price-setting formula and announced Wednesday night whether gas would go down or up Thursday morning. He once told me that he got calls from old ladies who'd ask him to bring down the price of gas because pork chops were on sale, and they needed to drive to the grocery store. I couldn't tell if he was joking. By a combination of name recognition and lucky political timing, the voters of St. John's East vaulted him from the driver's seat of a Jiffy Cab into a seat in the House of Assembly and a salary of nearly $100,000 per year. I suspect deep down, Murphy felt like he owed a lot to Michael, the leader who helped make that happen. On Tuesday afternoon, he wasn't really looking at me when he talked. His eyes were red, and he said he didn't sleep the night before. He said he was "Judas" and said that it was just stupidity to send the letter. "I should have been a little bit of a better thinker." I don't know what Michael said or did to flip him from being a guy who signed a letter calling for her resignation into a guy 100 per cent behind her, but it clearly took its toll on him.

After the interview with Murphy, the communications staffer led me to the next office down the hall, where MHA Gerry Rogers was ready for her interview. It was clear that the staffer planned on sitting in on the interview, the same as he did with George.

"I usually don't need babysitting," Rogers said archly.

"A lot of things around here seem to be different today," I said.

Rogers is sharper than Murphy, and the message she delivered was a bit more polished — but it was still a muddled mess. She said she believed the party had a lot of "work that we have to do" although she wasn't entirely clear what exactly that work consisted of. Years later, she told me that the personal animosity between Dale Kirby and Lorraine Michael was poisonous, and it was hurting the caucus' ability to function. She said she signed the letter hoping that it would be the jolt needed to sit down and confront those issues directly.

None of this was communicated clearly, at all, though. At the time, all I could get out of her was that she believed that the party needed to sit down and have a big group talk about how to renew and rejuvenate itself in preparation for the 2015 general election. And Rogers thought that talking about leadership had got to be part of that "hard work" that needed doing.

"Yes, but fundamentally, do you believe Lorraine is the best choice to lead the party?" I asked.

"At this point, I don't know. This is the work that we have to do," she said.

No other politician in the NDP is as slippery when she doesn't want to be pinned down.

"I'm hearing people who are really strong supporters of Lorraine and feel that she has taken this party to where it is today, and I'm hearing from people the same thing, but that now it's time for a change," Rogers said. "I've apologized to her for the clumsy way that I think we handled this. We could have handled this better."

It wasn't exactly a ringing endorsement, but she apologized for sending the letter, and that was enough to fit Michael's narrative that the whole caucus wasn't *actually* out to get her, even if the letter certainly made it look that way. When I asked about Dale Kirby, the party director of communications airily said that he hadn't been in the office today; he wasn't being offered up for media interviews quite so enthusiastically as the other two.

Divide and conquer.

• • •

For all the zeal of the NDP communications folks Tuesday, they didn't manage to fend off the looming disaster of Wednesday morning. For a moment, it looked like the wounds were healing, and everything was getting back on track. Then George Murphy did a 13-minute interview with CBC Radio's St. John's Morning Show. It was a complete meltdown. He cried on air. He accused Kirby of threatening him. He said he was held hostage, with Kirby saying if he didn't sign the letter, then it would be leaked to the media.

Host Anthony Germain didn't hold back, either. Here is some of their conversation:

GERMAIN: You strike me, of all of the members of caucus, as being the taxi driver, the gas prices guy, the man of the people. And yet you showed absolutely no backbone in this, nor did Gerry Rogers, and you allowed this to go ahead when you could have stopped it.

MURPHY: Yes, and you know, that's something that I have to live with for the rest of my life, and I have been deeply affected by it to the point where I feel that I am an ineffectual MHA now. To the point where I have to consider my own future. But you know, my family has to come first in all of this.

° ° °

MURPHY: Right now I am totally ineffectual. I can't get work done, and I have to get back on track and reconsider my future.

GERMAIN: To be clear on your position, you are completely distancing yourself from this email, if I take it correctly? You do not think Ms. Michael should subject herself to a leadership review?

MURPHY: No, absolutely not.

GERMAIN: Have you spoken to Gerry Rogers about this?

MURPHY: Well, you know, Gerry didn't want me to do this. To put myself out front. And it's as simple as this for me, that I have to save people's honour here.

GERMAIN: What would you say to Lorraine Michael?

MURPHY: I love her to death.

° ° °

MURPHY: As far as I'm concerned, there's an MHA out there that I simply can't trust now. I can't. And I have trouble living with myself.

GERMAIN: You're referring to Mr. Kirby?

MURPHY: Yeah.

GERMAIN: How are you possibly going to sit together?

MURPHY: You know, that's going to be a mystery question as regards to what happens here in that process. But you know, I have no trouble in saying that because of all of this, I have no trust, and it's going to take a long time for that to be built up, if that's ever going to happen.

...

GERMAIN: I could tell when you walked in this morning that you haven't been sleeping. You have a very long face. I can tell that this is a personal struggle for you, and I do appreciate that you came in. However, you are an elected representative—

MURPHY: I am.

GERMAIN: Of the people in your district. How much damage do you think was inflicted yesterday? And by virtue of the fact that you've just said that you can't trust Mr. Kirby, how much damage has this done to the NDP? I mean, the Liberals, from a political level, they must be doing cartwheels.

MURPHY: Oh, I'd say that they're laughing.

...

GERMAIN: You're the guys who are supposed to do stuff differently, and here you are signing a letter, apparently spearheaded by Mr. Kirby, to put a bullet into the most popular opposition leader in the country according to opinion polls.

MURPHY: Yeah, and like I said, a bullet was not my intention. Not at all. What we wanted to do was get together and have a renewal. Some people might even call it a new PR program or something. You know, where are we going to be going from here? What do we have to do on the inside in order to dress things up and make things better and go on to 2015? So that's where my belief came from that I was signing. And you know something? I should have read the fine print. I really should have. But the simple fact is that we tried to stop it. And now I'm probably going to pay the political price.

● ● ●

As Murphy was on the air, Kirby was listening in, and he took to Twitter.

"Wow @GeorgeMurphyMHA. That is simply not true," Kirby wrote.

Moments later, he directed a public tweet at Germain, saying, "@AnthonyGermain I would like to comment on this if possible" and then two minutes later, Kirby posted, "@AnthonyGermain ask George to produce evidence."

After a break for the news, Kirby phoned in, and he was patched through, live on the radio:

GERMAIN: George Murphy says the whole idea of trying to get Lorraine Michael to step down was your idea. Is that true?

KIRBY: Knock me over with a feather. Absolutely not, and I certainly would like to see Mr. Murphy produce some evidence to that effect. On October 11 I, in fact, was approached by Mr. Murphy ... He was quite upset. He was more or less told that he ought to stop. He would cease and desist speaking about natural gas issues to the media, and he was very upset about that. He had an outburst in the office on the previous day. I sat down with him and had a long conversation about this. I mean, he has 20 years of working with the Consumer Group for Fair Gas Prices, and he, in fact, was the No. 2 person for the Department of Natural Resources critic position, so it was his job to critique that (natural gas). So we were concerned that Ms. Michael had provided this direction. And we didn't think that it was correct, and —

GERMAIN: So, when you had this conversation with Mr. Murphy, did you say, look, hey we can actually get rid of her?

KIRBY: Well, it didn't happen like that, Anthony ... He suggested — *he suggested* — that the caucus meet, you know, outside of our normal routine, outside of the office in the Confederation Building, and have an off-site meeting to discuss how we would go forward. At that two-hour meeting we all agreed on the course of action we took. There were no threats by me. There were no threats by me that, you know, if you don't send this letter, I will leak it to David Cochrane or anything like that. That's absolute foolishness ... And at some point on Sunday we had a debate about whether to send it or not. I indicated to the caucus that I would email it to Lorraine Michael myself if they didn't want to do that. OK?

GERMAIN: OK...

KIRBY: I can provide an email to that effect. If Mr. Murphy contends that I said I would leak it to the media if they didn't send it, then he ought to produce the evidence to that effect — because that is an absolute lie.

GERMAIN: Alright. That is his contention. But you mentioned you had this two hour meeting with the caucus. When was that?

KIRBY: Um, that meeting was on October the 15th and the letter was signed on October the 16th, and I witnessed the signature of each one.

GERMAIN: Now, what Mr. Murphy said in the last hour — let's say I take what you're saying at face value — perhaps he seems to have had a change of heart. He contends that Gerry Rogers had a change of heart, but that there was nothing they could do to stop you—

KIRBY: It's really sad what's happening to the New Democratic Party this week, you know? If I was leader of the New Democratic Party — and I certainly have no aspirations to that effect — on Sunday after I read that email, I would have called an emergency meeting of my caucus. I would have called every member of caucus. I would have emailed them. I would have texted them. I would have gotten in a room with them. It's pretty easy. Four of us are in St. John's. One of us is not in St. John's, (but) we have telephones. I would have convened an emergency meeting of our caucus to discuss this situation. Instead, Lorraine Michael has decided to wait six days to have all of this foolishness go on, and I believe that Mr. Murphy is an agent of that. And it is really sad to me after 16 years of volunteerism and working in this party, to see these people tearing this down because they can't see anything other than—

GERMAIN: But Mr. Kirby, isn't that a bit rich? I mean, here you precipitate a leadership crisis and then you criticize the leader you want to try to get rid of with how she's actually dealing with you?

KIRBY: I stand by what I said. If this is a crisis situation, we ought to have met by now to discuss this. We should have met immediately.

GERMAIN: And who has caused this crisis?

KIRBY: Well, all of the names are on the letter. They signed it. It's in English. They understood what they were signing. People talking about how they didn't understand all the details and all of that is utter foolishness. We believed and I still believe that we need a different way forward. I mean, this last week, if nothing else, has indicated that. *sigh* Well, I can't imagine a premier waiting six days to convene her cabinet in a crisis situation. This is what we're doing. And like I said, this circular firing squad out in the media is serving no one.

GERMAIN: Mr Kirby, I appreciate you giving us a call.

• • •

After leaving the CBC radio studio, Murphy got into his car and called VOCM radio to do another interview — complete with the crying, threats, accusations of lying, and publicly questioning his own competence. Then Kirby called VOCM for a repeat performance of his own. While all of this was unfolding, Christopher Mitchelmore had largely been left out of the drama owing to the fact that he was 500 kilometres away in his electoral district on the tip of the Northern Peninsula. So he took to Twitter, saying, "I stand by my signature on letter requesting the NLNDP Executive to convene a Leadership Convention in 2014. This must be discussed w/caucus."

Then everything went quiet.

At some point on Wednesday, the NDP communications staffers managed to regain control of the situation — which, under the circumstances, amounted to telling absolutely everyone involved to shut the hell up. Politicians started talking about a self-imposed gag order, saying that they wouldn't be speaking publicly until after their scheduled caucus meeting, which would happen on Friday.

The meeting happened at a secret location to prevent journalists from showing up to stake it out. The meeting also involved a professional mediator, because apparently the five elected New Democrats were unable to speak to each other without some sort of intermediary.

It was a beautiful, clear fall Saturday afternoon when the NDP announced that the caucus meeting was over. Whoever set up the impromptu news conference didn't spend too much time thinking about the unintended metaphors. Lorraine spoke to reporters at the bottom of a little cul de sac on home turf, standing in the street in front of her house, which is in the shadow of the Confederation Building. Apparently the news conference would've been held in the NDP caucus offices *in* the Confederation Building, except that the building was experiencing intermittent power outages. So there Michael was — all alone, at the end of a road, on the outside looking in — telling reporters that she was still the leader of her party.

Michael was also calling for the party to conduct a formal leadership review some time in 2014 — essentially what her caucus members had asked her for on Sunday, before the party started tearing itself limb from limb. She said there was no sense in looking at what happened in the past.

"My suggestion was we need to move forward, and we put our energies today and yesterday into moving forward," Michael told reporters. "You move on by not being vindictive. You move on by saying we need to work together."

On Monday night, exactly one week after her first interview with the CBC, Lorraine Michael was back in the same TV studio for another one-on-one interview. She said following a tough meeting over the weekend, "we left the room on Saturday a caucus of five. We are still a caucus of five."

Michael was asked if she bore any fault in the way it all played out.

"Do you have any regrets about what's unfolded in this last week? Anything you regret doing yourself?" host Debbie Cooper asked.

"No. I regret that the caucus wrote the letter, but I did everything I had to do in response to the situation that was created, I believe," Michael said.

Less than 24 hours later, Dale Kirby and Christopher Mitchelmore would announce that they were leaving the NDP caucus, because they could not work under her leadership.

CHAPTER 3
NO UNFORCED ERRORS
NOVEMBER 17, 2013

Just before revealing the final results of the Liberal leadership election, Party President Judy Morrow took to the podium to make an announcement. She had to shout into the microphone and fight to be heard over the din of the crowd, but this was important information that the people needed to know: the winning ticket holder in the 50/50 draw won a measly hundred and twenty bucks. The announcement didn't draw much notice, but it told me everything I needed to know about the present state of the Liberal Party. The Liberals were making a concerted effort to be boring.

Up until the fall of 2013, silent auctions, live auctions and raffles had been a mainstay of every Liberal event I'd ever covered. When I drove out to Upper Island Cove to cover the Port de Grave District Association AGM one time, the silent auction items on the table in the corner included a can of white paint and a case of motor oil. Bidding was fierce on the live auction items out in Port de Grave too; people from the area were quite interested in winning one locally donated lot — one tonne of crushed stone.

Another lot — a dozen eggs a week for 52 weeks — also had several bidders vying for the prize. At a Liberal fundraising dinner I covered in St. John's, a friend ended up in a fierce silent auction bidding war for a jar of pickled sausages. At the 2011 party AGM, lying on the silent auction table was a "gift certificate" with a smiling picture of then-leader Yvonne Jones: "The holder of this Gift Certificate is entitled to a 1-2 hour session in our HYDRO WHIRLPOOL, SALT WATER HOTTUB for 4 people. Yvonne Jones, Leader of the Official Opposition, Leader of the Liberal Party of Newfoundland and Labrador will co-host." I wish I had checked back at the end of the day to see how much a dip in the hot tub with Yvonne went for.

Alcohol was an easy sell. At the 2012 Liberal Party convention, one of the district associations was selling raffle tickets. The prize was a 106oz "Texas mickey" of Lamb's rum, along with two 40oz bottles, a couple smaller bottles of Lamb's and one of those teeny tiny one-shot bottles. The enterprising raffle ticket salesman called it a "Rack of Lamb's." At a different Liberal event I covered for the newspaper, at one end of the silent auction table they had a case of Labatt beer up for auction. And in the event that the bidding on that case of beer got too pricey, there was another identical case of beer being auctioned off separately at the other end of the other end of the table — three metres away.

And then there are the 50/50 tickets. Usually it's not just one draw at Liberal events. Tickets are basically always $2 each or three for $5, and always selling well. Elected officials make especially good targets for the ambitious 50/50 salesman; if an MHA is caught flat-footed with only $20s in his wallet, he's liable to buy 12 tickets rather than risk the indignity of asking for change. Better still, if that MHA's ticket is drawn, he'll almost certainly donate the prize back to the party, rather than risk looking like he's greedy and selfish. If the event has a couple of friendly-but-implacable seasoned community fundraisers, a decent 50/50 draw can hit a few thousand dollars without too much trouble.

And yet on Sunday, November 15, 2013, the Liberal Party managed to raise a whopping $120.

A hundred and twenty bucks wasn't going to do much to eat away at the party's debt, which stood at around $800,000 on the weekend of the Liberal convention.[1] Party treasurer Jeff Marshall neglected to mention the debt at all when he gave his financial up-date Sunday morning to the 30 or 40 delegates who bothered to get out of bed to listen to it. I had to chase him outside and corner him in the hotel lobby afterwards, before I found out how bad things were for the party.

Marshall instead used his financial report to talk about how he saved the party thousands of dollars on Internet and telephone bills, and when the lease was up next year, he thought they could find cheaper rental office space. He also focused on the need to sign up as many people as possible to make solid, stable, dependable monthly contributions.

"Traditionally, in the past the party has lived on a kind of feast-or-famine kind of fundraising, where in one month we could be raising six figures, and in another month it could be much less," Marshall told me, after he admitted that they were $800,000 in the hole. "So what we want to do as a party — like any business or household — is you want to have a certain amount of cash flow so you know from one month to the next what's coming in so you can budget more effectively off of that."

This is what professional, mature party organizing looks like. It's just boring as hell. Also, it just hadn't been seen in the Liberal Party in a long while. But it's a lot better to be boring when it comes to this sort of thing. Boring means that everything is chugging along smoothly. Boring means that you're cashing cheques every month and paying your bills on time. Boring means that you're holding meetings and taking minutes and developing plans and following through on them.

Despite the party's best efforts, though, there were still little hints of the the old Liberal Party lurking around, if you looked hard enough for them. I could've sworn I saw one old guy selling raffle tickets at a table in the lobby; the prize appeared to be a homemade fruitcake.

---

[1] But apparently the Liberals hadn't been doing all that much to pay it down, anyway, because the debt was nearly $800,000 when I asked about it a year earlier at the 2012 convention.

• • •

Another vestige of the old Liberal Party which showed no signs of disappearing was the hospitality suites.

"Back in the old days, these things were about pouring as much booze as you could down delegates' throats so that maybe they'd come over your way on the second ballot," Liberal MP Gerry Byrne told me in a crowded suite on the second floor of the Delta Hotel in St. John's on Saturday night. Byrne was complaining wistfully about the utter pointlessness of all this free alcohol and finger foods. By the time thirsty party members converged on the Delta Hotel for the November leadership convention, the polls had already been open for more than a week; the vast majority of ballots were probably already cast online or by phone, and the final result was a done deal. The old-timey stuff that Byrne was fondly remembering — with the smoke-filled backrooms and boozing up delegates in the hopes of currying favour in a tight convention floor-fight — just wasn't going to happen this time around. This time, the results would depend a lot more on some old couple in around the bay, sitting on the floral print couch in their living room, logging their votes by phone.

But the three frontrunners had money to burn — the party imposed absolutely no fundraising limits or spending caps, so the money flowed freely — and old traditions die hard.

Like the Tories, Liberal gatherings often feel like a big drunken party with a little bit of political organizing on the side. During their 2011 convention at the Capital Hotel in St. John's, MP Scott Andrews threw such a raging party in his hospitality suite — bathtub full of beer and ice, people crammed into the room — that he was called down to the hotel manager's office. "Yeah, we got a bit of a talking to. It was like being called into the principal's office!" Andrews told me a couple years after the fact. I had heard from credible sources that Andrews was actually banned for life from the Capital, but he insisted it wasn't *quite* that bad.

At the 2013 Liberal leadership convention, I showed up to drink Pepsi and mingle, because the hospitality suites could tell you an awful lot about where things were at for the candidates.

I hit up Cathy Bennett's party first. She had set up in a room on the second floor of the hotel, with a little bar in the corner and finger foods laid out on a table. Campaign workers had taped little 4x6 photos from the leadership campaign to the wall — mostly badly-lit, amateur snapshots — the kind of pictures you might see in an album on your mom's Facebook page. Bennett had spent most of the campaign batting back accusations that she was a Manchurian Candidate for the Tories. She'd donated $6,400 to the PC Party over the preceding decade, and she'd only donated $500 to the Liberals during the same period. She also happened to be a Tory appointment to the board of directors of Nalcor, and she even sat as chair of the board for a while, during the time when the government was putting together its plan to develop the Muskrat Falls project. It was awkward, at best, that the rest of the Liberal Party was deeply skeptical of the Muskrat Falls development — if not outright opposed to the deal — and Bennett was forced to essentially defend the Progressive Conservatives' centrepiece policy priority, while she was running to lead the Liberals.

Bennett spent a lot of time traveling the province and spent just as much time making sure people knew that she was traveling the province. Every time I heard her talking, she was speaking about where she'd been and what she was hearing in conversations with "ordinary" people. Her campaign launched a Twitter hashtag "#48in48" where she hit up every electoral district over the course of 48 days. All of it — the hashtag, the photos taped to the wall, and nearly everything else about the campaign — seemed to say, "No really, I'm a Liberal and people want to vote for me, see?"

Bennett herself was still very much "on" and circulating around the hospitality suite, looking aggressively energetic and cheerful. Bennett built a personal fortune on a series of McDonald's franchises in St. John's, which grew into a little business empire handling everything from job recruitment to industrial fabrication. She had the sort of Type-A personality that made it feel like after she struck "Conquer the business world" from her life To Do List, she turned to the next item: "Build a personal legacy by beating the politics game."

She said she'd sold several of her businesses and delegated most of the work to clear the decks. She carried herself throughout the campaign with the demeanour of somebody who does not lose under any circumstances. If she didn't win on Sunday, that just meant that she'd keep playing until she won.

But for everyone else at the Bennett shindig, a weird fatalism had set in. I ended up nursing a drink and chatting with Nancy O'Connor, Bennett's media wrangler.

"We worked as hard as we can," she said.

Apparently in the last couple days everybody, including Nancy, was pulled off their campaign duties to work the phones and get out the vote. Nothing else mattered at the end. On the outside, it looked like a slick, organized, expensive campaign, but Nancy said towards the end it was pretty much just everyone in a boiler room making calls and making sure that every one of their identified supporters cast a ballot. Nancy said it was fun. When somebody on the phone would ask about Cathy's policy position on an issue, she'd just cover the receiver, lean over, and say "Hey Cathy, what do you think about X?"

• • •

Right next door, Dwight Ball's hospitality suite had the feel of a graduation party. He was relaxed and happy. Unless something went horribly wrong, he was the frontrunner and victory was pretty much a sure thing. Lots of MHAs and MPs circulated in the room, and people orbited around Ball, who seemed to have firm handshake and a few minutes of casual conversation for everyone.

Ball looks almost too much like a politician, with a strong jawline and a full head of coiffed, grey-white hair. He wears impeccably tailored suits, and perfectly knotted ties. It's difficult to overemphasize the subtle value of a well-fitting suit; it's the difference between an athletic, energetic can-do professional and a rumpled pretender who looks like he stumbled in and ended up speaking at the podium by accident. His handshake is firm and confident, without being aggressive. In politics, the value of looking the part cannot be overstated.

Ball didn't always look so comfortable in the spotlight. A year or two earlier, he'd give speeches and the punchy lines would fall flat. Speaking to the media, he'd get distracted by minutia, and go off on little policy tangents that had nothing to do with the questions he was being asked.

Ball had ended up as interim Liberal leader almost by default in December of 2011 after the disastrous fall general election. The Liberals came in third in the popular vote and barely eked out Official Opposition status thanks to some lucky electoral math. Ball himself only barely beat his Tory opponent, winning by a meagre 68 votes. He'd been an MHA before (barely) when he beat PC candidate Darryl Kelly by an even narrower margin — seven votes! — in a byelection in February of 2007. Ball sat in the House of Assembly briefly in 2007, before he lost the seat eight months later in the general election. But it was probably that brief House experience — and no political baggage — that made him the "natural" choice for interim party leader. Back then the party was in total shambles, and it also looked an awful lot like he was the only one who wanted the job.

In the 18 months on the job as interim leader, Ball's mantra seemed to be: "No unforced errors." He was frequently compared to both Dudley Do-Right and Guy Smiley — partly for his cartoonishly strong chin, but also for his relentless nice-guy persona. He seemed to lack the ability to really go for the jugular, even when Kathy Dunderdale or one of her ministers deserved it. But even if he wasn't scoring big points, he wasn't making any big mistakes either. Ball had been the steady, safe hand on the tiller that had kept the Liberals on the straight and narrow, even as the Tories took a nosedive on the right and the NDP was imploding on the left. It's boring, but it sure as hell beats self-immolation.

He seemed to grow a little bit during the leadership campaign, though. His campaign team came up with a poster with his smiling face in black and white on a burgundy background. He was wearing hipster sunglasses with thick white frames, and in big letters at the bottom it said "DWIGHT ON." It was goofy, but you also had to begrudgingly admit that it was pretty cool. I swiped one of the posters from the campaign table at the convention and took it home with me as a souvenir.

Ball showed a bit more edge during the leadership campaign, too. During one of the early debates, Ball turned to Cathy Bennett and said, "I welcome you to the Liberal Party." It was a small comment, but it was vicious. Under the smiley, big-tent, everybody-is-welcome veneer, Ball was saying to everybody that Bennett was just a Johnny-come-lately who was only running to be leader because with the Tories down in the polls it was the quickest shot at the premier's office. "I've been Liberal a long time, and I welcome people back to this party, but it's fair to ask the question: what makes people a Liberal today?" he said.

During the campaign, Ball racked up endorsements from every sitting MHA.[2] Ball also picked up the support of most federal Liberal MPs. In the end, his pitch essentially boiled down to this: I might not be a superstar politician like Justin Trudeau or Danny Williams, but I haven't screwed things up for the party in the past couple years at the helm, and now we're at first place in the polls. And the people who work with me seem to think I'm the best guy for the job.

The tacit endorsement of the people who work around Ball went well beyond his fellow MHAs. Throughout the campaign there were mutterings that the party structure had rigged the rules in a way that favoured Ball for victory. Moreover, a lot of the staffers who worked in the Liberal caucus office — salaries paid by the taxpayer — were also working on Ball's campaign. Throughout the five months of the leadership race, I received at least a dozen anonymous envelopes or cloak-and-dagger emails from people who accused Ball of using taxpayer-paid staffers on his campaign. One anonymous manila envelope that showed up at my desk appeared to show email chains of staffers using their government email addresses for campaign business. Other documents that came my way included photocopies of airline booking information, purporting to show that a researcher working on that taxpayers' dime was traveling with Ball to campaign stops.

None of the documents contained a smoking gun — the Ball camp insisted that staffers were taking vacation days for any campaign work they did, and there was no proof to the contrary — and none of the other four candidates would do on-the-record interviews calling him out. All of it left a bad taste in the mouths of the candidates and volunteers working to unseat Ball, but it also sent a very clear message: the party fixtures thought that Ball had brought

[2] Well, every MHA except Jim Bennett, who was running as a dark horse in the leadership himself, but would ultimately finish last place in the polling.

them this far, and they weren't interested in switching horses in the middle of the race.

In Ball's hospitality suite sometime past midnight, I fell in to a conversation with a couple of the hardcore senior strategists from the campaign — one from the Ball camp, one from the Bennett campaign.[3]

They were discussing the novel system that the Liberals had adopted to allow voters to cast a preferential ballot, and each electoral district would be given equal weight. Each electoral district would have 100 electoral points, and 2,401 of the 4,800 total points would win it.

"What's your worst case scenario?" Bennett's guy asked.

"1,905 (on the first ballot). Yours?" Ball's guy replied.

"Not as good as that," Bennett's guy conceded.

They both agreed that the X factor in the race was the third serious candidate in the race: Paul Antle. The thinking was that if Antle dropped off first, his supporters would go to Ball because they'd flock to a fellow Liberal instead of Bennett, the perceived Tory pretender. On the other hand, if Bennett was in third place on the first ballot and dropped off, her support might flock to Antle; both of the candidates were St. John's Townies, and both of them were pro-business types. If their supporters coalesced around one candidate as a consensus alternative to Ball, then that might be enough to unseat him.

Bennett's strategist said that wasn't going to happen.

"We'll be second unless everybody lied to Cathy," he said.

● ● ●

Paul Antle and his supporters were nowhere to be seen in all of this. While the other two frontrunners had opted for modest rooms on the second floor of the hotel, Antle booked a sprawling suite on the top floor, with a brass plaque that said "Executive Suite" on the door.

When MP Gerry Byrne entered the room, pining for the old days, he said, "Oh man, if I'd known about this, I would've changed

---

[3] The strategist from Ball's campaign also happened to be a taxpayer-funded staffer in the Liberal caucus office; go figure.

my vote." The wine and the food were more expensive up in Antle's suite, Byrne said. He'd already publicly endorsed Ball months earlier, but Byrne wasn't above drinking the good stuff and getting a decent bite to eat at Antle's expense.

The rumour was that Antle had just thrown money at every aspect of the campaign. Whereas the other two campaigns felt like they were fuelled by volunteers and devotion, Antle's machine seemed to run on cash. His targeted ads showed up in my Facebook feed all throughout the race, and everybody I talked to complained about relentless robo-calls from his campaign. He ended up spending $438,000 on the campaign — a staggering amount of cash for a party leadership race in a province of only half a million people.

But Antle's Liberal bona fides were solid; he'd been involved in the party for years, and he'd run and lost in a federal election a few years earlier. That Liberal cred and a solid campaign was enough to earn him second-place on the first ballot, and 8,178 votes on the final ballot. But Ball solidly trounced him with 59 per cent of the vote compared to 41 per cent for Antle.

• • •

By Sunday afternoon, it was a miracle that anybody was able to get excited at all.

The results were announced late in the afternoon, following speeches by party apparatchiks and an interminable ceremony where the party presented awards to four faithful and devoted members. Party President Judy Morrow even presented an award to a dead member who had been active in the party for decades. "Even at the time of her death, she was still actively signing up supporters for the leadership race," Morrow said. "On the day of her death, 20 membership forms were on her night table, filled out and ready to go. Even in their time of grief, a family member made sure her forms were sent in, because they knew that's what she wanted." Every party has their own version of Marjorie, I guess.

It was all just about filling time. VOCM, NTV and CBC were all doing live broadcasts from the convention, and they needed it to stretch out for at least a couple hours to make it worth their while. With an old style delegated convention, there would be lots of ongoing action — voting, endorsements, and efforts on the floor to change the momentum and lure wavering delegates. The Liberals had none of that, just a bunch of window dressing. In the room, there were little knots of supporters from each of the five leadership camps — Paul Antle's supporters had scarves with the campaign logo on it, Cathy Bennett's people had placards, Dwight Ball's people had Thunderstix, and so on. They dutifully waved their regalia and chanted when the TV cameras were turned on them.

Shortly after the awards wrapped up, Morrow came back out to make the announcement. The two long shots each got less than three per cent of the vote. Danny Dumaresque accepted defeat graciously, and Jim Bennett was bitter. Once the TV cameras left him alone and the mics were turned off, Bennett and his wife claimed to me that there were voting irregularities in Labrador, and if things had gone smoothly up there, Jim would've had at least 10 per cent support on the first ballot.

Cathy Bennett dropped off next, and more than 2,500 of her voters left with her. The ranked ballot meant that if a voter's first-choice candidate dropped off, the person's vote would be transferred to their second- or third-choice. Nearly half of Bennett's voters ranked her first, and listed nobody else as a second choice. They came to the Liberals for her, and when she was done, they were done too.

But after spending $255,000 of her own money in the race — along with campaign contributions totaling $156,000 — Cathy Bennett had done a valuable thing. She'd convinced everyone that she was a Liberal. On Sunday afternoon there was a lot of talk about her commitment to run for the party in 2015, and the general consensus was that she'd be a solid senior cabinet minister in a new Liberal government. Not bad for somebody who was an undercover Progressive Conservative in the minds of a lot of Liberal voters just a few weeks earlier.

Antle dropped last, and was diplomatic in defeat.

"Quite obviously, the choice was made by Liberals that they want Dwight as their leader, and I respect their choice," he told journalists in the convention hall. "We didn't leave any stone unturned, no phone call left unattended. We did everything we needed to do. I just think Liberals were very comfortable with Dwight. They were very comfortable with his performance over the last number of years, and I respect the outcome."

•••

Ball's victory speech was a culmination of his safe and steady political style. He thanked his supporters. He thanked his mom. He thanked the voters. And then, he delivered his big pitch: "I was incredibly inspired by my many conversations with thousands of people as I traveled the province — listening to their concerns, understanding their issues, sharing their hopes and dreams for a better Newfoundland and Labrador. This campaign has revealed a great thirst for change. People want democracy restored; they want honesty, accountability, integrity."

"My friends, the future of Newfoundland and Labrador is bright. We have the resources of a country contained in our province, and while we have challenges, we also have the wherewithal and the confidence to meet those challenges. The only thing standing in our way is a tired, arrogant government that has lost its way and forgotten who it works for."

A decade earlier, the PCs swept to power by convincing people that things were awful in Newfoundland and Labrador, and that the Liberal Party was driving things into the ground. Since then, the Liberals had been trying to do essentially the same trick. It hadn't worked. The Tories just weren't destroying things. During their 10 years in office, the price of oil went from around $30 per barrel to more than $100, and the Newfoundland and Labrador economy was booming. It's awfully hard to convince people that everything is going to hell when taxes are lower, government services are just as good, there are jobs aplenty and your house has doubled in value.[4] But despite it all, the Tories were looking long in the tooth, and the voters were turning on them. Scandals were catching up with them. They were seen as secretive, entitled and imperious.

---

[4] All of this was true in 2013, anyway.

With that in mind, Ball made a modest promise. He told people that he'd be a competent manager too, but he'd try to be a little bit more likeable doing it. All weekend, Ball had been the acknowledged favourite. For five months he'd been the steady frontrunner. For nearly two years, he'd been the slow-and-steady climber. Nothing spectacular. Just boring Mr. Nice Guy, and no unforced errors. Ball left the Liberal leadership convention with two years ahead of him to prove that "no unforced errors" could be enough to take him all the way to the premier's office.

"The truth about politics is that most of us really want the same thing. We want good health care. We want supports for our seniors. We want schools that encourage and enrich our children. We want safe roads, and an economy that sustains jobs. And we want the people that we elect to treat us with respect, manage our finances responsibly and be open and accountable."

Ball wrapped up with a call to party members to get organized and get ready for the 2015 election. He did media interviews. He didn't say anything remarkable. Nothing exciting at all.

CHAPTER 4
SECRECY

"As there was a feeling among the public that the city was far too secretive in its deliberations, I and my supporters devised the slogan 'You have a right to know,' which struck a very responsive chord. This is always a good campaign slogan: *You have a right to know*. Of course, I made a point after I got elected to try to make sure the public didn't know everything, but the slogan was a good one. *You have the right to know*. I recommend it. It fits almost anyone and any campaign, any time, anywhere!"

- John Crosbie, *No Holds Barred*, referring to his first run for political office in 1965

On that Sunday afternoon in November at the Liberal leadership convention when he took the reins of the party, Dwight Ball only mentioned one single, solitary policy idea in his victory speech. Amid the rhetoric and political platitudes, Ball only promised to actually *do* one thing if he won the next election and got his hands on the levers of power.

"The people of Newfoundland and Labrador are tired of being told what to think. They're tired of being told that they don't have a right to know what's going on inside their own government. That's why, my friends, the first order of business for the new Liberal government will be to repeal Bill 29," Ball shouted, and then he had to pause and wait for the applause and cheering to die down.

"This is the first day in ending the arrogance and restoring accountability. We will repeal Bill 29 and clean the dust of secrecy from government and all its institutions, including Nalcor Energy. A Liberal government will be open and will be accountable. A Liberal government will put the interests of people first."

The next afternoon, his first day in the House of Assembly wearing the mantle of *permanent* Leader of the Official Opposition, Ball drove the point home.

"Last year, this government passed the most secretive bill that this House has ever seen. Bill 29 has given this government and cabinet sweeping powers to hide information from the public," he said. "So I ask the Premier: Will you repeal Bill 29, and initiate a process of public consultation sessions on how our new protection of privacy laws should look?"

The answer from Dunderdale, of course, was a fairly emphatic no.

• • •

None of this was uncharted territory for Ball. He'd been banging the drum about repealing Bill 29 for the past year and a half. I mean, why wouldn't he keep pressing the issue, now that he was permanent leader of the party? Apparently it was working for him.

He was still suffering under the "interim-" prefix at the time, but he can rightfully claim that back in the spring of 2012 he led the fight against Bill 29 in the House of Assembly. It was the Liberals who were running the show during the four-day filibuster, right up until the whole thing ground to a halt amid accusations of racism in the legislature.

I was actually unwittingly roped into the 2012 brouhaha. I was sitting up in the press gallery posting live web updates on the late night debate when then-justice minister Felix Collins gave a speech that definitely felt to me like it was drifting into racist territory. All evening, members of the opposition had been citing a CBC news story that said the new law would make Newfoundland and Labrador's access to information law on par with Uganda and Moldova. Collins sneered and recoiled at the very notion that Newfoundland and Labrador could possibly be compared to "Mexico, Ethiopia, Nicaragua, Bulgaria, Uganda, Moldova, and Guatemala, countries where atrocities are every day, people kill women and children, where human rights atrocities are happening all the time." It would likely come as a surprise to the people of Bulgaria, for example, a European Union country and a member of NATO, that they're now relegated to the status of third-world hellhole by Collins, what with the atrocities and the children being killed every day. "I can only assume that the Liberals and the NDP equate Newfoundland and Labrador with Third World countries," he said in the legislature.

It's hard to capture the tone of his voice in printed quotations, but it definitely felt to me like he was balking at the very notion that anybody would suggest that any African or Latin American country could possibly be better than Newfoundland and Labrador on anything. Lorraine Michael called him on it, saying that his comments seemed to be racist. "I am in a state, first of all, of embarrassment to be standing in a legislature where a Minister of Justice and the Solicitor General has made the comments that have been made about other countries. I cannot believe that we are sitting in a legislature where we have actually seen the essence, and I am going to say it, racism. ... Mexico is a democracy. Mexico is a country that we have a trade deal with, for God's sake. What is going on in this legislature? I cannot believe what is going on. I am so angry right now. You thought you have seen me angry in the past, this is real anger."

Then all hell broke loose. Government House Leader Jerome Kennedy accused Michael of using unparliamentary language — verboten under the legislature's rules — and asked her to apologize. "Reasonable people can disagree on legislation, Mr. Chair, but to call a member of the Crown racist is simply not appropriate," he said.

This is the part where I got roped into it. Michael said the comments were racist. Kennedy said she called Collins a racist. Kennedy's trump card was the web updates I'd been posting on Twitter. I'd tweeted, "Lorraine Michael calling Felix Collins racist right now. Taking offense on behalf of Mexico, Uganda and other countries," and then a moment later, "Lorraine Michael is going NUTS. She is flipping out. Saying Collins' comments were racist."

On the floor of the legislature, Kennedy was on his feet, taking Michael to task and waving his Blackberry in the air and referring to me by my Twitter username. "I can quote from TelegramJames saying, 'Collins' comments were racist.' He is up there listening."

Up in the press gallery, I was cringing. I'd been paraphrasing debate, not posting direct quotes, and I was pretty sure that Michael hadn't come right out and called Collins a racist. "They're going to check against the record," I tweeted. "The chair (correctly) notes that Hansard, not TelegramJames, is the official record."

After a recess to cool things down, Speaker Ross Wiseman made his ruling: "We have considered the comments and the ruling is that the comments in reference to the commentary made by the Minister of Justice and Attorney General I have deemed to be un-parliamentary. I would ask the Leader of the Third Party to apologize for her comments."

Personally, I think this is a total disgrace. Whether Collins' comments were racist or not is a matter of opinion. But according to Wiseman's ruling, you can make potentially racist comments in the legislature, and that's acceptable. On the other hand, speaking up to call somebody out on offensive remarks can get you formally sanctioned. The fact that accusing somebody of saying something racist is considered a more serious offence than actual racist commentary is something that people should really stop and think about.

Anyway, the racism thing gave Kennedy the cover to shut down debate, and ram Bill 29 through the legislature. "We had every intention of allowing this debate to go to its fullest," he said, following Wiseman's ruling. "In light of the way this has deteriorated in the last little while and the fact that racist comments were just made,[1] Mr. Chair, I give notice that I will on tomorrow move, pursuant to Standing Order 47, [closure of debate]."

The next night around 1:30 a.m. debate came to a close and the bill passed. The debate had lasted close to 70 hours with virtually no interruption. In the foyer of the legislature, a small cluster of journalists interviewed Kennedy, Ball and Michael on how it all went.

Back then, Ball wasn't very good at talking to the media, and he tended to give long, rambling answers. I've reprinted the full response he gave when a reporter asked him what the effects of the new law would be, just to give a sense of how bad he was back then:

"Typically when you get governments that are — governments for a third term, in this particular case — you know, it's quite often that you see them not wanting to be as open. So when that happens,

[1] This quote is correct. I triple-checked in Hansard, the official transcript of what's said in the House of Assembly. Either this is a Freudian slip, and Kennedy admitted that what Collins said actually *was* racist after just denying it, or Kennedy misspoke, probably due to exhaustion after an epic round-the-clock filibuster. Judge for yourself.

of course, it leads to waste. It leads to government not being as accountable to the people and there's no question, we're going to see a lot more of that, I believe. When you have those checks and balances in place, and when you know that there's someone there watching, I guess, watching what's happening, and then to know that some of that information if an application comes you have to go through the due diligence, I do think it'll become much looser."

But even if he couldn't deliver a concise, declarative comment about the law, behind the scenes the Liberals recognized the political opportunity. Within hours, the Liberals issued a news release headlined, "Bill 29: A National Embarrassment" and a subheading that read, "Liberals vow to repeal Bill 29 if elected in 2015." A year and a half later, the same vow would be the climax of Ball's leadership victory speech.

• • •

Here's the thing about government secrecy and access to information: I've never met a Newfoundland and Labrador politician who really convinced me that they honestly believe the public has a right to know anything.

Sometimes, people in power believe that it'll be beneficial to put some information out there. Most of the time, politicians just figure that it'll be politically damaging if they act too secretive.[2] But personally, I've never talked to a politician who acted like the public has a right to know what the government is doing *as a matter of principle* — whether the information is politically damaging or not. The people I've dealt with — in all three political parties, as well as the federal crowd and the part-timers down at City Hall — all look at access to information as a strategic calculation. It isn't just a matter for elected politicians, either. No one is more thoroughly motivated to enforce government secrecy policies than the middle- and senior-management bureaucrats who have to carry out the orders of their political masters.

A perfect example of this attitude comes from the Royal Newfoundland Constabulary, who treat the public's right to know with

---

[2] Which, incidentally, is exactly what happened in the case of Bill 29.

thinly veiled contempt. Whenever there's a hit-and-run in St. John's, and the cops need help cracking the case, they fire off a news release to every journalist on their email list with "RNC Seek Public Assistance…" in the subject line. They're just as quick to trumpet their successes, when they nab a drunk driver or make a big drug bust. But when there was a prison riot and hostage situation at Her Majesty's Penitentiary in St. John's, the tone was different. RNC Constable Talia Murphy told reporters that it was an "institutional disturbance" at the prison. She wouldn't confirm that there was a hostage situation.[3] When I asked Murphy what exactly she meant when she said it was an "institutional disturbance," she looked me dead in the eye and said, "It was a disturbance which occurred inside the institution." The guards can lose control of part of the prison in the middle of St. John's, the cops can spend several hours negotiating with the rioters who have taken a hostage, the tactical unit of the RNC can go into the place with guns drawn, and the following morning, the spokeswoman for the force feels no obligation whatsoever to tell the public what happened, except to say it was an "institutional disturbance."

The same mentality infects the provincial government, and all three political parties. When the NDP caucus wrote a letter to Lorraine Michael, and the letter ended up in the hands of journalists, many New Democrats said the mortal sin was putting the whole thing down on paper. Never mind that when people are considering how to cast their vote in the next election, they might have a legitimate interest in knowing that no one in the party's caucus has full confidence in the leader. No, the real lesson here is that if you don't put it in writing, then you stand a better chance of keeping it secret.

There are a lot of documents in the government's possession that are kept secret — and rightly so. Nobody is clamouring for disclosure of hospital patients' private medical records, and I've never heard anybody argue that judges' trial notes should be available to the public. Even some of the more controversial access to

---

[3] Two months later, when the cops laid charges, they alleged that hostage taking was one of the crimes involved.

information exceptions generally have consensus support, at least in theory. As a journalist, I can respect the need to withhold certain commercially sensitive information when the provincial government is working with private companies, and I'm inclined to believe that the cabinet should be able to hold their deliberations in secret.

At first blush, the controversy appears to come in the nuances, and where you draw the line. I personally believe the actual substance of cabinet deliberations should be kept secret. I can understand why the government might want to extend that secrecy to all of the briefing materials expressly drafted to inform cabinet deliberations. But then there's the wildly broad provisions of Bill 29, which included any document which was used as source material for developing a cabinet paper. Similarly, Bill 29 allowed the government to withhold any documents which contain "consultations or deliberations involving officers or employees of a public body" — which is to say, they can keep basically anything they want secret. At least on the surface, the government secrecy debate is about the Progressive Conservatives insanely overreaching in order to cover their own asses and keep the public in the dark.

But that's not really what it's all about. Stop for a minute and think about the government's infamous ability in Bill 29 to dismiss "frivolous and vexatious" requests for information. That's actually a pretty sensible clause to have in an access to information law. For five bucks, anybody could make an access to information request. So, for $70, I could file access to information requests for every email sent and received by the premier and each of the 14 members of cabinet. For an even $100 I could make 20 requests, and include all the parliamentary secretaries as well. Throw in another five bucks, and I could request all of Speaker Ross Wiseman's emails for the past year.

Now, 99 per cent of these emails would be covered by one of half a dozen different completely legitimate exceptions to the access to information law — these are ministers of the crown who are dealing with sensitive information. But a small legion of government bureaucrats would be obligated to round up all the emails, go through them, read them all and provide an estimate on how much it would cost to redact all of the stuff that needs redacting in order to fill the request. That work could easily cost tens of thousands of dollars, when you consider the salaries of those bureaucrats charged with filling the requests. But I'd only be obligated to actually pay all that money once the work was done. So for about a hundred bucks, I could initiate a process that drains thousands of dollars in taxpayer resources, and then walk away without a care in the world. Two weeks later, for another hundred bucks, I could do it all again.

This is an imaginary circumstance, but talking to cabinet ministers privately, they have anecdotal stories that are just as silly. It makes sense to have a clause in the law that says if somebody consistently abuses the system, then the system can tell him to buzz off. It's a common sense clause, and I think a lot more people would be willing to see it that way, except for one critical problem: nobody trusts the government to use it in a common sense way.

I sure as hell don't trust the government. I've run up against too many bureaucrats who see almost no reason to release information, but they see all sorts of reasons to hold it back. As far as the bureaucracy is concerned, the public should only be informed by carefully-worded, on-message news releases. Any other documents must be withheld for a myriad of reasons — personal privacy, commercially sensitive information, cabinet secrecy, because the public won't understand the issue, because the public will understand the issue perfectly and they'll be very mad about the whole affair, et cetera. That's the thing about access to information: unless you really truly believe in the *principle* that the public has the right to the unvarnished facts, then there are all sorts of reasons to keep things secret, and precious few reasons to make things public. And like I said before, I've never met a Newfoundland and Labrador politician who really convinced me — on principle — that they believe the public has a right to know anything.

• • •

Dwight Ball sure talks a good game, but in the moment of truth he folded like a cheap suit. I have no doubt that as an opposition leader, when his caucus researchers kept getting their access to information requests rejected; he sincerely wanted Bill 29 repealed.

For that matter, I'm inclined to believe that he actually planned to repeal Bill 29 if he ever became premier.[4] But when it comes to the all-important *principle* of transparency, he faced the test on the day after he was elected leader of the Liberal Party, and he failed.

The Liberals didn't put any sort of financial limits in place for the leadership campaign, and Ball spent more than $300,000 during the race. A significant chunk of that came from donations. Partway through the campaign, when I went to him and asked him who was donating to his campaign, he wouldn't tell me. Suddenly, it wasn't about sweeping away the "dust of secrecy" as he put it in his victory speech. Suddenly it was hand-wringing, evasions, and a whole litany of reasons why he couldn't disclose the names of people who were giving him cash.

It wasn't really his fault, he said, the party put the rules in place and he had to live by them. It wasn't really the party's fault even, he said, because those bastards in the PC Party hadn't included leadership races in the elections act. It wasn't really a big deal, he said, because he would release the amounts of each individual donation, just not the name of which individual or corporation it came from. It's not really a matter of public interest, he said, because it's not covered under the Elections Act and therefore nobody is getting a tax credit for donating to him; if there's no public money involved, he said, then it doesn't matter who's writing cheques to help finance his political ambitions.

All of these justifications are bogus, in my estimation. There were no rules preventing Ball from posting a full list of his donors online. By blaming the party or the Elections Act, he was only saying that he wasn't being *forced* to disclose the list. Even if the rules didn't force him to do it, he could've told the public who was giving him money just because he thought it was the right thing to do. As for disclosing the individual donation amounts, well, Newfoundland and Labrador has examples in its recent political history of corporations or individuals giving a raft of small donations just to get around the rules. The tax credit? Utterly irrelevant. People

---

[4] We'll never know, though; the Tories beat him to it in 2015, just months before the general election.

don't want to know who's donating to a politician because the donors are getting a tax credit; they want to know who's donating to a politician because they want to judge if the person they're voting for has been bought.

The day after he won the leadership campaign, I sat down for an interview with him in his office, and he acknowledged that disclosing the names of his donors was the right thing to do. But in the same breath, he made it clear that he wasn't going to do it. "When you go looking for money from donors, I think the right thing to do is to let them know that the names would be disclosed through a full disclosure, and I think that's fair, and I think that's part of being open and transparent. That wasn't part of this campaign, and it's something that I think the Liberal Party needs to look at."

In that statement, his principles were on full display: protect the people who give you money. As for the principle of the public's right to know? Well, only if the donors say it's OK.

I'm singling out Ball here, but only because he's built his political brand on openness, transparency and accountability. I don't think he's any worse than any other politician in Newfoundland and Labrador. They're all like this. But that just means that they demand squeaky clean behaviour and high-minded, principled motivations from their opponents, but when it comes to their own conduct, they'll do whatever they think they can get away with. If Ball really, truly believed in the principle that the public has the right to know, then he could've held himself to a higher standard. He could've said from Day 1 that he would disclose all of the names of people who donated to his campaign, but then he probably wouldn't have pulled in as much cash from donations.

Runner-up Paul Antle did the partial disclosure thing — essentially exactly what Ball had originally promised to do. In total he spent $438,000, which was enough to buy him second place in the leadership race. Most of it was his own money, but Antle took in $163,650 from donors, including eight different $10,000 donations from corporations. The public doesn't know who those companies are. Antle said he started calling up companies and asking if he could publicly disclose that they'd given him money. "I have gone back to some of the corporate donors and asked them, and they said no," Antle said. "They said there was no requirement for disclosure, there was no tax receipt, and it's over, so we'd just prefer to remain anonymous."[5]

About a month after it was over, Ball released a nearly-complete list of the people who had given him money during the campaign. The single biggest donor to Dwight Ball's leadership campaign was Dwight Ball himself. He poured more than $200,000 of his own money into the race, but he'd also managed to raise around $90,000 from private donors. His finance people had gone back to each donor and asked for permission to disclose their name and how much they'd given. A total of 114 people who gave a combined total of $78,384 said yes. An undisclosed number of people said no, and so Ball wrote a cheque for $11,000 to repay those people. That way he could claim he'd fully disclosed the names of all of the people who contributed to his campaign.

In the weeks following the Liberal leadership convention, as people demanded to know about the campaign contributions, Ball was begging journalists for more time. He said that he'd offer up more information soon, but he still needed to finalize the paperwork. Oh, and after the campaign his finance chief went on vacation, so that was slowing things down too. Please, he said, I'll be open and transparent eventually — just not quite yet. All the while Tory politicians were gleefully sniping at him about it. In public, the Liberals did their best to brush it off, but in private they were getting awfully prickly about it. Then, when he couldn't get everyone to agree to public disclosure, Ball paid $11,000 out of his own pocket to make a political problem go away. Ball knows who gave him the $11,000 in repaid contributions, but in all likelihood, the public never will.

In the end, Ball appears to believe in the same principles that drive most politicians: expediency and winning.

The principles of transparency and accountability are only really useful when you're demanding that they should be applied to somebody else.

---

[5] It's worth noting that nearly all of Ball's donors said yes, and most of Antle's said no. That should tell you everything you need to know about the value of backing the winner in politics.

CHAPTER 5
THE BEGINNING OF THE END
DECEMBER, 2013

I started covering politics full-time in January of 2011, the same month that Kathy Dunderdale secured the PC Party leadership. I covered her just about as closely as any journalist in the province. I did more one-on-one interviews with her than I can count. Once, I played a game of cards with her in the premier's office on the eighth floor of the Confederation Building.[1] A couple times, I sat on Dunderdale's campaign bus during the 2011 election and chatted with her during quiet moments while we were rolling down the highway. And, at the risk of sounding immodest, I was one of the journalists (partly) responsible for dragging her party to the bottom of the polls, and bringing her political career to an end.

So I hope I've got a bit of authority when I say this: Kathy Dunderdale is a good person, and an impressive individual. But she was also a flawed politician, and she should never have been premier of the province.

I still don't have a firm accounting of the backroom deals and jockeying that happened within the PC Party after Danny Williams surprised everyone and quit in the fall of 2010. One moment she was interim premier, and promising not to run for the permanent job. The next moment she was reconsidering, and all of the other perceived frontrunners were emerging to endorse her. At the time, Dunderdale was seen as a capable lieutenant — solid senior management, and an inoffensive choice for interim premier. She'd held senior portfolios within the Williams government, but I never really heard her name tossed around as a serious contender to fill Danny's shoes. And then, all of a sudden, she was head honcho, and everyone had to get used to the sound of saying "Premier Kathy Dunderdale."

Nine months later, she ran a safe, take-no-chances election campaign, roundly defeating the Liberals who were in utter shambles, and the New Democrats who weren't much better. On that

---

[1] When I walked into her office for the game, the first thing she said to me was, "I'm gonna kick your ass!"

campaign, she spent a lot of time visiting schools. They couldn't cast a ballot for her, but she seemed to draw energy from the kids. I always got the feeling that they were the ones she was really trying to work for. The infrastructure projects, the focus on new schools and more affordable university tuition, the Muskrat Falls project — it all fed into that. She wasn't working to make Newfoundland and Labrador better today or tomorrow; she was working to make things better a generation from now. Every politician has a big ego — Dunderdale included — but I never really got the sense that it was personal glorification that was driving her. Whatever backroom gentleman's agreement among potential leadership contenders put her in the premier's office, once she was there, she got a taste of the power, and decided that she could use it for good, for the long-term.

She was a bit of a health nut. She loved to exercise — especially running. If you got her talking about her diet — no refined sugar or processed foods — or her running regime, she could keep you talking for hours. I was once drawn into a conversation with her and a couple other people in the hallway outside the legislature, where she was giving a rundown of all the details of her exercise regime. "And if I don't have a great ass by June, I swear to God!" she exclaimed.

● ● ●

Election night, October 11, 2011, was probably the high-water mark for her whole tenure as premier. It was all downhill from there. There were signs of trouble before October, of course, but it was easy to shrug those off as minor hiccups — just bumps in the road as she got comfortable in the premier's office. Everybody knew Danny Williams would be a tough act to follow. He was arguably the most charismatic premier Newfoundland and Labrador had ever seen. Nobody expected her to live up to that. But nobody expected Dunderadale to pick a public fight with the political demigod in the months after she took over. She snubbed Williams by not inviting him to the spring Throne Speech, and then he retaliated by refusing to show up to a tribute dinner organized in his honour, on the weekend of Dunderdale's coronation as the new leader of the

PC Party. She was weak on her feet in the legislature too, and just generally underwhelming. The government passed a ho-hum budget. Her poll numbers were generally flat, or slowly sinking, but nobody thought too much of it, because nobody expected the public support to stay at the stratospheric levels that Danny enjoyed. She coasted to an easy election win.

The election win was the most historically significant thing that Dunderdale would ever do. She was the first woman ever to hold the job, and she proved that she was more than just a party appointee. She shattered the glass ceiling for women in Newfoundland and Labrador politics, and proved that it wasn't just the boys who could play at the very highest levels of the game.

Dunderdale never shoved it in your face, but she's a fierce feminist. Before going into politics, she was involved in the Advisory Council on the Status of Women, and the Women in Resource Development Committee. As minister of Natural Resources, she was instrumental in pushing gender-based employment targets into big natural resources benefits agreements. Because of her, many women were able to get good, high-paying jobs in the skilled trades, and break into the traditionally male-dominated world of industrial fabrication and natural resource development. In speeches, she liked to mention how mining companies at first hired women because they were forced to, but then they noticed that the girls weren't as hard on the equipment as the boys were. Big, million-dollar pieces of heavy equipment needed less maintenance and fewer repairs when a woman was driving it, she said, and the mining companies learned that hiring ladies was something worth doing because it made good economic sense.

Symbolically, Dunderdale made history as the first woman to be premier. But she also made a lot of other moves, less visibly, to promote women in public life. She organized a conference in St. John's while she was premier to celebrate women. Again, it felt like she had the long view in mind. Sure, she wanted to make life better for women in the province today. But she always seemed keenly aware of her position in history, and the real goal was to empower women a generation into the future. When she finally said goodbye to politics, her farewell speech was peppered with references to women's issues: "In concluding, I want to recall the many women who could neither vote, nor run for office, who did not let that stop them from working tirelessly so women like me could vote, run, serve and lead. Let us give them the ovation they deserve. I, in turn, have derived enormous satisfaction from working to clear paths of opportunity for others. As the first woman to serve as premier, I hope I have stoked the fires of imagination in young girls in our province, and inspired them to consider running for public office. For the sake of our province and everything we aspire to collectively achieve, let us continue to teach our children there is no greater honour than to serve others. Let us teach them to take ownership of the challenges they see, and step forward to make a difference whenever they can."

She was in politics for the right reasons.

• • •

It's just a shame that she wasn't a very good politician. She was a good negotiator, it seems, but she did all her deals quietly, behind closed doors, without the kinds of righteous stands that boost polling numbers. She managed to wrestle a loan guarantee for the Muskrat Falls hydroelectric project from Prime Minister Stephen Harper — worth more than a billion dollars — despite years of mutual contempt between Newfoundland and Labrador and the federal Conservative government. Her government replaced ferries, built new schools, expanded services and cut taxes, all fuelled by economic prosperity and natural resource developments[2] — some of which she was personally involved in negotiating during her tenure as Natural Resources Minister before she became premier.

Her government signed a deal with the public sector unions where she held them to a five per cent raise over four years — less than inflation — which was a damn good outcome for the provincial treasury. But it came after a months-long, union-funded ad campaign attacking the government and sowing public discontent. Similarly, the Muskrat Falls loan guarantee was, on its own, an achievement. But the overall Muskrat Falls project never enjoyed

[2] Oil, basically. A little bit of a bunch of other things, but mostly oil.

much public enthusiasm, so the loan guarantee didn't really get people fired up. It went like that with all of her big wins: White Rose West,[3] Voisey's Bay expansion,[4] the fisheries provisions in the CETA free trade deal[5] and the provincial budgets[6] she helped to craft. It was never the good stuff that really resonated with the public.

The bad stuff, on the other hand, always seemed to get traction. And every time the government was confronted with a major political problem, Dunderdale and her ministers managed to make a bad situation worse. The most damaging scandals were the ones that were totally self-inflicted.

Nobody could blame Dunderdale directly for Burton Winters, the 14-year-old boy who died after getting lost on the sea ice off Makkovik in February of 2012. But when she brushed aside the need for a public inquiry into his death, she found herself on the wrong side of the issue. When she refused to meet with the boy's grandmother, she came across as heartless.

Similarly, Muskrat Falls wasn't a burning issue in the minds of most voters, but when Dunderdale's government tried to prevent the province's independent energy regulator, the Public Utilities Board, from studying the issue, it just seemed like they were rushing things through without proper scrutiny. Then the government backed down, and referred the project to the PUB anyway, but they set such a narrow reference question and tight timelines that it looked like the Tories were trying to rig the process and get a quick rubber stamp on the project. None of it did much to inspire public confidence. If you're 100 per cent confident that Muskrat Falls is a great development, why not let the independent regulator kick the tires and check under the hood? Around the same time, with an arrogance that came to define the Tory government, then-natural resources minister Jerome Kennedy famously dismissed the notion of a Muskrat Falls debate in the legislature. He said the opposition

---

[3] Since deferred due to a drop in oil prices.
[4] Hasn't happened as of the publishing deadline for this book, but it's looking promising.
[5] This one turned out to be sort of a train wreck. I'll deal with it in depth in a subsequent chapter.
[6] Ditto.

parties were so useless, they couldn't even ask valid questions. "The problem right now is that I'm not sure these opposition parties are going to provide quality debate on anything," Kennedy said in an interview with the CBC.

Close on the heels of the Muskrat Falls/PUB situation, the Tories introduced Bill 29 into the legislature, with the infamous "frivolous and vexatious" clause. That phrase came to symbolize the government's perceived attitude towards public opinion: Disagree with us? Your concerns are just frivolous and vexatious.

In the winter of 2013, *The Telegram* reported on leaked Blackberry messages that showed backbench MHA Paul Lane was orchestrating an effort to co-ordinate staffers and party supporters to rig news websites' online public opinion polls. The PC Party apparently wanted people to believe that their policies were popular, and they were so obsessed with it that they'd go to great lengths just to rig a stupid news website poll. When asked about the controversy, Dunderdale scoffed and said, "There's no story here."

That spring, Dunderdale was getting death threats. Jerome Kennedy, now shuffled into the role of Finance Minister, delivered a budget which laid off nearly a thousand civil servants and slashed provincial government spending. People were pissed. A Facebook group called "Kathy Dunderdale must GO!!!" became a space for people to vent about the cuts and Dunderdale's government in general. One commenter mused about Dunderdale being assassinated. Instead of playing the situation for sympathy, Government House Leader Darin King went on the attack and tried to get New Democrat politician Gerry Rogers thrown out of the legislature for being a member of the group. Rogers pointed out — to no avail — that she was unaware that she'd even been added to the Facebook group, and had never seen the offending comments. Doesn't matter, King said. By being a member of the group you're tacitly endorsing the death threats; you are responsible for any and all online associations, even the ones you aren't aware of. It went from bad to worse when the CBC scrutinized the social media accounts of several Progressive Conservative politicians, and found that Dunderdale was following "texasangel," a pornographic account that promotes x-rated videos on Twitter. Instead of admitting that she was wrong, Dunderdale torched her Twitter account and doubled down on the message that Rogers should be thrown out of the House of Assembly. The fact that King — who was also the justice minister — was effectively using guilt by association to convict somebody, without any sort of due process, was particularly chilling. On a more basic level though, it just looked like the Tories didn't know how Facebook worked.

On issue after issue, Dunderdale came across as imperious and haughty. "There's no story here" and "frivolous and vexatious" came to epitomize the way she responded to public criticism. She knew what was best, and if anybody disagreed with her, their opinions were brushed aside.

• • •

By September of 2013, when the Tories met at their convention in Gander, things were bad. By December, things had gone from bad to downright ugly. In the minds of most political watchers, it wasn't a question of *if* Dunderdale would resign, just a matter of when. Despite the NDP implosion, and a big flashy announcement about the Muskrat Falls project, the poll numbers for the Progressive Conservatives were just as lousy as ever.

A sense of bunker mentality was setting in, and you could feel it just by going to see Dunderdale in her office. I saw it first hand when I arrived at the Confederation Building for the traditional year-end interview.

To get to Dunderdale's office, the first thing you had to do is sign in at the security desk in the lobby of the Confederation Building. For routine visits to more mundane parts of the building, a simple signature in the logbook and a sticky "VISITOR" badge is enough. But to get to Dunderdale, security had to call up to the fourth floor offices and make sure you were expected. Then a guard needed to escort you into the elevator, swipe a pass card and punch in the floor number. Without proper clearance, you weren't even allowed to be on the same floor as Dunderdale.

When you arrived at the fourth floor, the elevator doors opened to reveal an eerily empty lobby. The lighting was warm and not too bright. There was a reception desk, but nobody sitting behind it.

For a second, you worry that security punched in the wrong floor. Across from the elevator, there was a locked door. Beside the door, a little grey console was mounted to the wall, with a speaker and a camera and a button. You pressed the button, and whoever was on the other end of the camera unlocked the door and buzzed you through.

On the other side of the door, there was a nondescript hallway and — oh you can't be serious! — another locked door. This door was identical to the last one, complete with another little grey console, another speaker, another camera and another button. For some reason, beyond the first two sets of locked doors and the locked down elevator and the security guards, there was actually a third set of locked doors on the way to Dunderdale's personal office, but after you've made it through all the other barriers, that last set of locked doors was a breeze. I'm sure the security analyst who installed it all had perfectly sensible reasons for each of these measures, but was unsettling to wade your way through it. This is Newfoundland, where a lot of people still don't lock their doors at night, and bumping into the premier at the grocery store is totally normal.

Dunderdale scoffed when she was accused of operating with a bunker mentality and an obsessive level of government secrecy. But during her final days in office, she sat in her office behind three sets of locked doors.

Once you're on the inside, it's all very comfortable. The person manning all the cameras is a middle aged lady — also named Kathy — who's got Open Line on in the background, and is happy to gossip about what's going on in the news. She says she sometimes gets phone calls from people who just start the conversation by saying "Is that you, Kathy?" Even in 2013, apparently, there were people who seem to think they can pick up the phone, call the premier's office, and the premier will be the one who answers. Kathy, the receptionist, said sometimes she'll just say, "Yes, this is Kathy," and the callers would spend a few minutes talking about how great she is, and how she's doing such good work for the province before they realize that it's not Dunderdale on the line. If there are any angry callers who don't think Kathy is so great, the receptionist doesn't mention them.

Before I finally got to sit down and do the interview, Dunderdale's director of communications warned me that if the premier seemed a bit "off," it was only because I was the fourth year-end interview she's done that day. The interview was supposed to start at 1:30 p.m. but Dunderdale wasn't even in the building until after 2 o'clock. The last interview down at the CBC ran long. When I finally followed Dunderdale into her office, she collapsed into a chair, and invited me to take a seat on the nearby couch.

She looked exhausted.

Earlier in the day, she told my colleague, CBC politics reporter David Cochrane, that she no longer read the newspaper, watched the TV, listened to the radio, or consumed local news in any form. She found it all too negative. She left it to her staff to brief her on what she needed to know.

I sat there and thought: honestly, I don't know why she hasn't quit already.

It had been a brutal two years for her, since election night. At a certain point, why stick it out? Why get your arms and legs torn off in public? Why not step aside and let somebody else take the pummelling for a while? Stubbornness? Did she really think that things could turn around? Was she just waiting for a time to exit gracefully?

I'm pretty sure she knew it was a lie when she looked me in the eye and told me she wasn't planning on quitting.

"Yes, I am going to be here," she said, claiming that she was planning on running in the next election.

One of the tough things about journalism is that we can't *force* people to tell the truth, and we can't always tell when they're holding back. It's not like I'm allowed to hook politicians up to a polygraph or waterboard them. I knew she wasn't being honest, but I really didn't have any choice but to sit there with a slightly incredulous look on my face. I'd love to know what Dunderdale was thinking that day in December. I wish I could get an honest answer — at least now that it's all over — about what she was planning.[7]

---

[7] A few months before this book was finished, I requested an interview with her. She declined, as she is perfectly entitled to do.

Was she still in denial? Did she know that she was getting ready to go, but just couldn't afford to say so publicly yet? Was it just an automatic response, at that point, after so many dogged questions about her political future?

Whatever the answer was, roughly one month later, Dunderdale would be standing in the lobby of the Confederation Building, reading her resignation speech. But before she got there, Dunderdale would have to slog through January, the worst month of her entire political career.

CHAPTER 6
POWER CRISIS
JANUARY 4, 2014

On Saturday morning, just after 9 a.m., the lights went off across Newfoundland.

Outside my bedroom window, the wind was howling and snow was coming down. My old St. John's house had shoddy windows and bad insulation. The room was cold. I decided it wasn't worth getting out of bed just yet, and like thousands of other Newfoundlanders, I reached for my cell phone.

Almost immediately, it was clear that this blackout was different. For a couple of days already, the province had been coping with rolling blackouts. This time, though, basically the entire island of Newfoundland was dark. Something big had gone wrong.

Oh well, I thought, it's warmer here in bed than it is out there. I rolled over and went back to sleep.

After a couple hours, the novelty started to wear off, and I had to stop making caustic jokes on Twitter because my phone ran out of power. I sat in my poorly-insulated living room, reading a book while wearing two pairs of socks and two sweaters, wrapped in a blanket, shivering. I fumbled to get a candle lit in my kitchen, and then made myself a sandwich for dinner. The stacks of canned soup in my pantry seemed like a brilliant stockpile of non-perishable food, but without a working stove to heat it up, the soup wasn't terribly appetizing.

"Goddamn bastards," I muttered to myself, and laughed.

For three years, I'd been writing stories about the province's electricity system, and the massive Muskrat Falls hydroelectric project. I'd pored over documents and questioned experts. Utility managers talked to me about system capacity and reliability, and minutia about how the power plants run and how they route electricity through the grid. But on Saturday it all failed, and like thousands of other Newfoundlanders, I was in the dark. I didn't have a clear sense of who was to blame, but as I fumbled to get the candles lit, my stiff, cold fingers told me that some goddamn bastards had messed up badly.

• • •

Nobody really thinks about the electrical system as long as it works. You flick a switch, and a light comes on. Nobody ever stops to think about the massive turbines spinning electromagnets inside a hydroelectric dam somewhere. You don't spend any time contemplating the amazing feats of engineering involved in the most basic elements of the electrical grid. You drive by a transformer yard on your way to work, and never bother to think about the piles of complex equipment that allow the system to function.

Nobody thinks about how it works, because most of the time, it all just ... works. And even when the system breaks, people don't spend too much time thinking about it. The lights go out, and for the most part, people just sit around waiting for them to come back on. Presumably, somewhere out there, *they* are working on it. *They* run the grid. When a piece of equipment gets old, *they* replace it. When *they* send you a bill in the mail, you just pay it, because you assume *they* came by and knew how to read the meter on the outside of your house, and *they* didn't make a mistake. Nobody gives it much thought, because even when something goes wrong, *they* fix it and the lights come back on. Since the fall of 2010, politicians had been trying to make Newfoundlanders and Labradorians care about who *they* are, and what *they* do. For the most part, the politicians failed.

Up on a river somewhere in Labrador, there's a waterfall called Muskrat Falls, and in a filing cabinet somewhere else, there's a set of very detailed plans for how to build a big hydroelectric dam there. In the filing cabinet beside it, there are plans for building a power line from Labrador, under the ocean, across the island of Newfoundland all the way down to St. John's. They say they need to build all of this to keep the lights on. They say this is the cheapest way to generate electricity for the province. They say, all told, it'll cost about $7-8 billion.[1]

Those, I think, are the facts that everybody agrees on. The rest is yelling.

Aside from the tiny group of people who were doing the yelling, I never really got the sense that people loved or hated the Muskrat Falls plan. By god, it wasn't for lack of trying, though. When the blackout hit, according to *The Telegram* archives, I had written 268 stories that dealt with Muskrat Falls in some way or another. No other political issue in the province even comes close to the size and scope of the massive, multi-billion dollar hydroelectric project. For one thing, it's easily the largest infrastructure project in a generation, possibly the largest project ever undertaken by the Newfoundland and Labrador provincial government. For another thing, it will define the energy system of the province for decades to come, which in turn will help shape the economic potential of the province. For another thing, it will reach straight into ordinary citizens' wallets, since Muskrat Falls will be a major factor in how much it costs to turn the lights on and keep the heat running in homes and businesses across the province. The Muskrat Falls project will affect every single citizen of the province in a myriad of subtle and pervasive ways.

In the House of Assembly, on Open Line radio, and in the newspaper, the Muskrat Falls debate raged. If you were to listen to Pre-

[1] At least, that's what they said in early 2014 when I originally wrote this. Until the dam is built and the electricity starts flowing, those dollar figures are subject to change. And even that number was subject to some dispute back in 2014, depending on how you tallied up the totals.

mier Dunderdale, it was the greatest thing to ever happen to the province. No superlative was too sweeping. There was no problem it wouldn't somehow help answer. When she formally sanctioned the project, with a rhetorical flourish, she claimed that for the past six decades, Newfoundland and Labrador had somehow been less than a full province within Canada, but Muskrat Falls would fix that.

"Historically, our province has been challenged economically and socially, both before and after confederation. However, in recent years, we have been moving toward a more promising and prosperous future. Today we take a significant step in that journey and move completely from the shadows of confederation into full and meaningful partnership as a regional leader in clean energy generation," Dunderdale declared.

On the other side of the debate, the critics claimed the project will lead to a hellish future where Newfoundlanders and Labradorians live in a sort of indentured serfdom, suffering under the crushing burden of debt and high electricity prices. They claimed that the geology of the waterfall means that the dam will burst, sending a deluge of water downstream to destroy the town of Happy Valley-Goose Bay. The line will break during an ice storm. The icebergs dragging along the ocean floor will sever the cable going under the Strait of Belle Isle. Ratepayers of the province will pay exorbitant prices for electricity while the government exports surplus power to Nova Scotia and the United States for pennies on the dollar. A small core of policy wonks and frothing partisans pored over every page of regulatory filings, obsessed over every aspect of the project and insisted that it was all doomed to fail.

But right up until the blackout hit, I couldn't shake the feeling that really, nobody cared. Unless electricity rates really did double in the space of a few years — as then-Liberal Leader Yvonne Jones claimed repeatedly in the spring of 2011 — people would pay whatever they were charged, because really, what other choice would they have? So long as the lights stayed on, and the rates weren't cripplingly expensive, the whole thing was just so much political noise.

But then, the lights went out.

• • •

It started, innocuously enough, with an emailed news release.

"Due to unseasonably cold conditions and very high load forecasts for the next 24 hours, Newfoundland and Labrador Hydro is requesting that customers on the island take steps to conserve electricity where possible," the bulletin from NL Hydro said.

But behind the scenes, the situation was dire.

One of the province's largest power plants, the Holyrood thermal generating station, was not working properly. Due to a missing fan motor, one of the three massive engines at the plant could only operate at around 35 per cent capacity. A couple of smaller emergency gas-turbine backup power plants were also broken down, and couldn't produce power. Meanwhile, the weather was turning bitterly cold. The temperature hovered around -20 C on Thursday, and fierce winds made it feel much colder. Across the province, all the tens of thousands of houses running on electric heat kicked it into high gear. By the evening, the electricity demand was just too much, and the power plants couldn't handle it.

Newfoundland has two utility companies. NL Hydro — a subsidiary of Nalcor, a Crown corporation — owns most of the power plants, and the big, arterial transmission lines. Hydro hands off the power to Newfoundland Power, a private corporation. Newfoundland Power owns the poles and the wires that transmit the electricity to your house. Thursday evening, Newfoundland Power was in the unenviable position of having to deliberately cut power to whole neighbourhoods' worth of customers because NL Hydro's equipment was broken, and they couldn't provide enough juice.

Then, the storm hit. Around 30 centimetres of snow and howling 100 kilometre per hour wind didn't make the situation any better. On top of everything, while the storm was still raging, at around 9 a.m. Saturday, a transformer at the Sunnyside terminal station caught fire. Sunnyside is right on the narrow isthmus leading onto the Avalon Peninsula. To get electricity from the big hydroelectric dams in central Newfoundland to the hundreds of thousands of people living in and around St. John's, all roads lead through Sunnyside. Dunderdale would later say, "We had a monkey wrench in the system, and then when we had the fire at Sunnyside, the monkey went into the system."

The only thing most Newfoundlanders knew was that the lights were out, and there was a big, big problem. Newfoundland Power would report that roughly 190,000 customers lost power on Saturday morning. Since utility "customers" are individual homes or businesses, many more Newfoundlanders were affected by the outage.

A week later, once the dust had started to settle, Nalcor CEO Ed Martin would essentially argue that all of those things happening at the same time was just really, really unlucky. A brutal winter storm, an electrical grid strained to the max, two broken power plants and a poorly timed transformer fire at a critical transfer station — Martin said they could've coped with any one or two of those on their own, but all together was just too much. Newfoundland is known to get cold, but the deepest freeze of winter usually doesn't happen until late January or February. Newfoundland power plants break down from time to time, but usually three of them don't all break down at the same time. Sometimes, when they're run at capacity, transformers catch on fire, but usually the grid isn't so fragile that a single transformer fire can cut off power to half of the people of the province.

Months later, though, an independent investigation conducted on behalf of the Public Utilities Board would conclude that NL Hydro didn't do necessary maintenance on the equipment that failed, and poor planning and bad forecasts meant that the electricity system wasn't ready to deal with the storm. Maybe the blackouts were inevitable, but it certainly looked like the people at NL Hydro dropped the ball, and if they'd done a better job, at the very least the blackouts would have been shorter.

I got lucky. I only lost power for 13 hours in my apartment. In my drafty old house, it got cold and dark and bloody unpleasant. But the power came on before my pipes froze, so I made out better than a lot of other people. A personal care home lost power in St. John's, and it didn't have a backup generator. All the old people had to be evacuated — oxygen tanks, wheel chairs and all. In Mount Pearl, a man died from carbon monoxide poisoning. He was found in a shed where he was running a backup power generator; he was rushed to the hospital before being pronounced dead. Eight other people had close calls; they needed to be taken to hospital and treated for carbon monoxide poisoning, but didn't die. Many homes were without power for 72 hours or longer.

• • •

Up until Sunday afternoon, Newfoundland was dealing with an electricity problem. That's when Kathy Dunderdale emerged to speak to journalists — flanked by top utility brass and cabinet ministers.

Then it became a political problem.

She was already under fire. For four days, the rolling blackouts and electrical system chaos had been going on, and she was nowhere to be seen. There were (false) rumours that she was in Florida on vacation. There was a sense that wherever she was, she wasn't taking charge of the situation and handling it like a leader should.

When she finally did turn up, Dunderdale firmly declared that the situation wasn't a crisis, even as more than 35,000 homes were still in the dark due to power shortages, and many people had been without electricity for more than 24 hours. Moreover, Dunderdale linked the not-a-crisis directly to the Muskrat Falls project, saying, "There is a solution coming," in the form of a shiny new hydroelectric dam. To drive the point home, her energy lieutenant, Nalcor CEO Ed Martin, said that he could not guarantee 100 per cent reliability from the electricity system; the Holyrood power plant was so old that these sort of things are just, y'know, going to happen from time to time. When she was asked about her personal situation, Dunderdale said that she lost power for more than 12 hours, but she had a propane fireplace, so she was OK. That may have been the truth, but it also doesn't exactly conjure up the image of a dynamic leader that's taking charge of the situation.

When I asked Ed Martin how he felt, having essentially failed at his mandate to provide reliable electricity, Dunderdale laughed at the question. It was just a little scoff, as if to say "That's a ridiculous, biased, off-base question." The TV cameras didn't catch it, and it was nearly silent, so the microphones didn't pick it up either, but I was looking her right in the eye when it happened.

Dunderdale didn't feel like Nalcor failed in its mandate; she felt like it was a company run by damn fine people doing their very best in a really tough situation. The notion that people would look around and view the not-a-crisis as a colossal screw-up by the province's electrical utility struck her as ridiculous. Call it compromised journalistic objectivity if you want, but when I was fumbling with cold, stiff fingers to get the candle lit in my apartment the night before, I definitely felt like somebody had dropped the ball in a big way.

The Sunday afternoon news conference was the final nail in Dunderdale's coffin. Everything else was epilogue. More than any other media appearance I've ever covered, that one showcased Dunderdale's fatal flaws as a politician. It was a train wreck. In those casual, low key conversations when you bump into her in the hallway, Dunderdale is sharp, personable and warm. When the lights are on her, though, and she's staring down the barrel of a TV camera, it's a different thing entirely. She comes across as arrogant, dismissive and nasty. Great politicians talk *through* the TV cameras, and *through* the reporters in the room to speak directly to the citizens they represent. Dunderdale talks to the journalists standing in front of her, and sometimes, it's clear she doesn't like them very much.

Dunderdale's political career was probably already doomed before the power outages happened, but any slim sliver of hope fizzled away during that 45-minute media appearance. CBC and VOCM radio both broadcast the whole thing live over the air, and the rest of the country got a taste of Dunderdale's leadership too, because CBC News Network broadcast the video live too.

After it was over, I almost felt bad for her. It was a feeling I was used to, during the three years I covered her as premier. As a journalist, what do you do? Do you print the quote as she said it, knowing that people will interpret it differently from what she meant? Do you deliberately choose to paraphrase her, and try to convey what she was trying to communicate, instead of what she actually said? So often, listening to Dunderdale speak, I felt like I knew what she was *trying* to say, and I knew what people would actually *hear*. The gulf between those two things in the Sunday news conference was the most brutal example of what an awful communicator she is, and why her leadership was utterly doomed.

Let's look at a couple specific examples:

1. "It's not a crisis."

What people heard: With the province entering its fourth day of unreliable electricity, things were feeling pretty damn serious. You can argue about the semantics of the word "crisis," but by brushing it off, Dunderdale sounded like she was trying to downplay the severity of the situation. In follow-up comments on Monday and Tuesday, Dunderdale would actually make the situation worse by allowing that individuals might have been in "personal crisis" but the province as a whole wasn't in a crisis. If you're sitting at home with frozen pipes, or a grandparent who was just evacuated from a personal care home, that sounds a lot like somebody saying, "Well, maybe *you* can't cope with the situation, but as a province we're getting along just fine."

What she meant: If you look at Dunderdale's comments in totality, she clearly has a very specific definition of the word "crisis." For her, a crisis is when things are out of control. A crisis would be a bad storm knocking out power lines faster than the utility crews could stay on top of things. A crisis would be a situation where the government was in over its head, and struggling to regain the upper hand. On a close read of her comments, she seemed to keep coming back to this point. It wasn't a crisis because the government was still in control of the situation. They'd been dealt a bad hand with the cold weather, the broken power plants, and everything else, but for Dunderdale, it wasn't a "crisis" because the government was playing that bad hand the best way possible, and they were still firmly in control of the situation.

2. "It's about Muskrat Falls."

What people heard: If you wrap your car around a telephone pole, you're bleeding, and you're trying to call up a tow truck, the last thing you want is for a guy in a suit to walk up to you and casually say, "Hey, looks like you're going to need a new car. I can sell you one at some very attractive financing rates." In the immediate wake of the not-a-crisis, people just wanted the electricity to start working again. What's more, the Nalcor folks who are responsible for building the dam at Muskrat Falls are the same people who just screwed up. It's pretty hard to trust somebody to competently build a $7.7 billion megaproject when they can't even seem to run the current system without messing up and plunging hundreds of thousands of people into the dark.

What she meant: Stepping back from the immediate not-a-crisis, Dunderdale's comments would have been valid, and perhaps even politically advantageous. For three years one of the Tories' core messaging lines had boiled down to two questions: "Do we need the power? And is Muskrat Falls the least-cost alternative to get that power?" (HINT: According to the Tories, the answer to both of those questions is "yes.") Opposition politicians disputed whether demand for electricity was really rising in the province, despite bigger TVs, bigger houses, more industrial development, and 90 per cent of new homes being heated by electricity. The January 2014 crisis emphatically demonstrated that demand for power is going up, and the existing infrastructure wasn't good enough to handle things. Dunderdale made that exact point in the Sunday news conference: "Just think about all the things that we've talked about over the last four years in preparing a case for Muskrat Falls. We've talked about the challenges of keeping 40-year-old infrastructure up and running. We've talked about high demand and the growth in demand. I mean, people argued with us — strongly — that there's not a growth in demand in the province, and yet, at the height of the storm, we had a demand of 500 megawatts of electricity more than any other time in the last five years."

3. "After 2017, hopefully we'll never find ourselves in this kind of circumstance again."

What people heard: It's really hard to listen to that sentence and hear anything other than: Until 2017 when Muskrat Falls is built, this sort of thing is going to keep happening. That's pretty thin gruel for somebody who's just been without power for the past 24 hours. Ed Martin didn't exactly help the situation by telling people that his power plants are liable to break down. "Unfortunately, they are old assets, and we're at a point where the load has increased significantly. And we're on top of it, we're going to stay on top of it, but honestly I can't promise the same reliability coming out of Holyrood that we may have had 10 years ago or 15 years ago or even five years ago."

What she meant: The comment about 2017 was actually making a fairly narrow point about redundancy built into the system and the two connections to the North American electricity grid. By running lines under the Strait of Belle Isle to Labrador and across the Cabot Strait to Nova Scotia, after the Muskrat Falls project was complete, Newfoundland would have two tie-ins with the North American grid. If domestic power plants broke down, Dunderdale was saying that electricity could be imported from the mainland. All throughout the not-a-crisis, Dunderdale and Martin insisted that the confluence of events that forced them to do the rolling blackouts was extremely unlikely. The only point Dunderdale was making with the 2017 comment was that even if it all those unlikely things happened again, the province would have an extra safety net through the connections to the North American grid.

4. "I have a propane fireplace which has been really helpful. … I had a source of heat, so I was comfortable."

What people heard: While everyone else was suffering, and things were going to hell across the province, Dunderdale was at home by a warm fireplace. Call it petty, but people don't like shivering in the dark and knowing that the premier isn't suffering along with everyone else. But worse, in a crisis (or even in a serious not-a-crisis), people expect their leaders to be doing *something* about it. A politician can't go out with the power line crews to fix blown transformers, but they can try to take charge of the situation. Tory backbencher Paul Lane offered to give constituents rides to the

Mount Pearl warming centre, set up as a refuge for people without electricity. Dunderdale, apparently, was just sitting at home by the fire.

What she meant: There's really no positive way to spin this one. I guess if that's what happened, she had to tell the truth about it, but if transformers are on fire and hundreds of thousands of people are without power, I kind of expect my premier to be at an emergency management meeting or something.

• • •

The power outages would continue through the rest of the week. On Thursday, a full week after the rolling blackouts began, Dunderdale again called reporters to the Confederation Building to announce that she was setting up an independent review of the province's electrical system. The province's energy regulator, the Public Utilities Board, also announced that they were doing an inquiry. And for good measure, Ed Martin announced that he'd be heading up an internal Nalcor investigation.

The damage was already done though. Public confidence in Nalcor was shot. For the government, it was even worse. Maybe people didn't really care much about Muskrat Falls one way or the other, but they knew that it was central to Dunderdale's political identity. And after three straight years of talking about every little detail of the electricity system, Dunderdale was at the helm when it all fell apart during the coldest week of the year.

And was it a crisis? Even a kid could tell you that it was. In fact, a kid wrote to Dunderdale to tell her exactly that.

On Sunday, as the province was reeling from widespread blackouts, a young citizen wrote an email to the premier.

"Hello Ms. Dunderdale I am writing you (concerning) your statement on the not crisis," the email said. "I assume you have not been out in a freezing house without power for 36 hours like my family and I have but it is absolutely a crisis."

I got my hands on the email in an access to information request a couple months later. The writer's name was blacked out for privacy concerns. But after criticizing Dunderdale's decision to let liquor stores reopen while the electricity system was still on wobbly legs, the email concluded by saying, "We are all very disappointed. Thank you (redacted) Age 11."

CHAPTER 7
SWITCHING SIDES
JANUARY 20, 2014

"I'll be holding a news Conference at 11am at Smitty's Mount Pearl to discuss my political future. Hope to see you there :-)."

When a politician uses the phrase "my political future," journalists sit up and take notice. When a politician starts sending messages out directly to reporters, instead of going through normal PR channels, journalists take notice of that too. When a politician personally contacts reporters via Twitter direct message, says he wants to talk about his political future and ends it with a smiley face... well... That's the sort of news conference you show up to.

On Sunday night, if you'd asked me to make a list of the 48 politicians in the House of Assembly and rank them in order of, "Most likely to switch parties," Paul Lane probably wouldn't have cracked the top 30.

But sure enough, on Monday when I arrived at Smitty's, there was a crowd of grinning Liberals. So many new "supporters" were there that Lane was busy hauling out more chairs from a storage room and setting them up himself. Lane had booked the little private room off to the side of the family chain restaurant. On the other side of the partition, people were squeezed into cheaply upholstered booths, chowing down on eggs Benedict and mass produced pancakes while the TV cameras set up for the big announcement. Apparently the private room at Smitty's is the weekly meeting spot for the local Rotary Club, because Lane did his announcement from a tacky podium with far too many ornamental embellishments on it, emblazoned with blue letters reading, "ROTARY CLUB OF WATERFORD VALLEY." When he made the announcement, thank God he resisted the urge to ring the Rotary bell, or bang the gavel that was lying on the podium in front of him.

Once the media was in place and the room was filled up, Lane spoke for close to 20 minutes, offering a lengthy explanation for why he made the move. He said it was about leadership, transparency, and the fact that the government wasn't sticking up for "everyday people."

Essentially, he said, the government had lost touch.

"While it is extremely important to continue to develop our natural resources and diversify our economy, it is equally important that government focus on issues that matter to the everyday person — issues such as affordable housing; ensuring all of our seniors are living with dignity; decreasing the lineups at food banks; providing school busing for our young children, particularly in busy, high-traffic areas; ensuring that our citizens have reasonable access to health care services; and as we've recently been reminded, ensuring our citizens have a stable and well-maintained electrical system."

You'd be hard-pressed to find a Tory who would take a stand against the dignity of senior citizens, and I'm not sure what exactly the government had done to inhibit "reasonable access to health care," but apparently in Lane's mind they weren't doing enough.

An odd touchstone for Lane's one-man political revolt was Bill 29. Lane said that even though he voted for it, and even though he still supported a lot of what was in the legislation, he now regretted standing behind it because his constituents thought that it made the government more secretive.

"Since the passage of the infamous Bill 29 and the subsequent media firestorm, many of the constituents I speak to question government's motives around various issues, and point to Bill 29 as a reason to be skeptical around decisions being made, and the real and/or perceived lack of transparency," he said.

But the hardest hits were saved for Dunderdale, and her lack of leadership and compassion during the blackouts. He said that in the midst of a crisis, she was, "once again, nowhere to be found" and that when she did finally emerge to speak to the province, instead of offering empathy and comfort, she spent her time quibbling about the precise definition of the word crisis.

"For me, this was the final straw," Lane said.

Dwight Ball's speech was shorter, and probably more honest. He spoke for less than two minutes, and welcomed Lane to the party. Mostly, he described how it all came together in the same way you might expect a regional sales rep to describe how he managed to land a medium-sized account selling printer toner.

"First of all, the door was opened with Paul last Monday when we had our first chat, and then we decided that— a number of issues that Paul brought forward and discussed with me. We then took some time because we wanted to consider what the next move would be — if indeed the fit was there. On Saturday morning we did indeed circle back and had a lengthy discussion, as Paul said. A couple discussions again yesterday, and we decided then that this morning would be the appropriate time to make the move. We certainly welcome Paul as a member of the Official Opposition."

Lane and Ball took questions for another 20 minutes or so — most of it was Lane squirming, as he awkwardly tried to justify going back on basically every single thing he'd said in the previous two years. Lane hadn't just been a Tory, he'd been the bruiser of the caucus, who was sent out to relentlessly spew talking points, pick fights with opponents and blindly support every government policy. He seemed to relish the role, and in the House of Assembly he went over and above to impress his political masters. He turned his maiden speech in the legislature into a partisan screed against the opposition parties. "As I look back over nearly two decades of Liberal governance, the one word that comes to mind is: Neglect. ... The mismanagement of the previous Liberal administrations had placed our province on the verge of bankruptcy."

During the Bill 29 filibuster, Lane took to his feet to attack the opposition parties for proposing an amendment which would limit the scope of total secrecy when it comes to cabinet documents.

"There is only one reason why this amendment would be put forward. It is simply to delay the debate, keep it going, keep it going, keep it going, and grandstanding, Mr. Chair. That is the only reason it is being done, so that people will be watching from home, CBC, the other media will be covering it. They will be covering it in the newspapers, Mr. Chair. It is just an opportunity for these people across the way to grandstand and try to score political brownie points but while they are doing it, Mr. Chair, I think they are being very disrespectful in my humble opinion."

Less than two years later, Lane was standing in front of a bank of TV cameras and journalists, saying that he was quitting the PC Party at least partly because of Bill 29, and the stuff about cabinet secrecy in particular. When I got him on the phone the day after his big announcement, I read him that quote and asked him how he could heap so much scorn on the opposition parties in the legislature, and then turn around later and admit they had it right all along.

"I know there were points of time (during the filibuster) I was doing, like, 18 or 20 hours straight. And there was, in an effort to keep it going, amendments made where someone would add in just a period or a comma," Lane told me. "Based on the information I have now, based on the feedback I've gotten from my constituents, I believe that was a mistake."

• • •

If you're the sort of person who's tempted to see politics as an affair of ideology and principle, then Lane's decision must look like rank opportunism and hypocrisy. But on ideology, you'd be hard pressed to jam a razor blade in between the Liberals and the Tories in Newfoundland and Labrador. Danny Williams and then Kathy Dunderdale led an ostensibly "conservative" government that nearly doubled public spending in the space of a decade. What exactly is right-wing about nationalizing a private corporation's assets, as the Tories did in the case of Abitibi-Bowater's paper mill and hydroelectric dams in Central Newfoundland? How many other conservative governments across the country are maintaining a post-secondary tuition freeze over more than a decade in office?

No, in Newfoundland and Labrador politics, the only thing that matters is "in power" versus "in opposition." You're either one of the Hatfields or you're one of the McCoys.

For a certain sort of person like Paul Lane, you start out as an active member of the community, coaching high school sports teams and sitting on charity fundraising committees. Eventually, you decide that where you can really leave your mark is in politics, so you run for city council. After a little while, you decide you're getting pretty good at this politics thing, and maybe it's time to try to make the jump to the big leagues.

Unfortunately for Lane, he made the jump at just the wrong time. After eight years of riding high under Danny Williams, the PCs had just made the switch to Dunderdale when Lane ran. And then pretty quickly after election day, it all started to fall apart for the Tories. The dream for a guy like Lane is to "make a difference" in government — to be seen as a guy who went into the legislature and delivered something for the people of his community — maybe a new hockey rink, or a fire hall, or something like that. But it's pretty damn hard to make that kind of thing happen if you're turfed out of office after four years sitting in the back benches. And the worst of it is, the guy who replaces Lane in Mount Pearl South would probably be somebody cut from the exact same cloth — some other community-minded former municipal politician who just happened to write "Liberal" on his nomination forms, because that's the way the wind was blowing in 2015.

So Lane jumped from the Tories to the Liberals, hopefully assuring himself a safe ride in the next provincial election, and probably a cabinet seat to boot, if the Liberals won. This way he got to extend his political career from four years to eight, or maybe even twelve, and get his hands on some real power so that he can "make a difference" some way, somehow. I suspect that's the only reason he was doing the rough-and-tumble Tory partisan shtick, anyway. Good soldiers who lead the charge get promoted.

If you look at Lane's defection through this lens, then it wasn't just understandable, it was a damn savvy political move. Not only did he leave a sinking ship, he managed to do so at the last possible moment when there was any political cover. He ditched the Tories, and blamed it all on Dunderdale. Two days later, Dunderdale would resign. If any other backbenchers in the Tory caucus were looking wistfully at their re-election chances and thinking of defecting, they missed their window. Lane caught the last train out of town, *and* he got to look like the guy who delivered the final nail in Dunderdale's coffin.

Not a bad political play, y'know, as long as you don't care about principle and ideology.

● ● ●

After it was all over at Lane's floor-crossing announcement and people were starting to disperse, Marjorie erupted. She'd been sitting towards the back of the room for the announcement. I don't know what, specifically, set her off, but she was livid with David Cochrane.

"The nerve of ye! The gall! I hope your tongue falls out. I hope you rots!" she shouted. "I can't believe it. You're rotten to the core, you are!"

I talked to her when she calmed down a bit, and Marjorie told me that she was there to support her friend, Paul, but she wasn't switching parties.

Did she feel hurt that he was abandoning the party?

"You have to do what you have to do," she said. "It's a rotten life as a politician. It's rotten."

A little later, once the room cleared out a bit, I ended up sitting with Liberal MP Scott Andrews, who summed up the situation with casual detachment.

"Politics is changing. It's like a hockey team. Trades happen," he shrugged. "It's not the way it used to be; people aren't dyed-in-the-wool."

• • •

As the smoke cleared, and I tried to wrap my head around the Paul Lane desertion, only one part of it didn't make sense to me. Sure, if you're Lane, I understand why you'd want to jump ship. But if you're Dwight Ball, why do you take him? The Liberals were already at the top of the polls, and had all the political momentum. The government was already hanging on by a thread. Dunderdale was already the most unpopular premier in the country. What exactly does Lane bring to the table? As a backbencher, he wasn't in the inner circle; it's not like he knew where the bodies are buried. Sure, the defection earned the Liberals an extra seat in the House of Assembly, and it probably hastened Dunderdale's collapse. But the longer it took for her to fall apart, the more damage the Tories did to themselves along the way.

A few weeks later, after Dunderdale had gracefully exited stage right, Ball picked up a couple more caucus members in Dale Kirby and Christopher Mitchelmore. The announcement was much less shocking. Pretty much ever since Kirby and Mitchelmore ditched the NDP at the end of the caucus revolt, people expected they'd wind up with the Liberals sooner or later. At the announcement, Ball talked about how the Liberal Party will welcome just about anybody — because at that point, what else could he really say?

To me, though, it looked like Ball was sending a pretty clear message to anybody who was paying attention. He was willing to do and say whatever it took to bring down the government. In December, he wrote a cheque for $11,000 to make a political problem go away. Earlier in January, at an event on the west coast, he made a multi-million dollar promise to put a PET scanner in the new Corner Brook hospital, based on sketchy research. When I called up his director of communications a couple days later, she wasn't even aware that he'd made the promise; it looked to me like he just did it on the fly, because it's what the crowd wanted to hear. And then Paul Lane came knocking at the Liberal Party door, and Ball said, "Sure b'y, come on in."

It didn't matter that he'd probably win anyway, even without Lane. Ball had a chance to score a point, and do a day's worth of damage to the Tories, so he took it. There was no bigger picture, no strategic play, no long game. Ball was just saying anything, doing anything, just swinging wildly, over, and over, and over again.

It's not about principle. It's not personal. It's just politics. It's just about the relentless pursuit of victory, and doing whatever it takes along the way.

CHAPTER 8
END OF THE ROAD
WEDNESDAY, JANUARY 22, 2014

In the lobby of the Confederation Building, the overwhelming emotion in the air was relief.

When it was all over, and I was talking with *The Telegram* columnist Pam Frampton, we agreed that Kathy Dunderdale's resignation announcement felt a bit like a funeral. It was like everybody was gathered together to say goodbye to a beloved friend who'd been fighting a terminal illness for a long time. Dunderdale appeared to be fighting back tears as she smiled tightly and gave her own eulogy. The assembled crowd of supporters and staffers applauded warmly. Ringing the upper level of the lobby, people leaned on the railing to get a better view.

Huddled behind a massive bank of TV cameras, listening to her speech, I let my journalistic objectivity slip away for a second, and I breathed a sigh of relief. For months, everyone in the political world had been holding their breath, waiting for her to go, as the government lurched from one disaster to the next. And through it all, she'd struck that imperious tone, that stubborn insistence that she wasn't going anywhere. Nobody believed her, of course, but in quiet conversations, people muttered darkly and worried about just how awful things could get if she really did decide to cling to power.

A caucus revolt? A mass exodus of staffers and caucus allies? Utter annihilation on election day? The future looked ugly.

And then, finally, it was over. She was gone.

In the lobby of the Confederation Building, as supporters waited for the speech to start, I saw smiles on lots of people's faces. Her caucus came out first, crowding around the podium, flanking Dunderdale on both sides. There were plenty of smiling faces among the politicians, too.

It's not that they hated her, but they were happy to see her go. She'd be happier in retirement. Instead of spending her days being denigrated in the media, she'd get to spend more time with her grandkids. And she was going gracefully, on her own terms. There was the faintest glimmer of hope that the rest of the Tories could turn things around.

And really, that's at least part of what they were all smiling about. Things could have gone much, much worse. Dunderdale stayed on just long enough to show everybody how ugly things could've been if she stayed even one second longer.

• • •

The day started early, with reporters arriving at the Confederation Building before 9 a.m. to stake out the lobby.

If I ever meet the architect who designed the Confederation Building, I'll give him a big hug and a kiss on the cheek. It's a dream for journalistic stakeouts. The lobby is big and open, and you can just wait for politicians passing through. Politicians' parking spots are all located right up against the building, and they're labeled so that you can tell at a glance whether the premier is in the building or not, just based on whether there's a car in her parking spot. The big, black Chevy Suburban SUV was already parked in the premier's spot, which meant that the plainclothes cops protecting Dunderdale had already driven her to the office. She must have come in very, very early to avoid the throng of media.

Nearly all the traffic in and out of the building comes through just a couple sets of doors, and they lead directly into the lobby. An enterprising or desperate reporter can loiter in there and know that the cabinet minister they're looking for will pass through sooner or later. To get to the upper floors, you've pretty much got no choice but to ride a bank of elevators located front and centre in the lobby, too. In this case, it was finance minister, and soon-to-be interim premier, Tom Marshall, who was accosted by the media. As he made the long walk across the lobby, weaving between chairs that were being set up for the impending announcement, reporters shouted questions at him. "We'll see what happens," he shouted back, with a shrug and a wave of his hand. "It's Newfoundland politics. It can change on a dime!"

Near the elevators, a knot of TV cameras and reporters lurked. In another corner, more TV guys set up different cameras and ran lines out to the satellite trucks to do live reports back to the studio. In the middle of the lobby, workers set up a sound system and unpacked rows of chairs for the announcement. In dribs and drabs the Tory caucus filed past the journalists and into the caucus room. Nobody looked especially grim, but nobody offered any comments to the media either. Just before 9:30 a.m., Dunderdale smiled and strode quickly past, surrounded by a small cadre of staffers.

I don't know what was said in the meeting, but it lasted about an hour. Meanwhile, the lobby filled up with people in dark suits — mostly political staffers and civil servants, by the look of it, with some supporters and members of the public peppered in. At least half of the people in the crowd — probably more — were women. Around the upper level that ringed the lobby, more public servants leaned against the railing to take in the whole scene. Somebody hissed, "They're coming!" and the caucus started filing out through that one narrow door.

• • •

The resignation speech itself was thoroughly underwhelming. It felt like a first draft attempt at the legacy that Dunderdale was hoping for, but mostly it just served to emphasize how disappointing her three years in office were. She claimed ownership of the Muskrat Falls deal — negotiated when Danny Williams was premier, although she did a lot of the grunt work to make it a reality. She said she was "especially proud" of the CETA free trade deal with Europe, even though that was negotiated primarily by the federal government.[1] She talked about "ratcheting down debt" even though the government ran deficits for two of the three years she was in office and interim premier Tom Marshall would post another budget shortfall a few months later, in the spring of 2014. Dunderdale spent three years in the premier's office, being savagely pummelled in the court of public opinion. And when she left office, she had precious little to show for it.

After all the build-up, the months of speculation and dread, Dunderdale was gone after speaking for less than 15 minutes. She offered no reasons for leaving. She just said it was time to go, and left it at that.

"Ancient Hebrew scriptures teach us that there is a time for everything, and a season for every activity under the heavens. I have discovered that this also applies to public service. Just as you know when it's time to step up, you also know when it is time to step back, and that time for me is now."

As reporters jammed their microphones into the faces of Tory politicians, one after another they said that she was a great leader, a passionate, caring, strong, capable woman. They also said again and again that she was leaving on her own terms. In case anybody was wondering, they said, this wasn't because of Paul Lane. There was no caucus revolt.

She was still well-loved among PC Party members, although most of them were clearly relieved that she was gone.[2]

●●●

Two days later, at a short ceremony in Government House, Tom Marshall was sworn-in as the province's 11th premier.

---

[1] And… well… the CETA thing didn't turn out so well for the province, but we'll get to that later.

[2] This would change over time. A couple years later, some Tories would bitterly remember Dunderdale's time in office as "a nightmare" that irreparably destroyed their standing in the province. But at the time when she left, there was no sense of vitriol or animosity. Hindsight is a funny thing.

Dunderdale was nowhere to be seen.

In his speech, Marshall formally said his first act as premier was to praise Dunderdale and thank her for her three years of service. But everything that came after that seemed to be a gentle rebuke of her leadership, and her governing style.

"Let the motto of my administration be the words in Deuteronomy that Moses used to set the highest standards for all who would serve in public office: Justice, he said, justice shall you pursue. So it is therefore very important for me that all Newfoundlanders and Labradorians shall share fully and fairly in the benefits of our newfound prosperity, and have a voice in the way it is distributed. So let us ensure that the fight against poverty and inequality intensifies in our province, and we never forget the needs of those who are aged, who have disabilities, who are infirm, and who live on low and fixed incomes."

° ° °

"We are not the province we were a decade ago. Opportunities have never been brighter. But we have to ensure — we must ensure — that they are available to all of us. By the same token, expectations have never been higher, but I am fully prepared with my colleagues to rise up to meet those expectations. I only ask that you work with us and that you open up to us. If we're doing something right, tell us. If we're doing something wrong, and need to do better, tell us. We will never promise what we cannot deliver, but what I will promise you is my full attention, my best judgment and my tireless service."

The part about income inequality and justice for all was weirdly similar to Paul Lane's floor-crossing call to address the lines at food banks and senior citizens struggling to get by in the oil boom economy. And the line about asking the public to tell the government what it's doing right and wrong seemed like a direct shot at Dunderdale's perceived recalcitrant attitude towards public criticism.

Within days of the swearing-in, Marshall would talk to cabinet about reviewing the province's access to information law, with an eye towards undoing the damage of Bill 29. When a reporter asked him point-blank if he had any thoughts about how damaging Bill

93

29 had been to the PC Party's credibility, Marshall said, "Any thoughts? Not that I can express in good company."

Marshall was only supposed to be a caretaker premier. He was only supposed to be on to the job for five months. But right from the get-go, he was sending a clear message to the people of the province: Dunderdale is gone, and things are going to be different now.

CHAPTER 9
YOU PUT ONE FOOT IN, YOU PUT ONE FOOT OUT...
JANUARY, 2014

It didn't take long.

After Dunderdale finished her resignation speech, soon-to-be-premier Tom Marshall was mobbed by reporters. But once we'd chewed through him, the hungry pack of journalists started casting about for other prey. Dunderdale was gone. Twenty minutes after her speech was finished, she was old news. The next big thing was the leadership race. Who was going to step up?

We cornered Fisheries Minister Keith Hutchings up against a pillar in the lobby. Natural Resources Minister Derrick Dalley got mobbed too. Justice Minister Darin King — one of the more wily members of the PC Party caucus — practically dove into the elevators to escape the journalists after Dunderdale's speech was over. Child, Youth and Family Services Minister Paul Davis wasn't quite so quick, and the CBC managed to grab him before he could escape. It was all totally pointless, of course. No self-respecting politician would say anything about running to replace Dunderdale just moments after her resignation speech.

Before we wade too much further into this, I should tell you that leadership speculation is one of my top journalistic pet peeves, right up there with with funding squabbles between levels of government and any story primarily about people getting angry on the Internet.

On January 22nd, Dunderdale quit. On March 14, when the dust settled, everybody knew who was in and who was out. By March 15th, all of the speculation, the anonymous sources, the evasive answers and fevered analysis counted for exactly zero. There were three men in the leadership race, and all the might-have-beens and almost-but-not-quite candidacies didn't matter even slightly. But between January 22 and March 14, it got very, very silly.

How silly? Let's take a minute to consider the case of Senator Fabian Manning. Despite his ability to dupe a few journalists (including yours truly) into thinking otherwise, with the benefit of hindsight, I think its safe to say that Manning was never *ever* a serious potential leader.

To say that Fabian Manning had a rocky history with the provincial PC Party is like saying that sometimes it's foggy in St. John's. Once upon a time, Manning was a rising star among Progressive Conservatives, right up until he ran afoul of then-premier Danny Williams and got thrown out of caucus. After he was run out of provincial politics by Danny, Manning ran for the federal Conservatives and won a seat in the House of Commons representing the riding of Avalon. This didn't sit well with Danny, and a few years later, when Fabian was running for re-election, Danny made it his mission to make sure Manning lost. Williams made it clear to people that he thought that Manning went up to Ottawa, became Prime Minster Stephen Harper's stooge and betrayed the province. People bought it, and Manning got beaten handily by the Liberal candidate. That year, thanks to Williams' "ABC: Anything But Conservative" campaign against Harper, the federal Conservatives were entirely shut out of Newfoundland and Labrador.

In case there was any doubt about whether he really was Harper's stooge, Manning put the matter to rest 2 1/2 months after election day when he accepted an appointment to the Senate. After the Newfoundland and Labrador electorate had roundly rejected him as a representative, Manning would be headed to Ottawa to … you guessed it: represent the people of Newfoundland and Labrador. A lesser man would've just accepted the patronage appointment quietly, and if his ego was bruised by an electoral drubbing, he could at least console himself with the $132,000 salary and lifetime job security. But not Fabian. This man really, *really* wanted everybody to know that he was Harper's stooge, and he was Newfoundland and Labrador's Conservative man in Ottawa, even if the voters didn't want him there and they thought the Harper Conservatives were a pack of arseholes.

Manning spent more than two years as the face of the Harper Government in Newfoundland and Labrador. He made funding announcements, handed out oversized novelty cheques, and scrunched his face into a smile for photo-ops. Even this would've been forgivable behaviour for a good, partisan soldier. Harper needed a man in Newfoundland, and Manning was a man who was being paid $132,000 by the taxpayers to represent the Conservatives so … I mean, *somebody* had to hand out those oversized cheques, didn't they? It's not like Harper had an MP in Newfoundland who could do all those grip-and-grin photo-ops.

But then, in the spring of 2011, Manning quit his post in the Senate to run for Harper again, trying to win back his old riding of Avalon. By 2011, Danny had moved on to picking fights with other people, and he wasn't bothering with the ABC campaign anymore. Plus, Manning must've told himself, voters love a guy who delivers money, right? And here, I've been delivering money to the good people of Newfoundland and Labrador for the past two years! Aw shucks, let's give this a go!

Manning lost.

Apparently voters didn't want to cast a ballot for a guy who'd built his political brand on being Stephen Harper's stooge.

If you want to pinpoint the moment when Fabian Manning's political career ended once and for all, that moment came on May 25, 2011 — just 23 days after he was soundly rejected by the voters of Avalon for the second time. On May 25, Manning accepted a second appointment to the Senate from Harper, and went right back to stooging.

Two years later, at a time when the Senate was in the news with allegations of illegal activity, cronyism and entitlement largesse on taxpayers' dime, Manning revealed that he was considering a run for the PC Party leadership. If nothing else, you've got to admire this guy's chutzpah, eh?

"I've learned some valuable lessons. I've got some political scars that no one else would ever, ever have," Manning told me. No kidding, brother, you've got some political scars alright.

At around the same time, I was chatting about politics with a friend who lived in Manning's old Avalon riding. She managed to sum up voters' feelings towards him in a single sentence: "He's got a face made for smacking."

• • •

If the public trajectory of poor old Fabian's political career seems kind of sad, then the behind-the-scenes story of his stillborn leadership bid is downright hilarious. For reasons that will be obvious, it should be noted that I wasn't physically present to witness any of this, but much later when I asked Manning about the story I'd been hearing, he laughed ruefully and said, "Yeah, I remember that."

Just after Dunderdale resigned, Manning happened to find himself on a plane with Newfoundland comedian Mark Critch. Because of the Senate gig, Manning spends a lot of time flying back and forth to Newfoundland. Critch, who works on the CBC show *This Hour Has 22 Minutes*, spends a lot of time coming and going from the province too.

So there they were, Critch and Manning, on a flight together in the days after Dunderdale quit. And so Critch decided to have a bit of fun.

"Fabian b'y, you've got to run for the leadership!

"Everywhere I go lately, I'm hearing talk about how the province needs Fabian Manning to get back in the game!

"People keep saying to me: 'what the Tories need to turn things around right now is Fabian Manning.'

"Just the other night I was at A&W and people were saying, 'Man, I wish Fabian Manning would run for the leadership. He's the sort of man we need as premier right now.'"

Manning politely laughed it off, but apparently he didn't think Critch was joking. Somehow, he managed to convince himself that at a mythical A&W out there somewhere, people were talking politics, and saying that Fabian is the sort of guy who really should be running the province.

The plane lands and they go their separate ways. And once Manning is out of earshot, Critch pulls out his cell phone and calls CBC political reporter David Cochrane.

"Dave, you'll never guess who I just bumped into! I was on a plane with Fabian Manning, and get this! He's thinking about running for the Tory leadership!"

So then Cochrane calls Manning to see if this is legit. And Manning says the same thing that every politician says when somebody asks them if they're planning on running for anything. I imagine he probably said something like: "Well b'y, I'm hearing a lot of interest from people. I'm getting a lot of calls. I've got to think about it. I've got to talk it over with my family. I'm just flattered that people are interested. I'm keeping all my options open."

So on January 27, Cochrane posted on Twitter: "Senator Fabian Manning tells me he is 'exploring options' when it comes to NL PC Leadership race. Not ruling it out."

● ● ●

Of course, eventually Manning announced that he was bowing out. "Believe it or not, an 11-year-old daughter has a fair amount of effect on her father," he told me. Being utterly unelectable probably had a bit of an effect on him, too.

Between January 22 and March 14, a total of 15 people announced that they were seriously considering a run for the PC Party leadership. Twelve of them weren't serious enough about it to actually file nomination papers and get into the race. I suspect that most of the almost-but-not-quite candidates have a backstory just as sordid and ridiculous as Fabian Manning, but frankly, I never spent any time trying to find out. People who don't run, don't matter.

Here's what matters: When the dust settled on March 14, there were three men in the race — well, two and a half, really.

Nobody from the Progressive Conservative Caucus in the House of Assembly bothered to get into the game.

Bill Barry, a businessman in the fish processing sector from Corner Brook, was first out of the gate. He styled himself as an outsider, and at his campaign launch, he swaggered in to the Beatles' "Revolution" blaring in the background. In his first campaign speech, he said that most of the members of the Tory caucus were completely useless. He promised to repeal Bill 29. The following day, *The Telegram* editorial about Barry's leadership bid was headlined "Maverick in the race."

Right off the bat, I liked Barry. My first contact with him was a text message I received the day after his campaign launch. In those early days, Bill Barry's director of communications was Bill Barry. When I got in contact with him for a story I was working on, I got a text message: "Hello James....... If you wanna interview... what's a good time for ya??????? Bill Barry"

Hoo boy, I thought, this guy doesn't stand a chance, but he's going to be fun to cover while it lasts.

A few days later, when I sent him a message about a story I was working on about the demographic challenges facing the province, I got a similarly unfiltered response: "Were in BIG trouble...from 1992 to 2035..pop will decline by 100'k...and the crew left will average 50..........we have the worst demographic profile in Canada.......and no focus on this mater ...or not enough..." Phone interviews with him involved fewer ellipsis, but the same feel of a guy who was just spouting off, calling it as he sees it.

The thing people like Barry don't respect is that politicians rely on talking points for a damn good reason. As much as people lament "politics as usual" and wish for somebody to break the mold, it's not a coincidence that dull, on-message folks in dark suits keeping getting elected. Talking points work. Speaking your mind to a reporter who's recording the conversation ... well ... that's dangerous.

Unfortunately for his political aspirations, though, Barry managed to do something to piss off former premier/Tory demigod Danny Williams. It doesn't matter what the perceived slight was; it doesn't matter if Danny's grievances were legitimate or not. All that matters is that Williams found a few reporters and TV cameras, and growled, "He doesn't stand for anything that I support." Those kinds of words from Danny Williams can have a fatal effect on your political future — just ask Fabian Manning.

After his brash entrance, Barry spent more than a month as the solitary candidate in the race. Everybody knew he wasn't going to win it — Danny Williams said so, after all — but nobody knew who the not-Barry consensus candidate would be.

Frank Coleman, also a businessman from Corner Brook, waited right up to the 11th hour before he got into the race. He didn't return reporters' calls, and refused to do any interviews on the day he filed his nomination papers. Behind the scenes, it was widely understood that Coleman was Danny's man. As soon as he got into the race, like dominoes, most of the other serious contenders announced that they were getting out, and a few of them announced that they were endorsing Coleman along the way. Such is the power of people thinking you've got Danny Williams in your corner.[1]

Wayne Ronald Bennett was the other guy. Bennett was a retired naval officer and a town councillor in Howley — a town on the west coast with a population of 221, according to the most recent census figures. At first, the only person who took his candidacy seriously was Wayne Ronald Bennett. This was a campaign to become the next premier of the province; the entry fee was $10,000. Nobody believed that some wingnut from the sticks was going to get into the race. Eventually, he felt that he needed to post a picture of his $10,000 certified cheque on Twitter in the days before the nomination deadline, just to prove he had the money. Then he took the picture down after a bunch of people reminded him that posting all of his banking information on the Internet might not be a good idea.

Of the three candidates, Bennett had the most political experience by a country mile. Not only was he a town councillor who'd managed to get a few of those 221 Howley residents to vote for him, he'd run in a federal election. Back in 2008, when Danny was doing

[1] Williams, for what it's worth, never overtly came out and endorsed anybody. In fact, he generally downplayed the idea that he was throwing his support behind Coleman. I would have liked to put the question directly to him, but Williams declined to do an interview for this book.

his Anything But Conservative thing, some political geniuses had an idea: What if we create a new political party, and get Danny Williams to endorse us! Thus, the Newfoundland and Labrador First Party was born. They ran candidates in the 2008 federal election, but the brilliant plan fell apart when Danny inexplicably concluded that they weren't a credible outfit. After the Newfoundland and Labrador First Party picked itself up and brushed itself off following the savage electoral beating of 2008, they called a news conference to announce a change in party leadership. The new leader was — you guessed it! — Wayne Ronald Bennett. Under Bennett's leadership, the party was deregistered by Elections Canada because they couldn't come up with 250 signed membership forms to prove that they were still a going concern.

One day after the PC Party approved his leadership nomination papers and formally accredited him as a candidate, Bennett surprised everybody by endorsing the NDP candidate in a critical byelection to fill Kathy Dunderdale's newly vacated seat. Bennett was a fringe candidate without any real political legitimacy, and zero chance of winning the PC Party leadership, and I've already wasted too much ink talking about him.

The delegated convention was scheduled to be held on the first weekend in July. The race was on.

CHAPTER 10
"FOURTEEN IS UNDECIDED."
MARCH 22, 2014

It was a thing of beauty to watch Cathy Bennett and Marc Garneau go to work on the beige house on Woodwynd Street, in St. John's.

There was a middle-aged lady in the driveway, as Bennett and Garneau closed in. The lady did her best to fend off the pair of politicians — she said she didn't live in the district, this is her daughter's house — but Bennett was undeterred.

"Do you have any grandkids?" she asked.

"Yes, five."

"Oh! Then I'll talk about full-day kindergarten," Bennett said, moving past the lady to take the door.

A minute later, there was a little social happening on the front step. Bennett deftly focused on the voter, the woman who lived in the house. Garneau ran interference, chatting with grandma and grandpa; they wanted to know what it was like to be an astronaut, and he was more than happy to oblige with stories about his trips into outer space.

And then, the moment of truth: Do you know how you're going to be voting on April 9?

There was a little pause; the energy of the whole conversation hinged on this answer.

"Not PC, I can tell you that," the lady said.

Good enough! Everybody happily went back to gabbing about astronauts and all-day kindergarten.

Out of nowhere, Liberal Leader Dwight Ball appeared, moving in for the kill with a toothy grin and a firm handshake.

"I know this is gonna be a big one!" the lady said, and then, as if to offer a little bit more assurance, she gestured at Bennett and added, "She told me everything I needed to hear."

Bennett and company got everything they needed to hear too. Mark her down as a Liberal and on to the next house. They artfully extracted themselves from the situation and keep moving.

•••

If you want to understand politics — *real* politics — the little Woodwynd Street cul de sac in St. John's is a good place to start.

The lady in the house was right; the Virginia Waters byelection was a big one.

St. John's is historically Tory territory, and in recent years, it's also been kind to the NDP. So if the Liberals could win here, in the solidly urban district of Virginia Waters, it'd be a major boost of momentum for the party. Symbolically, it wouldn't hurt that Virginia Waters was Premier Kathy Dunderdale's old seat.

Cathy Bennett may have failed in her leadership bid, but clearly it did enough to raise her personal profile so that she could call out the big guns. Along with Garneau and Ball, Liberal MP Scott Andrews was cheerfully heading from house-to-house as well for the campaign blitz.

Between houses, Bennett went over to Noah, a disaffected former New Democrat who was now volunteering for the Liberals.

"Twelve is not home. Fourteen is undecided," Bennett said to him.

Noah dutifully marked it down. He had a sheaf of paper with names and barcodes, and he was writing in "L" or "NL" or "NH" "UD."

Noah was keeping track of the four of them, as the politicians went door-to-door sussing out the Liberals, Not Liberals, Not Home and Undecided voters.

Noah was harried, and got a panic-stricken look on his face as Scott Andrews bounded up to a door and started knocking, before anybody could tell him that Bennett and Garneau had already done that house.

"It's like herding cats, eh?" I said to Noah.

"Herding kittens," he said, shaking his head.

The undecided old man at No. 16 got to hear the pitch again from Andrews, but remained undecided anyway.

Oh well, you can't get 'em all, and really that's not even what you're trying to do.

"Every fifth door, you might have that one person that says, 'Jeez, I've got a question about forestry and wood products and how much it cost me for that cord of wood,'" Andrews said, gesturing at the pile of cut wood stacked in the front yard of a house. "So you might pick up a little bit of that." For the most part, though, Andrews said door-to-door campaigning is not about policy, and it's not about winning votes. It's about *identifying* votes.

Really, Noah was the most important person on the team, because he was the one holding the clipboard. The other four were just over-glorified pollsters, figuring out which houses will vote Liberal, and which ones won't. Generally speaking, voter turnout in Canadian elections has been steadily dropping for decades. In a byelection, like the one going on in Virginia Waters, turnout will typically be even lower still, because people don't get inundated by the same onslaught of political coverage that you'd get with a normal election.

When the votes were counted, that trend was borne out; 49 per cent of eligible voters cast ballots in the byelection, fewer than either of the past two general elections.

If only half of the eligible voters will actually cast a ballot, forget about winning new supporters. Just make all of the people who support you show up at the polls. Call 'em up early on advanced polling day and try to lock it down then. And on election day, make sure your scrutineers track who's come through the polling station. If somebody said they're going to vote for you, and they haven't voted yet, call 'em up. An hour later, call 'em again. Can't make it to the polls? Like hell you can't, we're sending a car over; we'll drive you there.

People who don't know politics assume that on some basic level, elections are about convincing as many people as possible to vote for you. But that's not quite correct. Actually, elections are about making sure that you have the most votes when they get counted. Sometimes that means putting your smiling face on lawn signs, and trying to win people over. Other times it means running vile, vicious attack ads — don't put your smiling face on those ones! — hoping to turn off casual voters, and drive down overall voter turnout. If turnout is low, but you can get your hardcore committed people to the polls … well … winning is winning, right?

The high-profile blitz on Woodwynd Street was enough to garner a bit of media attention, but most of the time, it's much more low key. Usually it's volunteers with clipboards and numb fingers systematically working their way from street to street, and then doubling back later to hit up all the houses where people weren't home the first time around.

In fact, Andrews said, when the candidate actually goes door-to-door, it can be a bit of a liability, because it's harder to get honest answers.

"As a candidate, the information that you always bring back, you've got to cut it down, because people are always nice to the candidate," he said.

• • •

The PC Party knew the Virginia Waters byelection was a big one too, and it wasn't looking good.

The Tories were behind in the polls, not as well organized, and last out of the gate. Both the Liberals and the NDP had their candidates in place by early March, just a few days after Kathy Dunderdale formally resigned her seat in the legislature and departed from politics for good. It took the Tories nearly two weeks to beat the bushes and ultimately woo St. John's city councillor Danny Breen to put his name forward. Breen was a good candidate with a couple of municipal elections under his belt and a solid base of support, but he was campaigning with a severe handicap — the PC Party. A province-wide poll released during the byelection campaign put the Liberals at 60 per cent public support among decided voters; the Tories had half that, with 30 per cent.

Faced with that kind of uphill battle, the Tories reached out to the best fighter they've got: Danny Williams. It's important to understand just how wildly popular Williams was during his heyday in Newfoundland and Labrador politics. One of my colleagues at the CBC said that the 2007 general election campaign was like touring the province with Mick Jagger. Danny was a political rockstar, a saviour, an outlier. On the week that he announced his retirement from politics, back in 2010, Halifax-based polling firm Corporate Research Associates released a poll headlined, "Williams' Popularity As A Premier Unmatched In Canadian History."

Williams may also be the luckiest politician in Canadian history — he rode into office when oil was $30/barrel and by the time he retired, it was over $90/barrel. He got to take credit for the subsequent economic miracle, as the province's offshore oilfields started generating super-royalties and pumping billions of dollars into the provincial treasury. But in politics, it's better to be lucky than to be good, and Williams got out of Dodge before his luck turned. He presided over a massive increase in government spending — at one point, he gave the public service a 20 per cent raise over four years, and added thousands of people to the provincial bureaucracy — but by the time those chickens came home to roost, it was Kathy Dunderdale's problem.

Williams was a charismatic fighter and a no-nonsense business guy who was going to whip the government into shape. He was big on nationalistic rhetoric, and instilling a sense of pride in the people of the province. His political opponents weren't just wrong, they were branded as traitors. He made you feel like he was the smartest guy in the room, whichever room he was in. People loved him for all of it.

When he left, Dunderdale inherited a political party that was sitting at 75 per cent in the polls. Behind the scenes there was some sort of rift between Williams and Dunderdale in the months after he retired, and he basically sat out of provincial politics altogether for three years. Dunderdale won the 2011 election anyway on leftover Tory goodwill and then watched all that public support crumble. Fast-forward to March of 2014; Dunderdale was gone, her seat in Virginia Waters was vacant, and the Tories really, really, really needed to win this one.

Virginia Waters was a district that Dunderdale won handily in the last general election, even though she spent barely any time campaigning there.[1] But a few months earlier, the Tories lost the seat of former finance minister Jerome Kennedy out in Carbonear-Harbour Grace, and they desperately wanted to avoid another high-profile defeat. On Facebook and Twitter, you could watch as reams

---

[1] In the 2011 general election, she was on planes and buses, touring the province with a gaggle of staffers and reporters in tow.

of Progressive Conservative cabinet ministers posed for pictures as they went door-to-door for Danny Breen. And then there was Williams, with his characteristic growl, telling reporters about the good old days when he was in charge, and how awful things had been under the Liberals, and about the economic miracle that he, personally, was responsible for.

"I think it's important, you know, and people need to remember what it was like 10-12 years ago in this province. I mean, as a result of the Conservative government, there's been tremendous changes in this province," Williams told the pack of summoned media after shaking hands and chatting at a seniors' lunch in the MacMorran Community Centre. "I just think it's important that the people of the province are reminded, basically, of how good the Conservative government has been for the province. You know, things have never looked better."

It got so desperate towards the end that the Progressive Conservative campaign staff issued a media advisory telling reporters where Danny Williams and Danny Breen would be eating lunch — fish and chips at Ches's. It wasn't a campaign stop; they didn't have anything they wanted to announce to the media. The place was almost completely empty, and the two tables of regular people eating lunch got awkward when Williams went over to chat them up. It was just a photo-op of two guys eating cod and potatoes, but the Tories were basically convinced that the formula for electoral success was getting photographed beside Danny Williams. I mean, it worked for nearly a decade, didn't it?

• • •

When it was all over, Cathy Bennett took to the stage at her victory party and declared, "It's a really important night for the province."

I wound up at the Liberals' camp on election night, because it's more fun covering winners, and my gut said that they were headed for a narrow victory. Right through the campaign, the Liberals had been better organized, and as I've said, that's what wins these things.

As the results trickled in, at the Progressive Conservative headquarters, volunteers marked poll-by-poll numbers down on big pieces of paper taped to the walls. The Liberals had the results updated on a spreadsheet projected onto a big screen at the front of the room. As the numbers were coming in, a lot of the old timers with long memories said that it all had a similar feeling to a pair of byelections back in 2001 on the Northern Peninsula. Back then, a couple Tories stole traditionally Liberal seats, and it marked the symbolic beginning of the Danny Williams wave.

While the results were coming in, I ended up chatting with a guy who was in a good position to assess the similarities: Tom Osborne. He sat in Opposition with the Tories prior to Danny's big win in 2003, and then served in the cabinet for a while. A whole lot of water under the bridge and a floor-crossing later, and Osborne was now sitting in Opposition with the Liberals — likely in line for a plum cabinet post, or maybe House of Assembly Speaker if the Liberals formed a government.

I asked Osborne if it felt like deja vu. He just laughed and said, "This is pretty cool."

In the end, Cathy Bennett won by 40 votes. The cheers were massive. The booze was flowing. Everybody hugged everybody else. At one point, Dwight Ball led Cathy Bennett up to the podium, and lifted her arm into the air like a referee in a boxing ring.

"This night really builds on a tremendous amount of Liberal momentum that has been sweeping across the province and across Canada, and I'm honoured to be part of that momentum in Virgina Waters," Bennett said in her victory speech. "You know, Liberals have worked tirelessly and showed such great support over the past several weeks to get us to where we are tonight, and I know that we're going to continue to grow the party, build our momentum and work together for the people of Virginia Waters and across the province."

Already, the Liberals were looking past the byelection. They had bigger targets in their sights.

"Ladies and Gentlemen, Liberals are preparing for the next election, and Liberals will be ready for the next election, and we are preparing to lead the province," Ball shouted with jubilation. "People expect more from our politicians. They expect honesty, they expect hard work, and they should. And the Liberal Party of

Newfoundland and our caucus — now of twelve! — we're going to make sure that happens."

• • •

Over at the PC Party camp, in defeat, Danny Williams was in fine form as the inspiring fighter.

He told the crowd that they were squeezed by two other strong candidates, and they were 15 points down in the polls just a few weeks earlier. Williams said in the last few weeks — subtext: after he got involved — they managed to claw their way to within 40 votes of victory.

"Next time around, we'll bury 'em!" he snarled. People cheered. It was the sort of speech that hit you deep in the chest and grabbed hold of you, if you were susceptible to that sort of thing.

Watching the video of it, I felt bad for the old man. Back in 2010, everybody agreed that he was the smartest man in the room because he was getting out while the going was still good. Most political leaders stay around until after the people turn on them. It's better to leave while you're still on top, rather than wait for the voters to show you the door. A few years later, it was time to reassess the verdict. He was still trying to pull the strings behind the scenes, but he wasn't having very much success doing it. First he handed things off to Dunderdale, and that didn't go as expected. Then he waded into the race to pick Dunderdale's successor, and that turned into an unmitigated mess. Williams threw it all against the wall during the byelection — a tough fight in a seat that would've been completely safe back when he was in charge — and he couldn't even win that.

So there he was on election night, gnashing his teeth and showing his claws, looking every inch the political lion he once was. But as the saying goes, "Winning isn't everything; it's the only thing." And Danny Williams couldn't win anymore.

The Virginia Waters byelection was a watershed moment. Whatever the Tories were in the spring of 2014, it was clear to me that they were doomed if they kept looking to the past. Danny Williams was good for about seven and a half years of government. If he'd decided to stick around, he probably could have stretched that out into 12 years, or even longer. If the only thing that the Tories had left was reminding people about the time Danny went to Ottawa, put Paul Martin in a headlock, and came back home with a $2 billion cheque, they were doomed. Since those good old days, the government put that money in the stock market and lost it all. Between Bill 29, the blackouts, the public sector layoffs and everything else, they pissed away all their political capital too. The Virginia Waters byelection should have been a wakeup call for the PC Party.

Instead, the party was already in the process of doubling down on a failing strategy, and its feckless, tired, stammering champion: Frank Coleman.

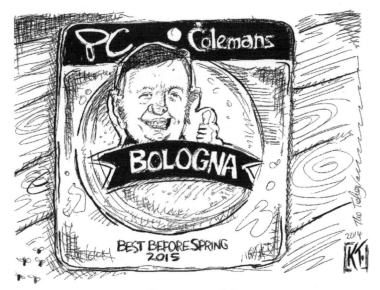

CHAPTER 11
I WAS THE COW
APRIL 2014

If you cover politics, you spend most of your time talking to losers. For any given election in any district in Newfoundland and Labrador, there is a 2:1 loser-to-winner ratio. Even among the winning cohort, there are plenty of losers who will never make it into cabinet, and loser cabinet ministers who will struggle, fight and fail to make it right to the top.

Frank Coleman skipped all those rungs on the ladder, and started his political career at the very top. But at the end of my first conversation with the man, I was absolutely certain that Frank Coleman was a political loser. There was zero doubt in my mind that given the chance, Coleman would lead the PC Party to a stunning defeat in the 2015 general election.

My very first question to Coleman was simple: Why do you want to be premier?

He answered in three parts, with so many half-formed sentences, rambling diversions, ums, you knows, that verbatim quoting would either be impossible or very, very cruel. So, here's a verbatim quote:

Me: So, why do you want to be the premier of the province?

Coleman: "Well, you know, I did give a very, I thought, uh, lucid explanation of why I wanted to do that on Wednesday. What I said was I felt a) this province has been really good to me and my family, and uh, I just felt it was, uh, you know, a great, uh, opportunity for me to contribute, No. 1. No. 2, uh, it's the right time in my career to do that, and No. 3, I actually, absolutely, uh, love what has happened to Newfoundland since, you know, uh, the early 2000s, and uh, I'd hate to see us go backwards. And, uh, you know, we've had such tremendous changes in our economy since then. I mean, more people are working. Uh. You know, we're no longer on equalization. You know, we're investing in infrastructure. You know, our credit rating is amazing — uh, historically high. Uh. You know, capital investment is at $11 billion and growing."

He kept going for a while like that, but I'm going to stop there, because it's painful to write, and it's painful to read. But really stop and think about that answer for a minute. He wants to be premier for three reasons:

1. Now is a "great, uh, opportunity" to get into politics and make a contribution to the province through public service.
2. He was at a point in his career where he could walk away.
3. The Tories have done awesome things in the past decade.

Is it possible to come up with a more uninspiring hodgepodge of reasons for going into public life? For starters, why should anybody care about where you're at in your career? This isn't about you, this is supposed to be about what you can contribute for the people of the province. And sure, it's a great opportunity; it's an opportunity to be premier of the province without paying your dues or learning the ropes first. But that doesn't tell us *why* you want to be premier. Nor does it tell us *why we should want you to be premier*. Neither does answer No. 3. That just tells us that you want to be associated with a decade of governing which you didn't participate in.

There's something deeply presumptuous about somebody who would waltz into politics without any experience, and then casually arrogate a decade worth of public policy accomplishments that he wasn't around for. And if you truly believe that the Tories have done great things in the past decade — the voters aren't convinced, but whatever — it's just as presumptuous to believe that you could go straight from private life into the most powerful office in the province and continue that record of success.

My interview with Coleman lasted a total of 23 minutes, and when I hung up the phone, without thinking, I blurted out: "Wow, that guy is hopeless."

It didn't matter.

Less than a month after I spoke to him for the first time, it was all over, and Coleman was premier-in-waiting for the province of Newfoundland and Labrador. Nobody ever cast a ballot for him; Coleman was set to become premier without ever contesting any democratic process of any type. But the backroom boys picked him out, and they paved the path to victory. People looked past his stammering mannerisms, his total lack of vision and energy. The folks who picked him out managed to ignore the fact that he had no political experience, and apparently his instincts were godawful too.

I have no idea what the mandarins of the PC Party were thinking. On the outside looking in, it was perfectly obvious that Premier Frank Coleman was going to be a mess. He was going to make Dunderdale look brilliant by comparison. The day after he "won" the leadership, a friend sent me a note: "So the PC chapters don't end with Kathy! This is good news for a book writer."

I replied: "I'm of two minds about the book: A close race would've been nice and exciting. But I'm OK with a train wreck too."

● ● ●

But before we microwave some popcorn and sit back to watch the unfolding train wreck, let's look at how we got here.

To understand how Coleman became the soon-to-be premier of the province, you just had to head out to the Society of United Fishermen hall in Heart's Content. The little hall is the sort of place with two portraits of the Queen — one at either end of the main room — along with many historical black-and-white photographs and SUF memorabilia hanging on the walls.

In total, 126 Tories registered to vote in the Trinity-Bay de Verde district delegate selection meeting, and a bunch more showed up to watch, all packed into the little hall. The voters sat on steel-and-wood church-basement chairs and patiently waited with ballots in hand for the thing to start. None of them wanted to talk to me about politics, though. When I asked one old lady who she was supporting, she told me that it'd be better if I asked her husband. The only information she offered up was that she had a wedding shower to go to at 8 p.m., and if the voting didn't start soon, she'd be leaving. When I approached another guy and asked him who he thought would make the best premier, he told me that there was too much fighting in hockey these days.

Frank Coleman was there, slowly wading through the crowded room, shaking hands and chatting with people. He told me that nobody really asked him about policy at the delegate selection meetings — mostly people just wanted to shake his hand, look him in the eye, and get a sense of what he was all about.

"When I'm going around right now, to be truthful, I'm really introducing myself, and it's not a really hard sell," he said. "Tonight I don't think I had any policy questions; it was really a meet and greet."

These sorts of meetings aren't really about vision or big ideas. The way you win a delegated convention is by stacking each little meeting with your own people — calling around in the weeks ahead of the meeting to make sure that reliable Tories will show up and vote for your supporters, so they can get elected as convention delegates and ultimately vote for you. After he made the rounds, Coleman ducked out before the voting actually got underway. He didn't need to be there; his people had already done all the heavy lifting for him.

Trinity-Bay de Verde was Finance Minister Charlene Johnson's district, and less than two weeks before the meeting she formally endorsed Coleman for leader. "I see in Frank a leader who understands the importance of fiscal stewardship and achieving balanced budgets while at the same time ensuring we are addressing the social needs of Newfoundlanders and Labradorians," she said in a news release. As Coleman was glad-handing around the room, Johnson was standing in his shadow.

When the actual meeting got underway, the four members of the district association executive formally resigned their positions, and PC Party chief electoral officer Robert Lundrigan called for nominations to fill those positions. The same four people — Johnson's people — were re-nominated, and no one ran against them. Each of them would get a vote at the leadership convention scheduled for July, and presumably they'd all vote with Johnson. Four easy votes for Frank Coleman.

Next, it was time to select the seven other convention delegates who would also head to St. John's. Unlike the executive, this part wasn't a fait accompli; it was loosely organized chaos. Lundrigan called for nominations from the floor, and people started shouting out names. On either side of the room at the front of the hall, two ladies stood beside big lined sheets of paper taped to the wall, and dutifully wrote down each of the names as the nominations came in. There was a moment of confusion when somebody shouted out Edna McCann's name. She was one of the two name-writers, and she clearly wasn't expecting it. Lundrigan asked her if she accepted the nomination.

"For what?" McCann asked, confused about what was happening.

"For convention delegate," Lundrigan said.

"Oh … Sure," McCann replied.

"OK, write down your own name," Lundrigan told her, and McCann dutifully added her name to the list.

When the dust settled, 15 people were nominated for the seven convention delegate positions. Nobody formally said they'd be supporting Frank Coleman or Bill Barry, but it wasn't too hard to read between the lines. Among the 15 names, Johnson's mother, father and sister were all nominated. And Johnson's aunt was one of the four people on the district association executive.

"They can make their own choice, but it's no secret that I've supported Frank and I hope they do the same," Johnson said to me as we were sitting in the hall after the votes were cast, waiting for the results to be announced.

On the surface, it looked like grassroots democracy, and overwhelming local support for Charlene Johnson —and by extension, Frank Coleman.

But look closely, and there were hints of something else at the meeting, too. Once the voting started, most people went to fill out their ballots behind cardboard privacy screens set up on tables at the head of the room, but plenty of people decided to skip the lines and just fill out their ballot on a windowsill, or in their lap, or pressed up against the wall. Because the nominations had only been shouted out from the floor a few minutes earlier, the ballots just had seven blank spaces, and voters had to write in whichever names they wanted from the list of 15 nominees. And some of the voters were getting a bit of assistance. I saw at least two people filling out their ballots holding a little card with names printed on it — tiny little computer-printed lettering on something about the size of a business card.

When I snapped a picture of one guy filling out his ballot against the wall with the aid of one of those little cards, somebody tapped him on the shoulder, and he whipped around. He pocketed the card. When I asked him about it a little later, he said he didn't know what I was talking about. "There's nothing top secret here," he said with a laugh. I asked Johnson about it too; she said that some of the older folks in her district are partially illiterate, so maybe that's why they had little cards. I guess I didn't look convinced, so she offered an alternate theory: Maybe it was Bill Barry's doing. She said that her people don't need to be prompted, because her district association sends the same people to convention every single year.

With all the ballots cast, Lundrigan and a couple of other people retreated into a back room to tally the votes. Two scrutineers representing Colmeman went in to watch the counting. Barry didn't have any scrutineers there. The hall cleared out pretty quickly. Most people left once their ballot was cast. In the end, it was entirely Johnson's crew that got elected as convention delegates. She said a few people she didn't recognize — likely Barry's people — got selected as convention alternates, but all the votes were aligned with Johnson.

• • •

Much later, after he dropped out of the race, I learned that by the time of the Trinity-Bay de Verde meeting, Bill Barry was starting to sour on the whole process. I heard that at an earlier nomination meeting in Bonavista South, the local MHA was allowed to give a speech before the votes were cast, and the speech amounted to an endorsement of Coleman. Barry was at the meeting, but he wasn't allowed to speak, because there wasn't supposed to be any campaigning happening. Barry was planning on going to Trinity-Bay de Verde, but after the Bonavista South meeting left a bad taste in his mouth, he didn't bother.

Less than a week after the the Trinity-Bay de Verde meeting, Barry sent an email to the media at around 4 a.m. He was bitter and dejected, and he wasn't going to go along with the charade anymore.

"I find it difficult to have many wonderful people offering me daily support and encouragement when the final outcome is preordained. Its less than interesting for me to play against a stacked deck," Barry wrote. "Bottom line; my heart is no longer in this process. I am NOT a status quo guy. Change; renewal and reality need to be the basis of our future Provincial agenda."

He said that people within the party were encouraging him to keep running, "but I have to ask ... Why would I and why am I being encouraged?"

Bill Barry was always destined to be a loser. The insiders didn't want him, and he was trying to beat them in a process that overwhelmingly favoured the insiders. Moreover, Barry didn't do himself any favours. At his campaign launch, he said that most MHAs in the House of Assembly — Tories included — were so brain-dead they wouldn't realize if "a bucket of S-H-I-T" was dumped over their heads. And whatever he did to piss off Danny Williams was clearly a mistake too.

But by the end, it was hard not to feel bad for him.

Coleman's campaign started rolling out a steady march of cabinet ministers endorsing his candidacy two at a time. All the news releases looked the same. It was perfectly obvious to anybody watching that the entire cabinet was behind Coleman, and the campaign was just spacing out the endorsements to keep up a steady drumbeat. When she endorsed him, Johnson praised his vision for the fiscal direction of the province, even though nobody could really remember Coleman talking in much detail about the province's finances. He said he wanted to fix the province's unfunded pension liability, but he said he didn't know how to do it. Nonetheless, in the news release where she endorsed him, Johnson said he was great on finance stuff.

Nobody endorsed Barry. It was like a high school cafeteria where all all the cool kids close ranks and leave one person on the outside, all alone. The Tory establishment didn't just beat Barry; they embarrassed him. This should go without saying, but in case there are any Tories reading this book, I'll spell it out loud and clear: Chasing Bill Barry out of the leadership race was a stunning tactical error. And yes, he was chased out of the race; he dropped out because staying around for another two months would have been absolutely humiliating, with zero upside.

Barry himself said it pretty well, when I sat down and talked to him over lunch, about a week after he quit the race. "I was told by a particular individual that I was providing a great service to the party. And I was thinking about, you know, the bull servicing the cow, and thinking that I was the cow."

The Tory leadership race was supposed to be the big chance for renewal — a chance to talk big ideas and get people excited about the party again. In the weeks after Dunderdale resigned, the thing I heard over and over again from rank-and-file Tories was that they didn't want a coronation. They wanted a healthy race. For about a minute, when there were a dozen potential candidates, it looked like the grassroots might just get their wish. But then Fabian Manning and all the others turned out to be a mirage, and everybody decided that they didn't want to go up against the anointed favourite: Frank Coleman.

"It's a party that's preaching renewal, but it looks like it's decided not to have any debates about what that means," Memorial University political science professor Kelly Blidook told me at the time. "Jeez, you can run a sham and you can make it look a little bit less like a sham than this. I mean, this is so obviously orchestrated at this point, right?"

When nominations closed, the only real challenger was Bill Barry, and he was already fatally wounded from the Danny Williams broadside.[1]

---

[1] Wayne Bennett was disqualified from the leadership race as a result of culturally insensitive comments he made on Twitter, and his inexplicable decision to endorse a New Democrat candidate. He was always an irrelevant, fringe candidate, and he doesn't factor into our story in any meaningful way.

So the party leadership race collapsed from the excitement of a dozen possible candidates down to just two: the favourite and the also-ran. Tories were forced to gamely insist that they were both capable contenders, and that the race between the two of them was exactly the sort of excitement and renewal that the party needed. Out in Heart's Content, Johnson told me that on a good night, maybe 20 people would show up to a normal district AGM. A hundred and twenty-six people casting ballots was proof, to her, that there was plenty of life still left in the PC Party.

"With so many people here tonight, it shows there's still a lot of interest in our party," Johnson said. "People still take us very seriously, support what we're doing and this will help build momentum as we go through for the next election."

If the party insiders wanted the kabuki theatre of a leadership race, they could've put up one or two cabinet ministers to run against Coleman. An ambitious MHA like Steve Kent would've provided a bit of opposition, and maybe a few provocative ideas.[2] Being on the inside, he might've even garnered an endorsement or two, to hide the appearance of a sham race. And Kent would've had a soft landing back in cabinet when it was all over — maybe even with a magnanimous Premier Coleman giving him a small promotion to show that there were no hard feelings.

The way it turned out, though, there was no excitement.

There was no debate.

There were no big ideas.

The average age in the Society of United Fishermen hall was well over 50, and most of them were there to cast a ballot and leave with the least amount of discussion possible. It reminded me of the policy resolutions session at the PC Party convention: a flimsy facade. At the convention, they went through the motions of debating policy, because that's what you're supposed to do at a convention. Out in Heart's Content, people showed up and went through the motions — shouting out nominations and voting — because that's what you're supposed to do during a leadership race. It didn't seem to occur to anybody that going through the motions might not be good enough.

[2] Dramatic foreshadowing...

To have *real* renewal, and *real* excitement, you need *real* debate. But the Tories didn't know how to do that. All they knew how to do was show up and vote the way they were told to vote, and just in case anybody got confused, all the names were neatly printed on little cards to make it easier.

• • •

Frank Coleman is probably a very nice man at home with his family, and chatting with him in the hall out in Heart's Content, he seemed like an affable, well-meaning guy. But when you were just chatting with her about the weather, Kathy Dunderdale was a really nice lady too. Nice doesn't cut it in politics.

Coleman was a rich guy who decided to go into politics, and he decided that the best place to start was in the premier's office.

He wanted to be premier of the province because — we never really did get a firm answer to that question, did we? He didn't offer a specific vision for the provincial government, except "more of the same" at a time when people were pretty fed up with the Tory status quo. "More of the same" was good enough to win the Tory faithful over, but from the outside looking in, it was a disaster waiting to happen.

And then, the disasters started happening for Coleman, literally one day after Barry dropped out of the race.

• • •

Coleman didn't show up to the 2014 Good Friday anti-abortion rally in Corner Brook, but his wife was there, and everybody in the political world knew that in any other year, he would've been there with bells on. The CBC did a story on the rally, and on Coleman's wife. Then the rest of the media jumped on board, and we were away to the races.

It seemingly didn't occur to the Tories that a vocally anti-abortion politician at the helm might be a political liability.

Pretty quickly after the story broke, Coleman issued a statement that was pure damage control.

"My family's participation in this event is a result of shared beliefs on the value of every human life. I do not seek to impose my

views on anyone and truly respect the gift of free will we are all af-
forded," he said. "As a leader, I believe in the rule of law. It would
be weak of me to deny my beliefs, and at the same time it is important that people understand I do not intend to impose my personal
views. I have too much respect for all the people of this province."

The controversy was short-lived. Abortion was a hot-button
issue two decades ago, but most of the world had moved on. In the
minds of most people, a woman's right to make her own decision
about abortion is a settled political issue. Frank Coleman wasn't
going to overturn that, and it would be nothing short of political
suicide to even try it, one year away from a general election with
the Tories already behind in the polls.

But the controversy definitely damaged Coleman. And it didn't
help that Bill Barry gleefully issued a staunchly pro-choice statement right in the thick of it all. The whole thing made Coleman
look like a die-hard religious holdout from an earlier era.

At the time, a massive swath of the electorate wouldn't have
been able to pick Frank Coleman out of a police lineup. Now, all
of a sudden, the only thing anybody knew about him was that he
was anti-abortion, and that was more than enough for a bunch of
people to decide that he didn't represent their values, and he
wouldn't get their vote.

Then, just as the abortion thing was dying down, the Humber
Valley Paving situation flared up.

Coleman used to own Humber Valley Paving, a company that
had multi-million dollar roadwork contracts with government. He
sold his shares in the company just before he made the leap into
politics — and he wouldn't say who he sold those shares to. On its
own, there's nothing scandalous about that, but when people found
out that the government let the company off the hook for a money-
losing contract to pave a section of the Trans-Labrador Highway,
it raised a few eyebrows. When reporters looked into it, and found
that the only two members of the company board of directors were
Michael Coleman and Robert Coleman, that looked a little bit suspicious. Then, Transportation Minister Nick McGrath revealed he
let the company walk away from the paving contract after he spoke
directly with Frank Coleman's son, Gene Coleman. And McGrath

admitted to reporters that he had never been directly involved in renegotiating a government contract before, but he was right smack in the middle of this one.

After a few days of stonewalling on the part of McGrath, interim Premier Tom Marshall referred the whole thing to the auditor general to study. It's possible to imagine Coleman himself might have stepped up and said something like, "I'm sure nothing untoward happened here, but I don't want any whiff of controversy dogging me when I'm sworn in as premier, so I talked to Tom Marshall this morning, and I asked him to refer this matter to the auditor general. Nothing is more important than maintaining the trust of the people."

That would've looked good.

That would've been politically astute.

That didn't happen.

Instead, it was Marshall alone that made the call, and so he was the one who looked like an upstanding, honest guy with nothing to hide. Too bad for the Tories that Marshall was retiring in a couple months, and all that public goodwill and trust would leave with him.

The Humber Valley Paving thing faded to a background irritant after it was referred to the auditor general, just in time for the next little controversy.

Coleman was a board member of a company that sold liquor in Alberta. In an interview, he was asked if he'd privatize the government-owned liquor stores in Newfoundland and Labrador. A seasoned politician would've said something like, "The system seems to work for Alberta, but frankly, privatizing liquor sales is not one of my priorities. When I get into the premier's office, I'm going to be focused on ..." and then he could've spent a couple minutes talking about his policy priorities, assuming he had any.

Instead, Coleman said this: "It works really well in Alberta. Uh, it isn't something that I've listed as a policy, uh, moving into this job. Uh, you know, as I say, it is a good alternative in Alberta. I think they, uh, it has been a rewarding experiment for them. Uh, it is something, I think, that the province of Newfoundland and Labrador could have a look at, but as I say, I don't know what the pros and cons are right now." That wasn't his whole answer; Coleman kept going for a while longer, musing about the possibility of privatizing the liquor corporation, and the possible benefits of going down that road.

It came as no surprise, then, when Opposition Leader Dwight Ball stood up in the House of Assembly a couple days later and demanded to know about Coleman's plans for privatizing the liquor corporation — "A corporation that contributes over $150 million a year to the provincial treasury and employs hundreds of Newfoundlanders and Labradorians," Ball noted.

Moreover, Ball wanted to know what the government was doing to ensure that there was no conflict of interest involved in Coleman's plan to privatize the liquor corporation, given that he was a part owner in a private liquor company which might start doing business in NL.

Of course, with only a year in office before the next general election, Coleman wasn't going to undertake something massive and controversial like selling off the province's liquor stores. He wasn't going to restrict access to abortion either, because that would be electoral suicide too. Frankly, I doubt Coleman had any plan to charge into the premier's office and enact any sort of dramatic policy agenda; he seemingly didn't even have a plan to answer basic questions from journalists.

• • •

Months later, the Humber Valley Paving report came back from auditor general Terry Paddon which concluded that Transportation Minister Nick McGrath had, indeed, acted inappropriately, and dropping the roadwork contract had been rushed.

In a passage that should have been prefaced with a bold, all-caps "READ BETWEEN THE LINES, PEOPLE," Paddon wrote:

"There is no documentary evidence to indicate what prompted two Ministers to call the Deputy Minister of Transportation and Works the morning of March 13, 2014 to enquire about [Humber Valley Paving], which, coincidentally, was the day before the close of nominations for the leadership of the Progressive Conservative Party of Newfoundland and Labrador."

The AG's report in September of 2014 ultimately cost Mc-Grath his job as minister, but it didn't matter for Coleman's political career.

The damage had already been done, for Coleman, and for the PC Party that apparently saw fit to pick him as their next leader. On April 17 when Bill Barry dropped out of the race, most people in the province didn't know the first thing about Frank Coleman. Then they found out that he might be a religious zealot who wanted to restrict access to abortion. Then they heard a lot of stuff that made it sound like he was involved in shady deals with taxpayers' money. And people heard he might sell off the liquor stores for some reason.

And through it all, Coleman developed a reputation for refusing to do interviews with journalists — a reputation he couldn't shake, no matter how many interviews he eventually said "yes" to — and that made him look like just another one of those secretive, out-of-touch Tories, contemptuous towards questions from the public.

• • •

It would be easy to feel bad for Frank Coleman. He was a guy who seemed to have the best of intentions at heart. He was polite and courteous whenever I talked to him. He wasn't a very good public speaker, and he certainly wasn't a larger-than-life ego like so many other Newfoundland and Labrador politicians. To look at him, he was a decent man who heard the the call to public service, and then he was swallowed alive by the rough-and-tumble reality of political life.

It would be easy to feel bad for that guy, but let's look past his appearance.

By actions, Frank Coleman was a staggeringly arrogant man, and a victim of his own hubris.

He convinced himself that, with zero political experience, he could be premier.

Politics is really hard. It's an ugly, ruthless, hyper-competitive world, and most people wind up as losers. It was pure delusion to believe that he could walk into that world and be greeted by anything other than brutal failure. He had no experience, so he commandeered the PC Party record and claimed it as his own. He caused controversy every time he opened his mouth, and then amid the ensuing firestorm, he looked around dumbly wondering what the hell happened.

Don't feel bad for Frank Coleman. Newfoundland and Labrador should expect better than a guy who wasn't even clever enough to think that politics would be hard.

He was a loser right from the beginning, and he got what he deserved.

CHAPTER 12
ORANGE WAVE CRASHING
MAY 17, 2014

Here's a partial list of the things New Democrats like: pensions, solidarity, health care, unions, shouting "shame!," photocopied pamphlets and hugging.

Here's what New Democrats don't like: Stephen Harper and giving short speeches.

On the Victoria Day long weekend in St. John's, New Democrats were in fine form, giving long speeches and hollering "shame!" with wild abandon.

It wasn't all fun and hugging, though; they were hunkered down in a windowless ballroom at the Holiday Inn to take care of a bit of old business.

For anybody paying close attention to the New Democrats, the May convention was stark evidence that the 2011 "Orange Wave" had crested, and the water levels were returning to their previous normal.

After their best-ever results in the 2011 provincial election, there were little glimmers of hope in 2012 and 2013 when it looked like the NDP in Newfoundland and Labrador might be on track to get its hands on some real power. Even if they were still the third party in the House of Assembly, in a couple polls they held the lead over both the Liberals and the Tories. At the very least, becoming Official Opposition looked very doable; heck, holding the balance of power within a minority parliament was a realistic possibility. People even idly talked about the NDP forming government, although that was always seen as a long shot.

Then the caucus revolt happened in October of 2013, and it all went to hell.

With her back against the wall, fighting for her political life, leader Lorraine Michael promised a province-wide convention and a leadership review. Seven months later, on the May long weekend, the party delivered on that promise.

It was too late.

In the intervening seven months, the party's poll numbers dropped off a cliff. Dale Kirby and Christopher Mitchelmore left the NDP caucus and joined up with the Liberals. The New Democrats fought their way through two byelections and came up embarrassingly short in both of them. In the House of Assembly, the rump caucus kept banging away at the same old issues, but they sounded tinny and out of touch with reality.

By the time May rolled around and the New Democrats converged on St. John's for their convention, the party had contracted to a diehard core. The New Democrats insisted that things weren't really so awful. And on paper, anyway, the numbers didn't look too bad. During the halcyon days of 2012 with the wind at their backs, the New Democrats were able to pull 165 people to their convention. During the dark days of 2014, they still had 125 people in the room. And they were 125 people who showed up on a long weekend — the first sunny, warm, beautiful weekend of the year after a long, punishing winter. Really, the New Democrats said, the convention was proof that the party had all the same energy, the same excitement, the same prospects for growth that it did before.

You really had to be there, sitting in the room and listening to the speeches, to understand just how far from reality they all were.

• • •

"If governments are taking away our rights, then it will be at their peril," Federation of Labour president Mary Shortall thundered from the podium Friday evening, as the convention got underway. "Governments can legislate away our rights, but they can never legislate away our anger, our determination and our solidarity."

Later on, leftie stalwart Bill Hynd got a warm reaction during a debate over free trade, when he declared, "CETA and evil have both got four letters, and to me they're both the same."

Judging by the cheers, it didn't occur to anybody else in the room that many voters are deeply ambivalent to unions, and that the combative us-against-them rhetoric of labour leaders can be a major turn-off to moderate voters. And never mind that a recent poll showed the CETA free trade deal between Canada and Europe had 81 per cent public support. Again and again, over the course of the weekend, it was abundantly clear that the NDP wasn't trying to appeal to the masses. The 2014 gathering was a chance for the small knot of hardcore social justice campaigners to get together and let their freak flag fly. The old warhorses and blind partisans were the only ones left in the party.

There's an old joke that I first heard a Tory tell me: "Tories go to their convention to get drunk, Liberals go to their convention to get laid, and New Democrats go to their convention for the pamphlets."[1] The NDP lived up to their stereotype. At the New Democrat gathering on Friday night, they spent what felt like about 10 minutes outlining the anti-discrimination and anti-harassment policy before they moved on to a report from the election planning committee, where an earnest-sounding lady described the committee's progress, and the work of the ten different election planning subcommittees.

You have to see it up close to appreciate just how different the culture of the NDP is from the other two parties. The Liberals and the Tories show up and go through the motions of conventioneering, but the New Democrats embrace it with gusto. They debate every motion, and they're sticklers for Robert's Rules of Order every step of the way.

The Liberals and the Tories are like the high school football team — people join for the parties and because it's cool. The NDP is more like the math club — the only reason you end up there is if you're really into math. It's not that New Democrats don't know how to have fun; it's just that fun for them is diligently and sincerely working to bring about social equality for disadvantaged members of the community.

For a lot of these people, listening to Mary Shortall bellow about collective bargaining amounts to a rockin' Friday night.

• • •

Just a couple hours before the leadership vote, Lorraine Michael took to the podium.

It was a good speech. It was exactly the sort of speech she needed to give. She admitted that she'd done wrong, and she took

---

[1] I'm sure when the Liberals tell the same joke, it's the Tories who are trying to get laid. Never mind. I've been to both, and it's the same vibe of drunken revelry.

a share of the blame for the caucus revolt. It was the thing that every New Democrat had been waiting seven months to hear.

"Did I make mistakes? Yes. Maybe the most serious was not to hear concerns in the caucus and the party about how to move forward. I missed the trees for the forest in what was needed to build a broader consensus in our party about the next steps. That was a mistake I just made. I am a big picture person — that's a very positive thing — the leader has to be a big picture person. You have to have a vision. And sometimes, as I'm there, I forget details because I'm so concentrated on the horizon. That's the reality. I don't want that to happen again, so I have to keep seeing the trees."

It wasn't much of a mea culpa — effectively saying "I was partly responsible for torching the NDP's public reputation, but only because I have such amazing leadership qualities," — but it was good enough for the New Democrat delegates in the room. After she got the sort-of-apology out of the way, Michael pivoted to her many accomplishments as leader.

She pointed out that in the months since the caucus revolt, the Tory government announced a moratorium on fracking, added transgender to the province's human rights code, enacted "Move Over" road safety legislation, started debate on public service whistleblower legislation, got the ball rolling on full-day kindergarten, cut small business taxes and increased financial assistance to college and university students. Each and every one of those measures started out as a New Democrat policy idea, and then it turned into a concerted advocacy campaign before it finally got adopted by the government.

It was an impressive list, and the delegates listening to her speech kept interrupting her with applause breaks as she rattled them all off. But the thing that nobody in the NDP ever acknowledges is that if you're in government, you could make all that stuff happen in a few months. The NDP, advocating from the fringes, spent *eight years* pushing for whistleblower legislation before it happened. The idea of replacing student loans with grants was more than a decade in the making.

For a little while, it looked like the NDP might get to taste real power at some point. It would mean abandoning some of the most extreme elements of the party and making way for a more inclusive message. It looked like Dale Kirby was trying to drag the party closer to the centre and, as much as anything else, that tension was what caused the caucus revolt. Of course, anybody familiar with the inner workings of the NDP will tell you that Michael and Kirby bitterly despised each other for years, and obviously that didn't help matters. The clash of vision was all tied up in a vicious little a clash of personality.

For a little while, it looked like the NDP would aim for a broader public appeal, and it would inch towards the centre. But with Kirby and Mitchelmore gone, and the party crashing back down to a distant third in the polls, Michael was regressing. If the rest of the population wouldn't love her, she'd revert back to the warm embrace of the hardcore union types and social justice campaigners. She would always know where she stood with those folks. They would always stick by her — a knot of true believers hustling for change from the fringes.

• • •

The actual vote took place just after lunch. It was the sort of disorganized circus which only the NDP could pull off.

First they held a vote to decide whether to throw the media out for the vote. They let the reporters stay, but half an hour later it was abundantly clear that they really should've kicked them out to avoid embarrassment.

The ballots were distributed. It was a secret ballot, but there were no privacy screens, so members were told to just sit at a table and sort of cover the ballot with one hand while you mark it with your other one.

Then the chair opened debate on the motion, and the first guy who got to a microphone said, "Um … why do we have a debate … when it's a secret ballot? I don't understand that concept."

Another person said that if they were going to debate Lorraine Michael's leadership, they should revisit the question of whether the media would be thrown out of the room.

Somebody else claimed that reporters moving around the room were trying to take pictures of people filling out their ballots —

which, of course, we were —and so the whole affair got sidetracked by a debate over whether to force the media to stand at the back of the room. That side-motion passed.

The confusion didn't stop there; there were ballot problems. Because the volunteers handing ballots out had just given one to everyone with a valid delegate badge, there was no voter's list and no way of knowing if people voted more than once.

"I thought only the PCs had this much red tape," one person grumbled, as organizers desperately tried to maintain control of the situation.

The ballot was pretty self-explanatory, albeit awkwardly worded. "VOTE NO if you don't want a leadership convention to be held" was on one line, with a "NO" box beside it. Below that, it said "VOTE YES if you want a leadership convention to be held" with a "YES" box beside it. Somehow, this confused a few people too.

One guy stepped forward uncomfortably to say that he needed a new ballot.

"I've got my ballot marked already because I thought the leadership convention was going to be held here today," he said. "If it's going to be held at some other time, then I've got a spoiled ballot."

At around this point, people started looking at each other incredulously.

Through it all, people stuck slavishly to their points of order, and correct rules of procedure. I mentioned in passing to one of the New Democrat bigwigs that no other party obsesses over the geeky minutia of procedure. She laughed. "Oh, we have to. Otherwise it'd be chaos. We'd have to taser people. And that goes against our whole peace and love thing."

Eventually, people started getting confused about why people were confused, and it looked like the debate would swallow itself whole. Somehow, after half an hour of befuddlement, the organizers manage to wrestle control back and the New Democrats got to voting.

A while later, after the ballots were counted, Michael sat quietly at a table up at the front of the room. A consummate politician, she probably wouldn't ever admit that she had doubts, that she believed the party might not stand by her, that she was scared. She sat there stonefaced until she saw me taking her picture, and then she painted on a smile.

Then the results were announced: 94 votes backing her leadership out of 125 cast — 75 per cent support.

Comedian, author and activist Greg Malone was sitting beside her. As she smiled with relief, he grabbed her wrist and lifted it over her head triumphantly. She hugged Gerry Rogers and George Murphy, and the three of them stood, hand in hand with their arms raised over their heads, as the party faithful cheered.

Everything was right in the world of the NDP.

● ● ●

I interviewed Michael the day after the leadership vote, and she was upbeat.

"I just know that there's real commitment in this room that will spread out to the district associations to work hard for our election and to continue the party growing in the province. I feel very, very positive and energized."

The problem here is that Lorraine Michael has a history of saying things that aren't true. It's tough to accuse her of lying, because that implies an intent to mislead. It's just that her words are out of touch with reality.

On the eve of the Carbonear-Harbour Grace byelection, Michael stood in front of the TV cameras and said, "I think we have a three-way race going on here; I really do. ... I'm really honest when I say I can't call tonight."

Hours later, the New Democrat candidate was utterly demolished, coming a distant third in the polls. If Michael was being really honest when she said the race was too close to call, she was really honestly deluded.

A few days before the leadership convention, I was interviewing Michael and she insisted that the caucus revolt hadn't done all that much damage, really. "We've had four or five people leave the party. ... Seriously, our membership is going up regularly. Every week our membership since October has been going up, and I feel really good about that."

It's impossible to independently verify Michael's claims about the party membership, but it's demonstrably false that only four or five people quit the party in the wake of the caucus revolt. Following the Great October Unpleasantness, MHAs Dale Kirby and Christopher Mitchelmore quit the party, of course, but also NDP vice-president Geoff Gallant stepped down from his position, and he started turning up at Liberal fundraisers. Around that time, other NDP candidates from the 2011 election quit, including Matt Fuchs and John Riche. Oh, and at least two board members in the party — Leigh Borden and Chris Bruce — quit their positions in the wake of the caucus revolt.

For anybody keeping count, that's seven people who held prominent positions within the party — either as candidates or executive board members — who publicly announced that they were parting ways. It might seem like I'm being pedantic, but if the premier or the leader of the Official Opposition made a claim that was so obviously and demonstrably untrue, it would be aggressively challenged. If Dwight Ball said some of the things that come out of Lorraine Michael's mouth, he would be met with ridicule. Instead, people just shrug and say, "Well, that's just the NDP."

Sitting with Michael in the NDP convention hall on Sunday afternoon, she was out of touch with reality. She made it sound like the Great October Unpleasantness was just a hiccup which the party had successfully put behind it.

"Right now in every region we have district associations, and we've had growth in every region, so we've just got to keep that going."

I just nodded, and let the comment go. If she wanted to claim that the party was growing in every region of the province, it didn't seem worth the effort to demand proof. It didn't matter if was true or not.

Lorraine Michael and the NDP were back to the political fringes; they were irrelevant.

CHAPTER 13
UNSPECIFIED ISSUES
JUNE 16, 2014

"Can I go on the air and just say, 'What the fuck?' Is that allowed?"

A few minutes later, Frank Coleman would walk through the doors of the little conference room at the Holiday Inn and announce that he was stepping aside as premier-designate for the PC Party. It was Monday afternoon, a little less than three weeks from when Coleman was supposed to bask in the glowing endorsement of the faithful Progressive Conservatives at the party's convention in St. John's. Instead, due to an unspecified "significant and challenging family matter" he was walking away. The news had leaked out a couple hours before the formal press conference, and as we set up our gear, journalists were having a difficult time digesting the news.

It's worth stepping back and looking at the big picture to appreciate how astoundingly dysfunctional this all was.

In the beginning, there was Danny Williams, who was wildly popular. Then Kathy Dunderdale took over, who was somewhat less popular, and got steadily less popular as time went on. Eventually, Dunderdale got so unpopular that Tories started desperately hoping she would step aside so they could turn things around. Dunderdale granted their wish and stepped aside. And after a totally-not-rigged-by-the-man-behind-the-curtain leadership race, lo and behold, Dunderdale was to be replaced by Coleman, a man so politically inept that he made her look half-good by comparison. Within three months of Coleman bursting into the spotlight, the long-suffering PC Party faithful — by this time having a bit of a spiritual crisis, and drifting towards agnosticism — had repeated the Dunderdale cycle, and were quietly praying for Coleman to go.

And then he went, and everybody stood around trying to figure out what the hell to do next.

The news conference itself was a pretty banal affair. Coleman walked in, poured himself a glass of water and put on a pair of glasses. He sat alone at the table and made his announcement, which would've been a bombshell except that it had already leaked out to the media.

It was "personal family issues." No details. Full stop.

"Family" makes it tough for journalists to ask follow-up questions. By and large, the Newfoundland and Labrador media will bend over backwards to avoid treading into the private lives of politicians' families. Some things are just off limits. Coleman's kids aren't elected, and they're not responsible for making government decisions. Coleman's marital life is his own business too, just like how Newfoundland media basically didn't mention the fact that Danny Williams got divorced while in office.

Resignations are tough for reporters, too. Even if it leaves a bunch of unanswered questions, once a politician has resigned, by definition they're not responsible for anything anymore, so they're not really obliged to answer questions. There's a limit to how hard you can grill a guy when he's quitting. We asked a few awkward questions, but Coleman steadfastly refused to give any details on why he was quitting, apart from the fact that it had something to do with his family.

With the event over, Coleman got up, walked over and shook hands with David Cochrane, and asked him how his infant son was. After a brief exchange, Coleman came over and shook my hand, and said it was nice to have met me. Not knowing what else to say, I responded, "It was nice to meet you too, sir."

It was a strikingly respectful moment from a politician — without a hint of cynicism or adversarial guile. Most politicians, by the time they call it quits, have developed a thick armour of contempt and defensiveness when it comes to the media. If Coleman had stuck around longer, he almost certainly would have, too. He was already being eaten alive by the media and the opposition, and it only would've gotten worse before the voters could discard whatever was left.

CHAPTER 14
NOT JUST A SPREADSHEET
JUNE 14, 2014

Saturday night in Gander, the Liberals were jubilant.

On top of all of the other reasons for them to be smug, just a couple nights earlier Kathleen Wynne beat the odds and secured another majority government — the fourth consecutive mandate for the Liberals in Ontario.

Amid the drunken revelry, I ended up chatting with a researcher in the Official Opposition office.

"Thirty-eight per cent!" he exclaimed.

To win a majority with 38 per cent, your voters have to be "efficient." That means you need to win narrowly in a bunch of ridings, as opposed to getting a whole pile of votes in some seats, and very few votes in other places. A majority government at 38 per cent is pretty good, and Wynne's government — with 30 more seats than the Official Opposition — was especially good.

This sort of thing doesn't happen by accident, and my drunken Liberal friend was happy to tell me what their secret weapon was.

"One word: Liberalist," he said. "Quite the fuckin' tool."

During 2013 and 2014, people mentioned Liberalist from time to time, but I didn't give it much thought. You hear pundits talk about a political party "machine" or how political "organization" is what wins elections — and that's true — but when you start digging into the nuts and bolts of political campaigning, people's eyes glaze over.

Liberalist is one of those super-important things that people never hear about because it can be really, really boring. But bear with me here, and hopefully I can make this interesting.

• • •

Right off the bat, let's revisit something very important I mentioned when we were talking about the Virginia Waters byelection: Election campaigns are not, fundamentally, about changing minds and convincing people to vote for you. It's not that election campaigns don't matter — they definitely do — but they matter to political insiders in a way that's dramatically different from how the public sees it. Campaigns are not necessarily about convincing the most people to vote for you. They're about making sure that when the ballots are counted, you *have* the most votes in the box. It may seem like a subtle difference, but tactically, it changes how parties operate in a big way.

This is a huge oversimplification, but basically, political parties spend the years in between elections picking issues, advocating policies and criticizing opponents so that they slowly, painstakingly define themselves in the eyes of voters. Good governance is (hopefully) a byproduct.

Generally, the strategists pick a small number of issues, and hammer away relentlessly at them — jobs and the economy, government accountability, health care, you name it. Between elections, most people aren't paying close attention to politics, so the strategy for politicians is to pick a topic, and just repeat it ad nauseam. That way, even if voters aren't paying close attention, they'll still pick it up as background noise, and the message will worm its way into their brain anyhow. The idea is that in the long run, it doesn't matter *what* Lorraine Michael is saying about health care on any given day. If she uses every opportunity to say that the government isn't doing enough to improve health care, then eventually, voters just get the sense that Michael is always talking about health care. When election time rolls around, the NDP hopes that some voters will subconsciously say, "Health care is important to me, and I always hear Lorraine talking about it. The other two parties just seem to squabble about things I don't care about, like Muskrat Falls and stuff."

When the election campaign is called, voters have in their heads a rough outline of what each political party looks like. People tend to pay more attention to politics during the campaign, and some of them might change their minds, but the general political landscape is set, and seismic shifts aren't terribly common. The party platform, leaders' debates, door-knocking, advertising, and the rest of it might push one party's support up by a few percentage points. A massive campaign gaffe — which, in turn, gets massively overblown by political journalists and pundits — could stand to knock a political party down by a bit, maybe even enough to change the outcome. But broadly speaking, the folks who were inclined to support you on the first day of the campaign are generally likely to vote for you on the last day of the campaign.

An August 2011 poll by Corporate Research Associates showed that the Tories had 54 per cent of decided voters, the NDP had 24 per cent and the Liberals had 22 per cent. On election day in October, the Tories got 56 per cent of the popular vote, the NDP got 25 per cent, and the Liberals got 19 per cent. Basically, no change.

There are, of course, wild election campaigns from time to time where huge numbers of voters change allegiance — the 2014 Quebec election is a good example, as is the 2015 Alberta NDP victory — but those are the exceptions. You might say that the 2015 federal election campaign that elected Prime Minister Justin Trudeau was a big swing in public support, but not really. At the beginning of the campaign around 30 per cent of the population supported the Conservatives, and pretty much everybody else supported "change" but they were undecided about which party best embodied that change. After two and a half months of mulling it over, around 30 per cent voted for the Conservatives, and most of those "change" voters coalesced around Trudeau as the best vehicle to defeat Stephen Harper. The NDP and the Liberals see-sawed back and forth a bit, but that wasn't a seismic shift in the political landscape. It was just all those "change" voters settling down after both the Liberals and the NDP spent many months laying the groundwork.

In a lot of elections, you don't need huge swings, though. In the first-past-the-post election system, small changes in popular vote can translate into big changes in the legislature. You only need to win by a narrow margin to get a majority government as long as you win by a narrow margin in a whole bunch of seats.

So the election campaign starts, and the basic political landscape is already in place. Leaders try to use the campaign period to damage their opponents and build their support a bit, now that the public is paying attention. They also travel around the province, hopefully drumming up a smidgen of extra support and favourable local media coverage by personally showing up in voters' communities. Meanwhile, the volunteers behind the scenes are hard at work identifying supporters, and making sure that they cast ballots, because it's no good having 35 per cent public support if a bunch of those people can't be bothered to actually show up at a polling place and vote.

• • •

With all of this in mind, let's look at how *not* to conduct an election campaign.

Flash back to the 2011 general election, on a big white tour bus with "GET ON BOARD" printed in red letters along the side, rolling down the highway. Liberal Leader Kevin Aylward was tearing through as many districts as humanly possible. The broader political landscape was not great for Aylward going into the campaign. Premier Kathy Dunderdale was still going strong on the leftover momentum from the Danny Williams years. The New Democrats were the hopeful beneficiaries of the "Orange Wave" which swept the federal NDP to Official Opposition status earlier in the year. Cynically, a few New Democrats would also admit privately that the death of revered leader Jack Layton in August probably helped to galvanize their support. The Liberals were off in the political wilderness somewhere.

Aylward didn't have a hope in hell of winning, but on this particular day, he did a pretty good job of making himself look busy.

The first stop of the day was Bellevue district, where Aylward did a bit of campaigning with local candidate Pam Pardy Ghent. Ghent was a woman who briefly achieved province-wide notoriety when she was sacked from a volunteer position on a provincial government advisory board after she made a joke on Facebook about Danny Williams having a small penis. This is what passed for a "star candidate" among the Liberals back in the shambles of 2011. On election day, Ghent got just 626 votes — enough for a distant third place behind the Tory and NDP candidates.

After leaving Ghent, Aylward got back on his bus and rolled along to the district of Trinity North for a visit with another dubious "star candidate" — Brad Cabana. Cabana was a political unknown until he arrived at PC Party headquarters one cold day in January and announced that he was planning on running for the leadership against Kathy Dunderdale. He was disqualified from running because of problems with many of the signatures on his nomination forms. In the ensuing unpleasantness, Cabana accused then-Environment Minister Ross Wiseman of sending a political staffer to his house to threaten him and his family.[1] Cabana quit the PC Party, joined the Liberals, and promptly ran for the Liberal leadership later the same year.[2] Around the same time, Cabana also developed a habit of taking people to court and losing. Over the course of a few years, he sued Dunderdale and Minister of Tourism, Culture and Recreation Terry French for libel, he filed a constitutional challenge relating to the Muskrat Falls project, and he got embroiled in a defamation lawsuit with Danny Williams. He represented himself in court for all of this, and none of it went well for him.

On the day when Aylward showed up, he and Cabana stood in the middle of a lonely road on Random Island, and talked about how the pavement was lousy and the government didn't do enough to fix it. Cabana got 344 votes — another distant third-place finish.

Aylward's bus rolled on to Bonavista South, where he visited a sawmill and chatted with another Liberal candidate. Nonetheless, on election day Johanna Ryan Guy would come third place — are you seeing a theme here? — with 13 per cent of the vote in Bonavista South. Tory candidate Glen Little won handily with 56 per cent.

Aylward spent the evening campaigning with Ryan Lane in the district of Terra Nova. Lane — you guessed it! — came a distant third on election day.

To sum up, Aylward stopped in the following districts:
Bellevue - Liberals lost by 2,379 votes
Trinity North - Liberals lost by 2,867 votes
Bonavista South - Liberals lost by 1,682 votes
Terra Nova - Liberals lost by 2,154 votes

And yet somehow, Aylward managed to miss Bonavista North *which was right next door* to Terra Nova and Bonavista South. In that

---

[1] That allegation was never substantiated.
[2] He lost. Shocker.

district, the Liberal candidate came in second place, and lost by just 205 votes. I've got to think that if Aylward had skipped all the other districts and spent the whole day in Bonavista North, maybe he could've influenced a couple hundred votes and helped win the seat. And why waste your time campaigning in districts that the Liberals didn't have a hope in hell of winning? What's the point?

Like I said, Aylward's adventure in 2011 is an example of how to do a political campaign badly.

•••

To campaign smartly, you need to have good information.

As Liberals tried to crawl out from under the wreckage of the 2011 election, they launched a "Renewal Tour" that really didn't amount to very much. Aylward went around the province with a couple of other recognizable Liberals — Siobhan Coady and Dean MacDonald — and they talked to people, and then they put together a report that was never publicly released. But one key recommendation in the Renewal Tour report was that the party should invest in some sort of voter identification software.

Fast forward to 2013, and the Newfoundland and Labrador Liberals had licenced "Liberalist" from their federal cousins. The software was closely based on a similar application used by Barack Obama and the Democratic National Committee in the U.S.

When the Liberal leadership race started in July, the Liberalist software formed the technological backbone of process. The five contenders relentlessly advertised, robocalled, mailed out pamphlets, canvassed and did just about anything else they could to sign up supporters. Every supporter had their information plugged directly into Liberalist. At the culmination of the campaign, the party used Liberalist for the online voting system.

Over the course of the leadership race, the top three candidates collectively spent more than $1.1 million — a staggering amount of money in a province with only 525,000 people — and nearly all of that money went into advertising and signing up supporters. Each of the leadership campaigns offered a competing, positive take on what it is to be a Liberal, and each campaign invited people to sign up by putting their contact information into the party's database.

Basically, the Liberals found a way to convince three rich people to spend hundreds of thousands of dollars and engage in a months-long advertising blitz promoting the party. And as they identified potential party supporters, a small army of volunteers busily pumped as much information as they could into the Liberalist database.

The system is more than just a spreadsheet of names and contact info for identified supporters. The program takes the official voters' list from Elections Newfoundland and Labrador, and then, using the software, the Liberals can attach additional data to those names. They can track everybody who took a lawn sign in an election, everyone who volunteered, everyone who donated, and everyone who said they were planning on voting Liberal when a volunteer knocked on their door during an election campaign. All of this information goes into a database which covers every district in the province, and it's web-based, so volunteers can access it from any computer that's connected to the Internet. By the 2015 election campaign, volunteers were going door-to-door with red iPads, so that if you said you were planning on voting Liberal, they could punch the data into Liberalist right while they were standing on your doorstep.

The system can generate lists — say, everyone in District X who took a lawn sign in the last election — and then the party can get in touch with those people and ask them for donations. Volunteers can phone identified voters on the day of advanced polls and urge them to vote in order to lock down that support weeks before election day. The party can also mine the data for information about what makes their supporters tick. Over the course of several elections, it will be possible to analyze the data and attempt to figure out what issues get people to give money, what circumstances spur people to volunteer on a campaign, and what factors cause past supporters to drift away from the party. Looking back on Aylward's ill-fated adventure in the 2011 election campaign, Liberalist could have helped him understand which districts to spend his time in, and which ones to abandon.

This is the sort of stuff that people don't really talk about when they discuss politics in the media. If it's mentioned at all, it's vaguely lumped together by discussing the "machine" or "organization" that a political party has. Part of the reason it doesn't get much attention is because politicians don't want to talk about it.

They want people to think that they get elected because of ideas and character and whatnot.

• • •

MP Scott Andrews ran the workshop on Liberalist for party members at the 2014 Liberal convention. Media was barred from the room, but I pulled Andrews aside later and asked him about it. He made it sound as boring as possible.

"It's a piece that you use and it records and retains that information over the course of time. It's just a big spreadsheet," he said. "The technology always existed. It was always a spreadsheet. It was always a paper list of a spreadsheet of voters. It's just modernized over time."

Far be it from me to suggest that a politician might say something that's not completely true, but based on what I've seen, this kind of campaign management software has the ability to change politics in huge, far-reaching ways. Political parties are building massive proprietary data sets of voter information that will only grow over time. With a few elections under their belt, political parties can track which issues motivate specific demographics of voters, and specific parts of the country.

Studying these databases could become a significant factor in developing public policy. If the Liberals notice that they send out an email blast to supporters on, say, Canada Pension Plan reform, and they get a lot of donations in response, they're likely to talk about that sort of thing more often. If the party campaigns heavily on environmental issues, and the database shows that a lot of lukewarm Liberal supporters didn't bother to vote in the election, maybe the party doesn't choose to prioritize environmental issues in the future.

This kind of information is new in politics; it's definitely not just a spreadsheet.

• • •

Just to get a sense of comparison, a few weeks after the Liberal convention, I asked Tory MHA Steve Kent what campaign software the PC Party uses.

"It doesn't," Kent told me. "I've run all my campaigns off an Excel spreadsheet."

The PC Party never had the benefit of a $1.1 million advertising blitz, and they never had the benefit of a bulked-up voter database from the party leadership either. During the summer of 2014, roughly 4,000 people showed up at delegate selection meetings for the Tory leadership, and party volunteers dutifully took down their names and contact information when they registered at the door. Near as I can tell, those sheets of paper just sat in filing cabinets at the party office, though. I never saw any evidence that it was used in any meaningful way.

TORY LEADERSHIP CANDIDATES REACT TO LATEST POLL!

CHAPTER 15
ZOMBIE PARTY IN SEARCH OF BRAINS
SUMMER 2014

It was almost enough to make you feel bad for them.

The Tories just couldn't catch a break.

They couldn't get the public to like them.

They couldn't get the public to trust them.

They couldn't win a byelection to save their life.

They couldn't keep the lights on in January.

They couldn't even run a leadership race without it all falling apart and everybody dropping out.

But when they re-ran the leadership race, they made it all the way to the convention without any meltdowns. And for a few glimmering hours on Friday night and Saturday, it looked like everything was going to turn out OK.

The convention floor was packed with Tories waving their placards and chanting. They decked themselves out in scarves and colour-coordinated t-shirts, buttons and bandanas.

Then it all went to hell.

• • •

Even before things got really ugly on Saturday night, the Great Progressive Conservative Revival was a total mirage.

In the convention hall, the Tories were full of enthusiasm and zeal. They were back, baby. Sure, they'd been pummelled in the polls and in the media for a few years. Sure, they'd lost four straight byelections. Sure, a parade of senior cabinet ministers were cashing it in for pensions. But never mind all of that, things finally looked like they were turning around.

After they picked themselves up and dusted themselves off from the Coleman debacle, the Progressive Conservatives ran something that looked like a real, honest-to-God leadership race. They had three non-crazy candidates that you could credibly envision as premier of the province. Danny Williams didn't tear a strip off anybody. More than a thousand people packed into the St. John's Convention Centre for the big conclusion. It was the biggest meeting space in the city, and still they had more people trying to show up than they could safely fit into the place. The fire marshal had to be called in to go over things, and organizers strictly policed who was allowed on the convention floor.

If you threw perspective out the window and just gave in to it, the energy of the PC Party leadership convention was intoxicating. Again and again I talked to cabinet ministers and party strategists who marvelled at the thing. All these people, they said, were enthusiastic supporters of the Progressive Conservative cause, and at the end of the weekend, they'd scatter back across the province to their home communities. The party delegates would be all charged up with partisan energy, the Tory mandarins told me, and they'd channel that energy into getting ready for the next election. It's pure fantasy to believe that a single exciting afternoon would light a fire inside a thousand Tories, and it would burn hot enough and long enough to turn the tide and win the next provincial election. But sometimes partisanship is about putting your faith in something, so I guess it's understandable.

Maybe there was a kernel of truth to it. Maybe it would've turned out that way, if only the Tories could have had their perfect little storybook convention. If only John Noseworthy could've admitted that 340 is a bigger number than 339, maybe everything would have been different. But even before it all went wrong, I had my doubts.

For one thing, consider the thousand or so Tories at the convention. On the Monday after the convention, more than twice as many Liberals — upwards of 2,400 in all! — voted in a single electoral district nomination race out in Port de Grave.

Other Liberal/Tory comparisons were just as unflattering.

Including volunteers, ex officio delegates, people who showed up to delegate selection meetings and everyone else, the Tories had fewer than 5,000 people participate in picking the 12th premier of Newfoundland and Labrador. The Liberals, by comparison, brought in upwards of 23,000 people to help in picking the leader of the Official Opposition.

The top three Liberal candidates also spent upwards of $1.1 million on voter outreach and advertising, and I don't think it's any coincidence that their polling numbers shot up around the same time. By comparison, the three Tory leadership candidates spent a combined $455,000 on the leadership campaign, and much, much less on advertising — they certainly weren't running radio and TV ads like the Liberals, and they weren't papering the province with glossy leaflets. Paul Davis reported spending a paltry $3,628 on advertising and signage for his campaign.

Instead, Steve Kent, John Ottenheimer and Paul Davis spent their energy criss-crossing the province attending delegate selection meetings, and doing the critical backroom organizing needed to win those contests. Behind the scenes, I'm sure that there was plenty of hard politicking going on as the leadership candidates pressed to get as many supporters out to the meetings as possible. But in public, all I saw was sterile delegate selection meetings like the one from April in Heart's Content where tired Tories would show up, sit around for an hour without talking about politics, cast a ballot and then leave before the results were announced.

Sorry if I belabour this point, but it's important: The delegate selection meetings *should* have been huge. They were the only chance for the regular people to have a say in choosing the new leader. They were the backbone of the process. Those meetings were *the* chance to bring lots of people into the party. They should have been energetic, competitive, wide open affairs. Instead, they were rushed and poorly promoted. Once those meetings were over by mid-August, the race was left to be decided by the few hundred PC delegates who were elected, and the ex officio party members.

As the race unfolded, I got the sense that the PC Party was just going through the motions without knowing why they were doing it. The deadline for nominations was July 7, and eight days later the party was already holding delegate selection meetings. The three candidates didn't really have any chance to define themselves or do any meaningful public campaigning before they were plunged into the delegate selection meetings. Those meetings happened before the candidates held any debates; in fact, John Ottenheimer's informal campaign launch didn't even happen until the day after the first delegate selection meeting.

It was like the Progressive Conservatives were a zombie political party, shambling along, aimlessly going through the motions.

In any logical democratic process, you have a campaign full of speeches and debates and events to let people get a sense of the candidates, and *then* you let people vote to pick a winner. By holding all the debates after all the meaningful voting was over, it's as though the PC Party understood that debates are a thing you're supposed to do, but they didn't understand *why* they're important.

The general consensus was that Steve Kent won all three debates held in early September. If those debates happened *before* the delegate selection meetings, maybe it would've inspired people to show up and vote for delegates who would support him during the leadership convention. Instead, the debates were meaningless theatre. By September, nearly all the delegates were pledged to one candidate or another. Kent came in third by well over a hundred votes on the convention floor. The debates weren't about informing voters or fostering public discourse; they were free infomercials for the PC Party broadcast on TV and radio.

Too bad for the Tories, by that point nobody cared.

In late August, the Irish Loop Chamber of Commerce arranged a dinner event just outside St. John's, where all three leadership candidates would speak. It wasn't going to be a debate, as such, but it would've been the first public event of the campaign with all three candidates present. Because it was going to be a dinner, and a fundraiser for the Chamber of Commerce, they were selling tickets at $60 a head. A week before the event, the organizers canceled because they'd only been able to sell 12 tickets.

• • •

The political mood of the province was summed up nicely by a cab driver I talked to in early September, while he was giving me a ride up to the Confederation Building for a news conference.

"Come on with the Liberals! Throw out those Danny Williams bag-lickers. That's all that's left in there now."

The Danny Williams juggernaut was a distant memory, and in the year leading up to September 2014, a steady stream of Williams-era heavyweights announced that they were moving on — first Jerome Kennedy, then Kathy Dunderdale, then Joan Shea. It got even worse just a couple weeks before the convention when Finance Minister Charlene Johnson and Justice Minister Terry French announced on the same day that they were retiring from political life. Caretaker Premier Tom Marshall had one foot out the door, ready for retirement just as soon as the party could get its act together long enough to pick a new leader and make it stick.

The byelection resulting from Shea's retirement was particularly embarrassing for the Tories. The Liberals had three different people vying to carry the banner in the byelection. The Tories had to beat the bushes for nearly two months before they could come up with one person who wanted to run for them. Marshall waited until literally the very last day before he called the byelection. When the polls closed and the ballots were counted, the Liberals steamrolled over the Tories with nearly 60 per cent of the vote.

A couple weeks later, a poll from Halifax-based Corporate Research Associates put the PC Party at 26 per cent among decided voters — on par with Kathy Dunderdale's lowest ebb — and the Liberals at 58 per cent.[1] The convention was supposed to be the

---

[1] The NDP, since their implosion, had levelled out in the mid-teens, and were a non-factor as far as most political watchers were concerned.

turning point. If everything went well, it'd be a seven-hour infomercial for the PC Party, streamed live online, and broadcast continuously on TV and radio. With a real, competitive leadership — subtext: not like the Frank Coleman Fiasco — Tory organizers I talked to painted fantastical pictures of people across the province glued to their TV sets, watching every thrilling development with bated breath.

Too bad the weather didn't co-operate.

It was sunny, and pretty warm for a mid-September afternoon in St. John's. Only the political die-hards and shut-ins were at home watching on TV. In the St. John's Convention Centre, the mood was electric, but fifty metres away down Duckworth Street, you never would've known that something important was happening nearby. Well, except maybe for the fact that it was impossible to find parking anywhere in the area.

The slate of candidates didn't help, either. It was basically the choice between a cardboard cutout of a politician, yesterday's man, and a guy that a big chunk of the population viscerally loathes.

Let's take a look at them one at a time.

• • •

Any other politician might have been uncomfortable holding a pig roast at his campaign launch, but not Steve Kent. Kent had "Farmer Jim" roast up a hundred-pound hog on the deck outside the Hotel Mount Pearl, and dozens of people lined up for their pork sandwich.[2]

Most politicians wouldn't have the gall to use a three-day-old child as a political prop, either, but Kent isn't most politicians.

There's a weird, off-putting desperation to Steve Kent. He was deputy mayor of Mount Pearl at 19. By his mid-20s, he was mayor. Before he turned 30, he was elected to the House of Assembly. At 36 he was a cabinet minister. I moved to Newfoundland in 2008, so I missed his adventures in municipal politics, but people throw around terms like "golden boy" and "Mount Pearl's favourite son"

---

[2] Full disclosure: In the name of thorough journalistic inquiry, I ate a pork sandwich. It was pretty good.

with only the faintest hints of biting sarcasm. Mind you, I also heard one dyed-in-the-wool Progressive Conservative describe him by saying, "He's a fat Patrick Bateman in glasses."

Basically, he provokes strong reactions.

Kent's constituents really love the guy, and when you deal with him directly, it's easy to see why. He works hard, and he tends to get results. He's also much more approachable than your average politician. During the leadership campaign, if I wanted to get Paul Davis on the phone, I called his PR person and set up an interview. It was the same general idea with Ottenheimer. With Kent, all I had to do was email steve@stevekent.ca. From what I can tell, that email went straight to his Blackberry, because I'd usually get a reply or a phone call back within five minutes. You could also reliably get in contact with him by sending a Twitter direct message. And if all else failed, Kent cheerfully gave me his cell phone number.

I've always kind of liked Kent, and during the leadership, I believed that he was the only candidate who stood a real chance of winning the next election for the Tories. The other two were dependable, sensible, steady-hand-on-the-tiller guys. That kind of politician is no use to anybody when you're 30 points down in the polls and a year away from an election. I don't know if Kent's scrappy desperation would have been enough to win the 2015 general election, but I'm quite sure he would've thrown it all against the wall trying.

A pretty good example of that ethos was on full display at the campaign launch. Three days earlier, his wife gave birth to their third child. In the sweltering room at the Hotel Mount Pearl, Kent was surrounded by a dozen or more members of his extended family, and right there by his side, his wife Janet was holding little baby Samuel in her arms.

For most politicians, family is a no-go zone. It's private, personal, and off-limits to the media. For Kent, it was the cornerstone of his first campaign speech.

"There is really no better feeling than bringing a child into the world," he declared. "I've had a great opportunity to reflect over these past few days. I've been thinking a lot about the future.

Not only the next couple of months and years, but I'm thinking about my children's future. I'm thinking about their children's future. I'm thinking about a prosperous future for generations of people in Newfoundland and Labrador."

I still have no idea what sort of family situation forced Frank Coleman out of the race, but I'm fairly certain if Kent was faced with the same issues, he could've found a way to turn it into a vote-getter.

The same thing that makes him a successful politician also makes him deeply unpopular. Step back from the people who know him well, and you find a lot of people who have never met Kent, but dislike him deeply. The same drive that makes him rise up so quickly is also unnerving. He's called a "brown-noser" and a "suck-up." People say he's too young to be in politics. Normal, decent people have an honest job for a few decades, and then go into politics later in life. What kind of weirdo is drawn to political life so young? How can you be grounded?

At the time of the leadership, Kent was already a remarkably successful politician, and still younger than most people are when they begin their political careers. But you also got the sense that no matter how successful he was, it would never be enough.

It wasn't good enough to be one of the youngest municipal politicians in the province. It wasn't good enough to be the youngest MHA in the legislature when he was elected. After years of hustling as a backbench MHA, he finally got a spot in cabinet, but that wasn't enough either. Just months after being invited to the cabinet table, he needed to run to be premier of the province at the tender age of 36.

People can sense this, even if they can't fully articulate it. I think deep down, they get the sense that Kent isn't in this for altruistic reasons. People like politicians who seem to be sincerely motivated by a desire to help others. You get the sense that Kent is in this because he wants something for himself.

I don't know what's driving Kent, but I always got the sense he's desperately craving ... *something*. Maybe it's simply power he's after. Maybe he's just craving validation from the voters, and the public at large. In any case, it's like there was a hole inside of him that he's trying to fill up with political success, and nothing was ever good enough.

•••

Paul Davis held his campaign launch one night before Steve Kent.

The FIFA World Cup was going on, and there were only two nights in the broadcast schedule that didn't have 6 p.m. soccer games pre-empting the supper-hour news. Davis announced on the first night. Kent took the second. In the bible of Newfoundland political staging, the 6 p.m. Big Announcement is a staple. The trick is to time it so that CBC and NTV take your speech live on the evening news. Davis hit his mark perfectly.

Everything about Davis's campaign launch was right by the book. He packed about 250 people into a room at the Paradise Rotary Youth and Community Centre — smack dab in the middle of his Topsail electoral district, but close enough to St. John's that a solid cadre of journalists could make it out. Natural Resources Minister Derrick Dalley introduced Davis, reading out a quote from former U.S. General Douglas MacArthur about "true leadership."

Davis strode up to the stage, through a crowd of clapping senior citizens, "Rant and Roar" by Great Big Sea playing in the background.

Once he got to the podium, he gave the sort of speech that any Newfoundland and Labrador politician could give, at any time, anywhere.

"We will continue to advocate for better health care, for better education and better social programming. We need to work together to identify opportunities. We need to listen to all generations of Newfoundlanders and Labradorians. We need to stay true to our culture which makes us so unique and so strong."

The only hint of personality in the speech was when he mentioned his fight with cancer, which conveniently doubled as an excuse for why he chose not to run for the leadership three months earlier, during the Coleman fiasco. He said he was still recovering then. The rest of the speech was bland platitudes and vague aspirations.

"I've learned to believe wholeheartedly in the importance of teamwork, the importance of working together. The value of surrounding yourself with individuals who have good ideas, common goals, that want to make a difference and make the lives of people better. One team. One direction. And I can tell you, there are no shortcuts to success."

Davis has always been at his best when he's a cardboard cutout.

Before he went into politics, he was a familiar face to most people in the province as the spokesman for the Royal Newfoundland Constabulary. When I started working in journalism in St. John's, Davis was the guy you'd call if somebody robbed a Marie's Mini Mart. He was very good at wearing a cop's uniform, standing in front of a camera and delivering a message without getting distracted by journalists' questions. At the same time, he earned his political stripes serving on the Conception Bay South town council before making the jump into provincial politics just a few months before Danny Williams retired as premier. After a short stint in the backbenches, Davis landed in cabinet. He was the sort of minister who was rarely at the centre of a controversy, which is usually the mark of a good manager. If you're running your department well, the fires get put out before anyone in the public notices smoke.

After Dwight Ball, Davis was the best-dressed man in the House of Assembly. And don't underestimate the value of that; looking the part is important in politics.

Through six years dealing with him in the Constabulary and then later in politics, I never got the sense that Davis was a big ideas guy. His twin campaign themes were "teamwork" and "listening."

Senior cabinet ministers and high-value organizers endorsed him. He was a cardboard cutout, but he managed to stay out of trouble, and he looked good doing it. In the PC leadership, he wasn't yesterday's man, and he wasn't hated by a sizable portion of the population, so right from the start he was considered the favourite.

• • •

Yesterday's man was remarkably spry out of the gate.

Frank Coleman dropped out of the race in mid-June, and even before the dust had settled, there was John Ottenheimer announcing that he'd run in the Tory leadership redux. Then he had to stand around awkwardly for a couple weeks waiting for the party to catch up and organize the leadership race he'd already announced that he was entering.

When he finally got around to doing some sort of a campaign launch, it was more than a month after he announced his candidacy, and it was a pitiful affair. It was attended by a handful of journalists, half a dozen politicians who had endorsed him, and the few supporters who didn't have anything better to do in the middle of the day.

He started by introducing himself, and going over his bio, acknowledging that in the seven years he'd been out of public life, a lot of people had probably forgotten him. Ottenheimer worked as both a teacher and a lawyer before going into politics; he sat in opposition for seven years before the Tories took power, and he was a cabinet minister right from the beginning of the Danny Williams government. He retired from politics in 2007, and by all accounts, he was a well-liked and well-respected guy.

The first time I ever saw him, though, was in 2008 when he was called back into the spotlight during the Cameron Inquiry. More than 300 women with breast cancer received wrong hormone receptor test results — which determine treatment options — over a period of eight years. Ottenheimer was health minister when the mistakes were discovered. At the inquiry, he said he wanted to go public right away, but he said he was convinced by bureaucrats to keep the matter under wraps until the internal investigation was completed. He claimed he never saw the briefing notes that were prepared for him on the issue. He didn't ask to see two reports by independent experts on the issue, and didn't want to know what recommendations they made.

I remember thinking that he came across as feckless and disengaged from the issues going on in his department in the midst of a crisis.

Years later, during his leadership run, I saw the same short, stout, directionless politician. At his campaign launch, he said if he was elected premier, he'd make childcare a greater priority. He couldn't say what he would do to make childcare more accessible or more affordable. He couldn't say how much his non-plan for childcare would cost. In the same appearance, he boldly declared the Public Utilities Board should be given a greater role in the Muskrat Falls project. The PUB was cut out of its normal regulatory function on the project by Premier Kathy Dunderdale, and the billion-dollar federal loan guarantee stipulated that the PUB couldn't be allowed to set electricity prices related to the power coming from Muskrat Falls. Ottenheimer said he wanted to bring the PUB back into the process in some way, but he couldn't explain what role it would have, since all the important stuff had already been decided, and couldn't be undone.

During the debates he seemed weak and unfocused. His speaking style in interviews and speeches reminded me of Frank Coleman — lots of ums and qualifiers and weasel-words. In the whole leadership campaign, he was the only candidate who ever ducked an interview request I made.

But in the delegate selection meetings, it was a different matter. Presented with a room full of Tories, Ottenheimer became an affable, back-slapping guy who could work a room with the best of them. Especially at the meetings in and around St. John's, his numbers were dominant. He racked up plenty of endorsements from current and former Progressive Conservative caucus members too, and word was that he had solid support among the ex officio Tories who would make up a significant chunk of the eligible voting delegates at the convention.

A closer look the the endorsements, though, revealed the cleavage in the party. Kent and Davis had support from the current crowd. Ottenheimer's support tended to come from the caucus members who were looking long in the tooth, or the old guard party apparatchiks who dated back to the early years of the Williams government, or even before that.

At least part of his appeal was that Ottenheimer got out of the game in 2007, so he missed out on the Dunderdeale slide. For the old timers, he represented a sort of renewal-by-way-of-reversion —

a way to flash back to the halcyon days of the Williams government, without actually having Danny back.[3]

• • •

I won't waste your time by recounting the details of the summer leadership campaign. Nobody in the province cared at the time, and I don't see why anybody should care after the fact. The delegate selection meetings happened. People showed up and voted and most of them left before the organizers announced the results. Clearly even the participants didn't care too much about the outcome. The debates happened, but by that point they didn't really matter. Ottenheimer released some YouTube ads that everybody thought were pretty funny. Kent released a barrage of policy positions. Davis kept saying "listening" and "teamwork."

Then everybody descended on St. John's for the big weekend.

• • •

Things started so well on Friday.

Organizers reported well over a thousand people packed into the St. John's Convention Centre. They had signs and scarves and buttons and ball caps and colour-coordinated t-shirts. Ottenheimer's delegates wore white. Davis's camp was decked out in blue. Kent went with yellow. People chanted and cheered as each of the hopefuls made a presentation to delegates.

The mood in the room really was lively.

The Tories had a spring in their step as they headed across the street to the Delta Hotel where each of the candidates hosted a "hospitality suite." I use that term loosely, because Paul Davis's "suite" was half of the partitioned-off hotel ballroom. The other half of the ballroom was Steve Kent's "Ultimate Shed Party."

---

[3] Despite Williams' repeated insistence that he had nothing to do with the Frank Coleman fiasco, there was a palpable sense at the September convention that a good chunk of the party was happy he decided to butt out. Whether Danny had been pulling the strings before, as so many people suspected, it was fairly clear he was gone now. Williams was a fun ride while he lasted, but once he was gone and the Danny Williams Effect was no longer playing out in the polls, Tories were getting plenty sick of him meddling behind the scenes. Williams endorsed no one in the re-run leadership race, and on the weekend of the convention, he was in Halifax for the premiere of a documentary about himself.

Kent's shed party had a literal shed built out of particleboard in the corner of the room. There were flags draped against the walls, a couple couches, folksy Newfoundland and Labrador tchotchkes hanging from the walls, and a big crab pot leaning against the outside of it next to the door. The shed also had a photo booth where you could go in and make silly faces and get your picture printed out while you waited.

Outside of the shed, I bumped into Kent and his wife, Janet. Slung from her chest was baby Samuel, now three months old, who was fast asleep despite the fact that a band was playing deafening Irish music on a stage just a few metres away. We chatted for a few minutes — had to shout, really, to be heard over the band. Kent was projecting confidence. He knew he'd won the debates, and he felt like he was running the best campaign. He'd definitely put the most work into his hospitality suite. He had The Navigators booked, which is just about as good as you can ask for in terms of authentic Newfoundland Irish folk music. Kent also had about a dozen pretty young girls wearing little black cocktail dresses standing in the hallway outside, inviting delegates to pop in for a drink.

Oh, and Kent had free booze.

Next door, Paul Davis had a cash bar, but he also had a bigger crowd. Kent's people had worked to decorate their room in that "Ultimate Shed Party" theme. Davis's team didn't bother to dress up the cavernous space, apart from taping a few campaign posters to the walls. At least the band playing in Davis's room — Shanneyganock — was every bit as good as Kent's band. On average, I'd guess the crowd in Davis's room was 15 years older than the folks at Kent's party.

Upstairs, Ottenheimer had booked an authentic "suite" for his hospitality suite — which is to say that the space was 90 per cent smaller than the Kent and Davis parties. But a small room makes it look that much more full, and Ottenheimer's suite was packed to the point that it was spilling out into the hall. Ottenheimer had free alcohol too, along with a guy sitting against the wall playing a button accordion.

The really amazing thing about Ottenheimer's party, though, was one door down the hall. Set up right next door to Ottenheimer, there was a second party going on. I walked into the place trying to figure out whose party it was, and incredulously looked down at a table of finger foods and cupcakes with Steve Kent's campaign logo on them.

You've got to admire a guy who's so competitive that he fights a party war on two fronts, eh?

During a lull in the action on Saturday afternoon, I ended up chatting with Justice Minister Terry French, who is widely known as one of the PC Party's best campaigners. For years, French was part of a small team dubbed, "The byelection in a box," because the Tories would dispatch them to any district in the province where a campaign needed to be run. French was Paul Davis's campaign manager, but he marvelled at Kent's organization, saying that it was far stronger than either Davis or Ottenheimer had going on. French told me that whoever the new premier was, he'd be an idiot if he didn't tap Kent to run all future byelections, as well as general election prep.

If it wasn't for the fact that so many people viscerally disliked Steve Kent, he probably would've won hands down.

CHAPTER 16
COUNTING IS HARD
SEPTEMBER 13, 2014

The big day started with a quick AGM, and then brunch.

Delegates who managed to shrug off their hangover and make it down for the annual general meeting were treated to the optimistic news that the Tories had more than $926,000 in the bank account. With an election less than a year away, that's pretty decent. Bragging rights over the Liberals — still $800,000 in debt — is good too. At brunch, Kathy Dunderdale was feted. She'd been keeping a very low profile since her resignation, but she briefly thanked the party for being a solid rock of support for her during her years in politics.

"I haven't missed one minute of political life, but I've missed you," she said to a room full of Tories.

It was a nice moment.

After Dunderdale, the party turned their attention to Premier Tom Marshall to say goodbye. Marshall was always a respected senior cabinet minister for the Tories, but in the months he served as premier he'd risen to the level of beloved elder statesman.

Within weeks of taking the reins as premier, he ordered a comprehensive, independent review of the province's access to information legislation led by Clyde Wells, a retired premier who also happened to serve as chief justice of the Newfoundland and Labrador Supreme Court. Along with former-premier cred — and a Liberal premier, at that! — Marshall stacked the ATIPPA review panel with a retired journalist and a former federal privacy commissioner. Taken together, their independence, integrity and gravitas was beyond reproach.

A month later, in his throne speech, Marshall announced that the Tories would finally make good on a seven-year-old election promise to enact whistleblower legislation. It was originally Danny Williams who committed to give civil servants whistleblower protection way back in the 2007 general election, and a year later, in the 2008 throne speech, the government promised to introduce a bill within a year. That promise was broken in spectacular fashion, with a parade of ministers stalling, dodging and dismissing questions for years, saying that "consultation" and "study" was needed before anything got passed into law. The whistleblower promise was a favourite topic for government critics — a simple reminder that the Tories talked a good game on transparency and accountability, but it was all talk and no action.

Marshall became premier in January, and he said, "We're going to do whistleblower." Less than six months later, it was the law of the land.

During the Frank Coleman Humber Valley Paving controversy, Transportation Minister Nick McGrath spent weeks blustering and deflecting criticism. The Liberals wanted the auditor general brought in to do a special report on the issue. McGrath said that the AG was free to study any aspect of government he wanted, but the Tories wouldn't order him to look at Humber Valley Paving in particular. Less than a week later, Marshall swooped in and ordered the auditor general to study the matter, issue a special report and determine whether there was any wrongdoing.

These were all easy political wins.

As premier, you swallow hard, admit you were wrong, tell somebody to get it done, and then take credit for doing it. After 10 years in government, the Tories had gotten a little bit too good at telling critics to buzz off, and they'd forgotten how to admit they'd made a mistake. Marshall was different. In eight months in charge, he led the Tories to make several high-profile mea culpas, which is the sort of thing that really goes a long way to blunt the perception that your government is arrogant and out of touch with the people.

It wasn't all symbolism, though. In the 2013 budget, the Tories laid off about a thousand civil servants, as part of their "10-year sustainability plan." The plan was a total sham. Year One called for core civil service layoffs. Year Two called for the government to turn the crosshairs on post-secondary education and health authorities. Year Three — election year! What a coincidence?! — was just marked "return to surplus." Years Four through Ten were just vaguely labeled as "Continued focus on innovation, economic diversification and debt reduction," as though the government had been completely ignoring "innovation" and "economic diversification" up until now, and needed a 10-year plan to remind them to do it. But those years didn't really matter, because they were after the 2015 election.

Anyhow, the sustainability plan and the thousand layoffs came from former finance minister Jerome Kennedy, since retired, a guy who was shuffled into a cabinet portfolio whenever the government needed to pick a fight with somebody about something. With Premier Marshall at the helm, though, the government suddenly decided that slashing and burning in the health care system and the university wasn't such a great idea. The government repackaged some old, smaller cuts to the health authorities, and told the university to study its operations and try to find "efficiencies" but that any savings they found, they could keep and put that money into other programs.

No big layoffs. No big budget cuts. Instead, Marshall's only budget as premier created full-day kindergarten and phased out provincial student loans, replacing them with non-repayable grants.

After the budget was put to bed, Marshall and Finance Minister Charlene Johnson turned their attention to the province's multi-billion-dollar unfunded pension liability. Marshall had spent years laying the groundwork during multiple stints as finance minister, and as premier he was able to bring it over the line in early September, just a couple of weeks before the Tory leadership convention. The unions agreed to a cut in benefits, an increase in the retirement age, and higher pension premiums. They also accepted joint management and joint liability for any future pension fund shortfalls. In exchange, the government kicked in billions of dollars to top up the fund, and preserved the defined-benefit structure that the unions wanted. It will likely take decades before we can judge how it all worked out, but on paper, the pension deal looks like a solution to an intractable problem that was plaguing the government for years.

On the Friday before the leadership convention, Marshall invited civil servants to the lobby of the Confederation Building to thank them before saying goodbye. It was only a brief speech, but Marshall managed to get two standing ovations, and half a dozen laughs out of the hundreds of bureaucrats who packed into the lobby. For those who know him, Marshall will likely go down as the funniest premier in Newfoundland and Labrador history. His best jokes were wry, obscure, sharp little off-the-cuff comments, but he routinely had the entire House of Assembly press corps laughing in the middle of a serious political scrum.

I won't try to retell any of Marshall's jokes here; print saps all of the flavour and comedic timing out of it. Just take my word for it, he was a damn funny guy.

After the speech, Marshall spent 10 or 15 minutes mingling with the civil servants he'd worked with for more than a decade. Dozens of people weren't satisfied with a handshake; they hugged him to say goodbye, and at least a couple looked like they were close to tears.

It was the same mood at the leadership convention brunch Saturday morning. Marshall was seated at a table at the front of the room, flanked by his wife on one side and Marjorie on the other side. After Danny Williams himself — who is a minor deity in Marjorie's eyes — Marshall is just about the finest human being in Newfoundland and Labrador. She was in such a good mood about things that she didn't threaten to kill me even once, and when she bumped into David Cochrane on the convention floor, she shook his hand and apologized to him.

At brunch, junior minister Sandy Collins introduced Marshall with a Maya Angelou quote: "People will forget what you said, people will forget what you did, but people will never forget how you made them feel." It was a pretty appropriate observation on Collins's part. You can debate the budgets he delivered as finance minister, and the moves he made as premier, but anybody who has spent five minutes or five years working with Marshall will tell you that he's a good guy. He's competent. He's humble. He's quick to laugh at himself, and at the ridiculousness of political life.

Marshall took to the stage and thanked the Tories for giving him the opportunity to be premier. He made some jokes, but he also talked about the serious burden of leadership.

"You never know what it means to lead until you sit in that big leather chair behind that big wooden desk in the Confederation Building, and it fully sinks in that the buck really stops here. I remember on the first night (as premier) there was a young man missing in Labrador. And you know, when you're premier, you wait up until you get the word they've found him. That's responsibility. You can't slough it off. Premiers know. Kathy knows. You can't slough it off."

After the speech, brunch was served and then hundreds of Tory delegates migrated across the street to the convention hall to pick a new leader. I think most of the party delegates knew that no matter who they picked, the new guy wouldn't be anywhere near as good as the one who was saying goodbye.

• • •

The thing they don't tell you about delegated conventions is how much bloody waiting around there is.

Once the convention hall filled up, each of the three would-be leaders had a final chance to give a speech before the voting started. Kent went first, and reminded everybody — yet again — that he had just recently given life to a child. Davis went second, and talked about how great the Tories had been for the past decade, and how they'd keep being great with him at the helm. He only referenced the party's dismal polling numbers briefly — saying that the pollsters were wrong, and the PC Party was on track to triumph despite objective evidence to the contrary. Ottenheimer went last, and took the opposite tack. It wasn't entirely doom and gloom, but he pointedly reminded delegates that the average voter had a pretty dim view of the governing party. He reminded people that they were perceived as arrogant and out of touch, and no matter how the Tories saw themselves, they needed to fix that problem if they wanted to win re-election.

Then the polling stations opened up, and delegates started casting ballots. Us media types circulated the room, picking up gossip and whatever little telling details we could find. The broadcast folks filled time with endless panel discussions and live interviews from the convention floor. I'd love to know the numbers on how many people were actually watching the CBC and NTV broadcasts. In the week after the convention, I talked to less than half a dozen people who tuned in — and my friends tend to be political nerds. Mostly, everybody just killed time and kept speculating.

It's a credit to the Steve Kent machine that right up until the end, there were observers predicting he'd be a surprise second place finisher on the first ballot. Paul Davis looked weak. There were rumours coming from the other camps that he was tough to work with. People whispered ominously about how no women had en-dorsed his candidacy. Via Twitter, a friend offered me a $20 bet that Kent would come out ahead of Davis. But as the ballots were counted, the mood in the Kent camp changed. Word trickled out from the scrutineers. It didn't look good.

Kent was ashen-faced as he re-entered the the hall, and made his way to the little raised platform in the section of the room re-served for him and his supporters. Family and senior volunteers filled up the platform, surrounding him. I don't know if he asked them to do it, or it was a spontaneous sort of thing, but his support-ers were making a conscious effort to protect their guy. At that mo-ment, protecting him meant blocking off reporters from filming his reaction to the bitter moment of defeat. Media packed in, as close as possible to the platform, trying to get the shot. Supporters packed in tighter, and organizers brought more people up onto the platform — off limits to journalists — to further block the view. Down below, supporters packed in tightly, trying to edge out the media. It was weird and intense. A CBC cameraman went and got a chair, and tried to stand on it to get a clear view of Kent. A big Kent volunteer wearing a headset charged through the crowd at the CBC guy, push-ing people out his way. The volunteer shouted "Safety concerns, sorry!" and snatched the chair out of the cameraman's hands.

None of it mattered in the end. I managed to snap a picture of Kent in the moment of truth. He had sort of a resigned smile on his face. So it goes.

After a few minutes of conferring with his team, he strode to the stage. It wasn't much of a speech; he thanked his supporters and congratulated both of his opponents. Then he endorsed Paul Davis, and asked his supporters to come with him and vote for Davis on the second ballot. If Kent wanted to say anything else, he was out of luck, drowned out by a primal cheer from the Davis con-tingent in the convention hall.

Kent wove his way through a crush of cheering supporters to-wards Davis's section. Davis had a little platform of his own, and the two men embraced and stood side by side, amid a mass of cheer-ing, chanting, waving supporters. Not far away, the Ottenheimer contingent looked sullen.

If you wanted to pinpoint a moment when things started to go wrong for the PC convention, this was it.

"Paul Davis can get right to work, right away, as premier of this province. He has a seat in the House of Assembly. He's got lots of recent experience at the cabinet table," Kent told reporters, standing in the middle of the Davis section of the convention hall. "He's got the confidence of many people within our cabinet and caucus — that was indicated by the level of endorsements he received from my caucus and cabinet colleagues — so he's the logical endorsement for me today."

Translation: Paul Davis and I are current politicians with the support of the caucus. Ottenheimer doesn't have a seat in the legislature, and he's mostly backed by has-beens.

As Kent was speaking to reporters, a Davis supporter unfurled a yellow "TEAM DAVIS" flag behind Kent, in full view of the TV cameras. Davis's campaign colour was blue. Ottenheimer's people were all wearing white. Kent's colour was yellow. The yellow "TEAM DAVIS" flag — and dozens of more like it, which were being distributed to delegates — seemed to indicate collusion. Did Davis know in advance that Kent would be endorsing him? Did they have a backroom deal all along? Why else would they have those flags printed up in advance? Was there a box of white "TEAM DAVIS" flags sitting in a closet somewhere, in case things had gone the other way and they were courting an Ottenheimer endorsement?

I'm not sure if it really matters whether there was an agreement in place that Kent would endorse Davis. Kent fought hard throughout the campaign, and everything I saw over the three months leading up to the convention indicated that he was a guy who was in it to win it. If he wasn't, why attack Davis during the debates? Why spend all that money on hospitality suites? If your only goal is to be kingmaker, there are easier ways to do it. Why does it matter whether Kent knew months in advance that he'd endorse Davis, or whether he made a spur-of-the-moment decision? The effect is still the same.

Ottenheimer's folks were definitely feeling jilted, though. I got the sense that they were expecting Kent to remain neutral. It set up a potentially nasty second ballot. The numbers on the first ballot put Ottenheimer in first with 289 votes, Davis in second with 253 and Kent far behind with 141 votes. If all of Kent's supporters went to Davis, it was a done deal, but not all of Kent's supporters were going along with it. On the floor, Davis and Ottenheimer supporters furiously tried to to woo over Kent's people. Backbench MHA Calvin Peach — a Kent supporter — donned a white shirt and endorsed Ottenheimer, bringing a solid block of his district's delegates with him. As the ballots were cast, nobody was sure what would happen.

"I'm confident, but I'm not comfortable," Ottenheimer campaign co-chair Shawn Skinner told me, moments before the second ballot results were announced. Davis's campaign manager, Terry French, told me that based on his head count, it would come down to less than ten votes. The PC Party was evenly divided, which is never the way you want this sort of thing to go.

Then, John Noseworthy made everything worse.

● ● ●

John Noseworthy, a former auditor general and a former PC Party candidate — he lost to NDP Leader Lorraine Michael in the 2011 election — was the party's chief electoral officer for the convention. As auditor general, he broke open the House of Assembly constituency spending scandal, which sent four MHAs and a senior government bureaucrat to jail. Noseworthy's integrity, at one time, was beyond reproach. Then he quit his job as AG to run for the PC Party, and that didn't go so well. Then after he lost the election, he got a no-bid government consulting contract worth nearly $150,000 from cabinet minister Joan Shea.

Despite his spotty past, he was a guy with a reputation for integrity, and a guy with a recognizable name, so he made sense to be the guy manning the ballot boxes and the counting room. And he was an auditor, so he was probably good with numbers, right? I guess the party expected him to be diligent, although maybe not *that* diligent.

The second ballot results were expected before 7 p.m., but there was a delay. We waited around, knowing it was going to be close. Finally, he appeared in the convention hall. On the weekend of the convention, Noseworthy had a polyp on his vocal chords, so he couldn't do any shouting. He made for the stage and spoke softly.

The only three words anybody heard were: "No clear majority."

Then it was bedlam.

The party announced that there would be a third ballot. The candidates would have one hour to get their delegates together for voting, and then the polls would be open for one hour.

Campaign volunteers were frantic. While I was sitting at the media table writing, one Kent supporter walked by, shouting into his phone: "Andrew! It was a tie! You have to come back." Dozens of delegates left after they cast their second ballot — it was over then, right? With only two candidates, one of them had to get more than 50 per cent, right? One couple was on the highway an hour out of town before somebody managed to get them on the phone. They turned around to come back.

There was even a rumour that somebody made a call and turned around the Bell Island ferry so that delegates could get back. A few days after the convention, I asked Service NL Minister David Brazil about it. Brazil was the MHA for Bell Island and Steve Kent's campaign manager. Brazil said the rumour wasn't entirely true. Yes, there were some delegates heading home on the ferry. They stayed on the boat when it made it over to Bell Island and then rode back. Brazil said while they were on the boat, they had to rifle through the trash for their torn-up convention credentials — no credentials, no entry, no voting.

As for the rumour about turning around the ferry halfway across the Tickle, apparently Transportation Minister Nick McGrath heard that rumour too. McGrath was an Ottenheimer supporter, and Brazil said there was an angry confrontation between the two of them on the convention floor. McGrath, furious, asked Brazil if he's made a call and ordered the ferry to turn around. Brazil said he shrugged it off, saying something like, "You're the minister; how could I do a thing like that?" The delegates from the ferry sped back to town — about a 20 minute drive — and made it back to cast their ballots with three minutes to spare.

• • •

While all of this was going on, I was trying to get answers from Noseworthy. He announced, "No clear majority" but he didn't actually say what the ballot count was. The candidates and their volunteers were scrambling to get delegates back, but up at the front of the room, there was another frantic conference happening among convention organizers. Noseworthy, party president Cillian Sheahan and a few other bigwigs huddled together in a roped-off section beside the stage.

It took about 15 minutes for them to settle things and announce what the vote counts were: 680 votes cast, one spoiled ballot, 340 for Paul Davis, and 339 for John Ottenheimer.

It doesn't take a genius to figure out that 340 is bigger than 339.

In fact, you have to do quite a lot of thinking and mental contortion to find a way that Paul Davis *isn't* the winner there. Noseworthy was the man for the job.

When I heard the results were announced, I assumed that Noseworthy was counting the spoiled ballot as a validly cast ballot. By that logic, you could theoretically conclude that Davis got exactly 50 per cent of the validly cast ballots, but he didn't get a majority.[1]

In actual fact, though, the explanation for the "No clear majority" was much more convoluted. It was insane. After much waiting and haranguing, reporters were ushered into a room upstairs where Noseworthy explained his logic. Forget the spoiled ballot, he said, there were 679 valid ballots cast. Based on that number, 50 per cent of the vote would be 339.5. By Noseworthy's tortured logic, Davis got 340 votes, but that wasn't enough to give him 50 per cent plus one, since he really only got 0.5 votes more than the 50 per cent threshold.

Confused? Don't worry, about a thousand other people at the St. John's Convention Centre were confused too.

Here's the really insane part: By insisting that the winner needed 50 per cent plus one — and inventing a rather exotic definition of

[1] On the spoiled ballot, I'm told, a Kent supporter clearly marked an X for both Davis and Ottenheimer. I didn't see it personally, though, so take that with a grain of salt.

"50 per cent plus one" — Noseworthy was creating his own rules out of whole cloth. The PC Party constitution is crystal clear when it comes to this stuff. Here's what it says:

PART V: CONVENTION PROCEEDING
Sec. 10: BALLOTING

...

F. Balloting shall continue until one candidate obtains an absolute majority of the ballots cast in a ballot.

G. *An absolute majority shall mean more than 50% of the valid ballots cast on any particular ballot.*

Got that? In his briefing with reporters, Noseworthy said that when the results were counted, they consulted a lawyer, and came to the conclusion that an "absolute majority" must mean 50 per cent plus one. That conclusion runs contrary to Section G, where the party clearly defines what "absolute majority" is supposed to mean.

Any idiot could read the constitution and figure out that Paul Davis won on the second ballot. Noseworthy, though, decided to go the extra mile.

● ● ●

As all of this filtered out, things were getting acrimonious in the convention hall. Both the Davis and Ottenheimer campaigns were fretting that they might lose simply because they couldn't get one or two delegates back to vote. Ottenheimer's supporters were happy that their hopes were still alive — barely — but most of the people I talked to clearly knew this would be a lousy way to win.

Meanwhile, Davis supporters were already laying the ground-work to claim that if Ottenheimer won, it was illegitimate.

Kent took to Twitter to say, "340 to 339 is NOT a tie."

Former finance minister and criminal defence lawyer Jerome Kennedy was pursuing the same line of thinking by different avenues. As a politician, Kennedy was notorious for going from zero to hyper-pitbull lawyer in the blink of an eye. At the convention, he looked furious and was arguing to anybody who would listen that Noseworthy had made the wrong call. Kennedy told me he was ready to go to court on Monday morning to fight the verdict if Ottenheimer won.

People knew it was getting bad.

"Dwight Ball is sitting down somewhere sipping a bourbon, loving life," one Davis volunteer told me. "You're going to see bloodletting before this is done."

I talked to Natural Resources Minister Derrick Dalley who, like Kennedy, was musing about a possible court challenge. I pointed out that a court challenge would tear the party apart, and it would be a bad scene. "This is already bad," Dalley muttered darkly.

• • •

In the end, I guess a few Ottenheimer supporters realized how ugly things could get if he won on the third ballot after clearly losing on the second. Nearly everyone who had left made it back to vote, and Davis picked up eleven delegates on the third ballot — enough to comfortably put him over the top. The final tally was 351 to 326, with one spoiled ballot. Some anonymous hero in the PC Party had a chance to help pick the premier, and instead spoiled his ballot, and then stuck around for another three hours so he could spoil his ballot again. It warms your heart.

As soon as "351" was announced for Davis, his supporters erupted, cheering. Davis made his way through the crowd, stopping to shake hands and hug supporters, as a knot of TV cameras and photographers clustered around him. He took to the stage amid throngs of people chanting "Davis, Davis, Davis!" and plenty of cheering.

He thanked his supporters and his family, and congratulated the other candidates. He thanked Tom Marshall for leaving the government slightly better than he found it. He thanked his supporters again.

"To every Newfoundlander and Labradorian, I make this promise," Davis declared. "I promise to lead with vision, to provide sound governance and to be accountable to every citizen in our great province. Under my leadership, the PC Party will be a party for the people with a focus on working together to take advantage of every opportunity, strengthen our communities and build a brighter tomorrow."

It wasn't a particularly impressive speech, but then, soaring rhetoric and inspiring ideas aren't what won him the leadership, so why change tack now? It didn't matter much, anyway. Thanks to Noseworthy's creative interpretation of mathematics, the results were announced around 10 p.m., late enough to kill even the most hopeful Tory's dreams of masses watching the thrilling conclusion on TV. Who the heck sits at home until 10 p.m. on a Saturday night watching political coverage?

• • •

I spoke to John Ottenheimer on the floor of the convention hall, a few moments after Davis' victory speech. He stood alone in an aisle between rows of empty chairs and discarded campaign signs. He said he accepted the result, and congratulated Davis. He equivocated when asked if he'd run for a seat in the next general election.[2]

As Ottenheimer was speaking to me, Davis moved to the back of the room, where the CBC had their massive live TV broadcast going. Somebody manning the sound system decided to take the CBC audio and run in through the big speakers in the convention hall, so that everyone could listen to Davis' first one-on-one interview as leader of the PC Party.

So there was John Ottenheimer, trying to look gracious in defeat. "I feel fine," he said. "I went into this with my eyes open, realizing that there could be any possibility in terms of an outcome." I didn't get much more than that out of Ottenheimer, because the booming voice of Paul Davis was drowning him out. I suppose I could have waited until Davis' interview with the CBC was finished, or Ottenheimer could have continued shouting, trying to be heard over the noise. Instead, I turned off my recorder, and walked away.

The bleak reality of politics is that losers just don't matter.

• • •

Davis was sworn-in on a Friday afternoon nearly two weeks later.

---

[2] He didn't run, in the end.

Steve Kent got his due for endorsing Davis. Kent was named deputy premier and became minister of health, arguably the largest portfolio in cabinet. Ottenheimer basically disappeared from the picture altogether, and along with him went any signs of bitterness and acrimony. There were tense moments on the convention floor, but if anybody was really left with deep and abiding resentment, it didn't flare up publicly. Maybe everybody calmed down and came together again. Or maybe the bitter Ottenheimer supporters just didn't show up to volunteer when the election rolled around. It's tough to quantify that sort of thing, especially at a time when the Tories had already bled so much support, and their organization was already so rickety.

Perhaps more significant than Kent or Ottenheimer, though, was former police chief Joe Browne who Davis hired as his chief of staff. Browne was Davis' boss back in the good old days when the two men were in uniform; now the roles were reversed. It led to a bout of jokes about Newfoundland and Labrador becoming a "retired police state," but among the journalists who covered crime back when Davis was Royal Newfoundland Constabulary spokesman and Browne was chief, the reunion was seen as a grim sign for the Tory government.

I remember Browne as being thin-skinned and at times combative with the media. I don't remember anything that indicated the two men would steer the government in a deferential, transparent direction that was more responsive to citizens. Back when Davis was the RNC media relations officer, reporters would have to call a pager. This was in 2009. Davis had a cell phone, but the number was a closely-guarded secret. The idea that the police would employ some sort of two-way communication was simply out of the question. No, the way it worked was that a reporter called the pager, left a number, and when he felt like it, Davis would call back and deliver the official message that the cops were delivering. Since Davis moved on to provincial politics and Browne retired as chief, the police have retired the pager in favour of email and phone contact information, listed on the RNC website.

Suffice it to say, I was skeptical that his actions would live up to the promise Davis made in his first words as premier, moments after being sworn in.

"I know that we're going to receive criticism, and I welcome criticism. People are entitled to their opinions, and they're entitled to disagree with us," he said. "People have told me that they're tired of politics as usual, and now that I have an opportunity to do things differently, I intend to do that. I am first and foremost a listener. The government that I lead will occupy the high ground and we will lead by listening to the people of the province."

A month later, his chief of staff was threatening to sue *The Telegram* for defamation, his star cabinet minister was dismissing widespread public outcry as irrelevant political noise, and Davis had a minister resign from cabinet in disgrace for what looked an awful lot like political cronyism.[3]

So it goes.

---

[3] This was one of those dubious political resignations. Nick McGrath said he was quitting voluntarily, but at the same time he said he hadn't really done anything wrong. On the other hand, Davis said he would've sacked McGrath if he didn't resign voluntarily.

THE BELLE OF THE BALL

CHAPTER 17
MR. BORING

November 17th, 2014 was a good day for Dwight Ball.

He got to escort MHA Scott Reid into the House of Assembly on the opening day of the fall sitting, with Rex Hillier looking on from the Speaker's Gallery. Both Reid and Hillier won seats in byelections, stealing them away from the Progressive Conservatives. When Ball took over as interim Liberal leader in the dark days of 2011, the party was a distant third place in the polls, and barely clinging to official opposition status with six MHAs. By November of 2014, six MHAs had become 14, and the Liberals had a 32 percentage point lead over the Tories in public opinion polling. By the end of the month, Ball would pick up two more caucus members, winning byelections in the seats formerly held by Premier Tom Marshall and Finance Minister Charlene Johnson.

The 17th was the first question period of the fall sitting of the legislature, and the Liberals threw out a smorgasbord of issues — whether the province's electrical system would be ready in time for winter, whether the government would reinstate a specialized court designed to deal with domestic violence, and whether the government would enact new mandatory reporting legislation dealing with children who die in provincial custody. Ball didn't land any knockout punches, but neither did newly minted Premier Paul Davis, and if you're leading by more than 30 points in the polls, a tie game means that you're still winning.

The rest of the day in the legislature was pretty unremarkable — the government and opposition spent a couple hours bickering about a piece of over-glorified housekeeping legislation, and nobody of consequence paid any attention. After things wrapped up at the Confederation Building, Ball headed down to the Sheraton Hotel for a party fundraiser. The Liberals charged $250 a head for the privilege of seeing Ball get interviewed by federal Liberal candidate Seamus O'Regan. It was a chummy affair without much in the way of depth, but it was telling for a couple reasons. For one thing, around 300 people showed up for the event, which means the Liberals grossed around $75,000 on the night. It was also worth noting that on the other side of town, federal New Democrat Leader Tom Mulcair was holding an event — free of charge — alongside MP Ryan Cleary. About 150 people showed up to the NDP thing.

The Q&A with O'Regan seemed like a weird event for Ball to organize, though. I mean, softball questions with a journalist-turned-politician? Isn't that the sort of thing Stephen Harper did with Mike Duffy? Is that really a comparison you want to draw?

The thing that really interested me about the fluffy Q&A, though, was whether I'd finally get a clear answer to a simple question: who the hell is Dwight Ball?

Ball was an enigma. Despite having been leader of the opposition for three years, in the fall of 2014 most people seemed to know a very short list of facts about him:

1. He was born in Deer Lake.

2. He was a pharmacist.

3. He wasn't a Tory.

4. He was going to be the 13th premier of Newfoundland and Labrador.

5. He had a big chin and great hair.

For what it's worth, the Liberals were making an effort to fill in the blanks, at least a little bit. They recorded a series of short YouTube videos of Ball talking about himself and his vision for the province — pearls of wisdom like, "One thing that the Tories have never understood is that oil is not a policy, it's a resource. And we will use that resource to invest in the economy of our province. My vision for the province when it comes to economic diversification is building a smarter economy — creating those pathways to success."

If that statement means anything much more than, "We'll throw money at an attempt to diversify the economy," then I certainly missed it. And spending oil dollars on economic development sounds shrewd, but when the province is already cashing the oil cheques and spending the money as fast as it comes in, and still running a $500-million deficit,[1] then you can only use oil dollars on economic diversification if you make cuts somewhere else. Sadly, Ball didn't make an upbeat little YouTube video about which programs and services he'd cut.

After watching him in action for a few years, this is what I'd come to expect — public statements laden with corporate jargon, caveats, weasel-words and very little in the way of specifics.

For a journalist like me, the best quotes come from politicians who give strident, declarative answers — "They're bastards, and they're lying," is a great quote. This is the kind of thing that Danny Williams might say. Dwight Ball is the anti-Danny. "I don't think the underlying numbers support their position; the marginal cost of providing that service means that the bids will likely come in much higher than budgeted," is the sort of quote Ball is liable to give.

Back in 2002, Opposition Leader Danny Williams angrily and repeatedly demanded that Premier Roger Grimes call an election. Williams was riding high in the polls; Grimes was a premier who'd

---

[1] Actually, it was more like a $900-million deficit, because oil prices were in freefall at the time. But in November 2014, people thought it was more like $500 million, so we'll stick with that number for the moment, and we'll go into more detail in the following chapter.

In an admirable display of consistency, and a less-admirable display of fiscal recklessness, even when the government was running a $1.1-billion deficit the following year, Ball still freely made campaign promises worth hundreds of millions of dollars in new spending.

never received a mandate in a general election. Faced with a similar situation, Ball took exactly the opposite approach. He knew an election was coming whether he demanded one or not. Instead of spending his time grandstanding, he was meeting in the back rooms, raising money and making sure that he had solid candidates ready to put their names on ballots in every district in the province.[2]

Again and again, in all aspects of political life, Ball's modus operandi was cautious, fastidious and low-key. Staff talk about him as a ravenous reader — the sort of boss who will already have read the report you're supposed to be briefing him on. By all accounts, he does his research and painstakingly examines all sides of a situation before making any sort of move. He doesn't commit to a position until he's damn sure that it's a safe move to make. It's that same "no unforced errors" ethos that he rode on through the Liberal leadership.

In sharp contrast to most of the other political leaders in Newfoundland and Labrador history, Ball presents himself as less than he is. There's nothing larger-than-life about Dwight Ball, except maybe his chin. His persona is that of a community pharmacist from Deer Lake, a nice guy who goes salmon fishing in the summertime and snowmobiling in the winter. His net worth is almost certainly

---

[2] On the matter of money, specifically, Ball was quietly making a lot of moves. At one fundraiser in the spring of 2014, 500 people packed into the Delta Hotel in St. John's. The party ostensibly charged $500 per person, but most of the tables were bought for $5,000 by the big companies of St. John's, and then the tickets were handed out to whichever employees wanted a free meal and a chance to hear Dwight Ball give a speech. Somewhere along the way, Ball and the Liberal party worked out a deal with the banks to write off part of the party debt, and a payment plan to take care of the rest. By November of 2014, the debt had dropped from around $800,000 a year earlier to roughly $360,000.

Here's the really remarkable thing about the deal to wipe out the Liberals' debt, though: Ball didn't tell anybody about it. I heard from some sources within the party, and then I asked Ball about the debt point-blank without warning.

"I don't think I've ever said this in an interview yet, so James, this could be your story," he said with a sheepish laugh, as though paying it off was some uncomfortable secret that shouldn't be discussed in polite company.

The debt was a stone tablet around the neck of the Liberals for years. The persistent snipe from the other partisans was, "How can you manage the finances of the province when you can't even balance the books of your own party?" Any other politician would've shouted it from the rooftops if he'd manage to put the party finances on track to paying off the debt; Ball just did it, and waited for somebody to ask about it.

in the millions. In addition to owning pharmacies and a personal care home, he had business interests in real estate development, self-storage, logging, venture capital and potato farming.[3] Sticking with the pharmacist persona sort of makes sense, though, given that pharmacists routinely rank among the most trusted professionals in public opinion polls.[4]

If you really want to understand Dwight Ball, you're not going to find any answers in a YouTube video, or at a fundraising Q&A event. If you want to understand Ball, you need to watch him for a long time, because he moves very slowly and very deliberately. You can't point to defining moments or iconic images, because he doesn't work that way. You have to understand Ball based on his results.

He started out as a community pharmacist in Deer Lake, sure. But then he bought another pharmacy in a neighbouring community. From there he branched out into a personal care home, and the rest of it. If he's screwed anybody over or made any enemies, I certainly can't find them. Aside from the Tories, who think he's an empty suit, I haven't really heard from anybody who hates the guy. Mostly, from what I can tell, the impression he leaves with people is that he's a banal, nice guy — maybe not worthy of being a premier, but not a bastard, either.

When I asked him about his life in business, he gave me a politician's answer: "If you really want to build community, there are a number of thing things that you have to put in place. And I know this all sounds a little bit fluffy to some degree, but it's who I am. It's important to me that you keep putting the services and infrastructure in communities if you want people to come to live. That was important to me. ... If more people live there, it supported the other businesses you had on the go, too. So it was really, in some ways, a bit of a business integration. That was why we went from a

[3] From the website of the potato company:
"Humber Valley Potato Company is an industry leader in producing fresh products with a full Potato Flavour. We produce premium fresh-cut oil blanched fries without the fresh-cut hassle. Our objective is to produce a product you can be proud to serve, and delighted to consume."
[4] Which means he's dropping quite a long way by switching from pharmacist to politician. A very, very, very long way indeed.

pharmacy to a personal care home to you know, assisted living units or affordable housing units. It was all about integration and leveraging one business off the other."

When I approached the same question from a different angle, I got an answer that sounds closer to the truth to me. He said that he started off in the health-care business because it was a safe bet. "When you look at pharmacies and you look at personal care homes, even though they're somewhat highly regulated, it was consistent. You didn't hit those highs and lows."

That same cautious, building approach he took to business showed up again once he got into politics. He ran in a byelection in February 2007 and narrowly won, only to narrowly lose the seat eight months later when the general election rolled around. Winning the Humber Valley seat back in the 2011 general election was one of the few bright spots in a mostly catastrophic result for the Liberals, and then months later when the party was at its lowest ebb, he agreed to take over the leadership.

From there, the results speak for themselves. The caucus steadily grew. The poll numbers slowly improved. It's difficult to put your finger on what exactly he did to turn it all around, but the party definitely turned itself around, and he was definitely at the helm when it happened. Adopting the voter identification software Liberalist was a good idea, for sure. The approach to fundraising worked, evidently. In hindsight, the decision to filibuster Bill 29 and make government secrecy into a signature issue seems like a no-brainer, but it's the sort of thing that could have pretty easily passed the Liberals by if the leader didn't recognize the opportunity.

On policy, the Liberals proposed plenty of stuff so they could say they weren't totally devoid of policy. They promised to reinstate the Family Violence Intervention Court which the Tories cut.[5] They promised to enact mandatory bicycle helmet legislation.[6] On health care, they promised to enact a handful of strategies to address mental illness and diabetes and put radiation therapy in the

---

[5] The Tories beat them to the punch and did that in the 2015 budget, months before the general election.

[6] The Tories enacted this one too, after the Liberals promised it.

planned Corner Brook hospital. Ball promised a business invest-ment tax credit and a few other things like that.

On the larger issues, though, Ball's policy stance was vague to the point of being ridiculous. In an interview in November 2014, I asked him how he would tackle the massive fiscal imbalance facing the province. At the time, remember, the government was running a $538-million deficit. I asked Ball, specifically, what he would do to fix the situation.

"I think you look at whatever options you have. There are a number of options on the table. In some areas you can save money. In some areas you can create new revenue streams," Ball said.

More often, when asked for specifics on a given issue, Ball was most likely to deflect by saying something like, "Well, I'll tell you what I wouldn't do, and that's…" and then turn the answer into an opportunity to bash the Tories.

The message basically amounted to him saying, "My specific policies don't matter; what's important is that I won't screw up as bad as the Tories have." At the same time, I think there's something else going on, too. When he's really pressed, Ball says he simply cannot give any detail about what he would do to fix the province's fiscal imbalance. In another interview in late December 2014, Ball said he couldn't talk in concrete terms about government finances "until we get into a situation where we can look at every single ex-pense line within government" and figure out what's really going on.

The most egregious example of this actually came from one of Ball's lieutenants. When finance critic Cathy Bennett was asked in the lead-up to the 2015 budget how she would address the deficit sit-uation, she said, "I haven't seen the books, and until I see the books and understand the complexity, I think it's really inappropriate for me to comment on what parts of the entire government public serv-ice we'd look at eliminating."

That's an awfully convenient stance to take. It basically amounts to saying that that there's just enough information to iden-tify a problem and criticize the government about it, but they don't have enough information to proffer a solution. A cynic might look at that quote about scrutinizing every line item in government and see Ball laying the groundwork for his first few months in power. It's not exactly a new trick for a political party coming into government to say, "Sorry folks, the old crowd was cooking the books. Once we got in and looked at the real numbers, we realized things are even worse than we thought. We're going to have to raise taxes and we won't be able to keep all our election promises. Sorry. Blame it on the other guys."

• • •

Ball's slow-moving caution eventually started getting him into trouble. If I've painted a flattering picture of him so far, it's worth noting that there were also signs of trouble brewing. If it hadn't been for the high polling numbers and a looming election, I honestly think that a caucus revolt against Ball would have been a real possibility.

Take, for example, an episode in early January 2015 when Premier Paul Davis announced he would move to cut the number of seats in the House of Assembly.

Ball's response was a train wreck.

The way these things usually work is that the premier or a government minister will hold a media availability in the foyer in front of the House of Assembly, and then Liberal and NDP politicians come out one after the other to deliver their response a few minutes later. This is a bad scene for Dwight Ball. Typically there's a few Liberal and NDP staffers lurking behind the journalists taking notes when the government politician speaks. So Mr. Slow-and-Boring has five minutes or so to frantically huddle and come up with a coherent response to whatever thing the government just announced.

So there was Premier Davis on January 16, announcing that he wanted to cut 10 seats from the House of Assembly, and he wanted to make it happen in just three months. And then a few minutes later, there was Dwight Ball saying words, some of which even stitched themselves together into full sentences, but nothing close to a coherent response.

Davis sounded like a leader. His basic message was: here's a thing that I think we should do; it's ambitious, but I think we can get it done. Whether you agree or disagree on the policy, taking decisive action looks good on a leader.

Fumbling around and obfuscating looks bad.
That's what Ball did.

• • •

Before we try to parse the political calculus of reducing the seats in the House of Assembly, I should say that I have a hard time approaching this issue as a dispassionate reporter. Cutting the number of politicians in the legislature is a godawful idea on many levels. It's cynical politics and bad policy. It does very little to benefit the citizenry and it makes politicians less accountable to the public.

As far as I can tell, the only reason they were able to get away with it at all is because of a simple and important truth about Newfoundland and Labrador politics: what happens in the House of Assembly doesn't matter.

It's the political equivalent of a tinpot dictatorship show trial.

It's a place where adults — some of them very sensible, intelligent, impressive people — debase themselves in the name of idiotic political games. It's a vapid, self-absorbed place filled with people who are mainly interested in scoring political points and playing little strategic games that are utterly meaningless beyond the walls of the Confederation Building.

I'll say it one more time, bolded and underlined: **what happens in the Newfoundland and Labrador House of Assembly doesn't matter.**

Perhaps the only useful function of the legislature comes from the opposition parties. The politicians who sit on the lonely side of the legislature are basically taxpayer-subsidized government critics. They serve as a check on the "elected dictatorship" which a majority government holds. Question period matters — a bit — insofar as it allows the opposition to force the government to respond to questions on the record, under the watchful gaze of journalists up in the gallery and broadcast live to whichever political ultra-junkies and shut-ins happen to be watching legislative proceedings in the middle of the afternoon. A call to VOCM Open Line probably comes with more bang for your buck for an opposition politician, because the audience is bigger. On the other hand, questions in the legislature offer a bit more gravitas, and the proceedings get transcribed in Hansard, so it's easier to throw the government's words back in their face later.

Actual debate on legislation is meaningless 99.9 per cent of the time. In the four years between the 2011 and 2015 elections I can think of a perhaps three or four times where the actual content of legislative debate mattered. The Bill 29 filibuster mattered — sort of — but only because the politicians were there, 'round the clock, for several days. What they actually said during those days didn't really matter until Felix Collins' (arguably) racist meltdown brought the whole thing to a halt.

The opposition matters, and for the sake of appearances, they do stuff in the House of Assembly. But by and large, it's the existence of opposition parties that matters. What happens in the House of Assembly generally doesn't.

And that's a bad thing. Democracy works best when it's messy and slow and it all happens in a public venue like the legislature. In a perfect world, I'd like to have committees that study issues, come up with policies, question expert witnesses and hash things out in public. I know this might sound dreamy and idealistic, but I really believe that it's possible to change minds and reach positive compromises if you stick half a dozen adults in a room and force them to talk about public policy issues, and that's the beauty of parliamentary committees. With a big enough cohort of legislators and a well-defined structure in place, you also get a marketplace of ideas and real honest-to-goodness debate. Individual politicians that really care about specific issues advocate for them and lobby the relevant powers for reform, or propose private member's legislation. In a legislature that's functioning well, you have at least two parties — hopefully more — that hold each other accountable.

The problem with all of this is that it relies on a certain critical mass of human beings to make it happen. There are only so many hours in the day, and thoughtful, well-researched policy debate takes time.

If you want a committee to intelligently study, say, post-secondary education policy, you need to give the committee members hours to read up on the topic, and then more hours to sit in a room and ask questions of expert witnesses, and then more hours still to discuss what they heard and draft some sort of consensus report. Then you need to get a different group of people to do the same thing with forestry regulation, economic diversification and a whole bunch of other topics. Sure, the same MHAs that tackled post-secondary education can also probably handle child care and arts funding and tourism marketing, but only if you give them the necessary hours for reading up on it.

Most MHAs live far enough from St. John's that you've also got to grant them extra time for driving or flying back and forth to their constituencies. On top of that, you have to give them time to handle constituency issues, or you've got to give them more staff who can handle the local stuff while they're away doing the House of Assembly work.

All of this is a tall order, even in a 48-member parliament.

This is part of why Newfoundland and Labrador doesn't have an active committee structure in the legislature at present. Dwight Ball has promised to implement standing all-party legislative committees as premier, but he also supported cutting the number of MHAs in the House. You can have one or the other, but in my mind, it's impossible to have both. With 40 MHAs, I suspect the best you can really expect is committees that exist on paper and in reality do very little meaningful work.

All of this will likely suit Ball just fine. Power is a zero-sum game, and the more power the legislature has, the less power the premier can exercise. That's the thing about cutting seats from the legislature — it actually serves to benefit the politicians who stick around. The thinking among the public goes: I hate politicians, so let's have fewer of them. The problem is that in reality, fewer politicians means power is concentrated in the hands of a smaller group of people. Moreover, it means that the work of government policy-making won't be done by the politicians you elect. Instead, it'll get done by politically appointed staffers and bureaucrats whose names you'll probably never know, and who don't feel the same direct ballot box accountability to you.

Smaller legislatures also mean smaller opposition parties, which are basically the only useful part of the current House of Assembly structure. Even if the government caucus goes from 30 to 25, you might not notice any real difference. But if the Official Opposition goes from four to three, that one person they lost would mean a world of difference when it comes to their ability to hold government accountable for their actions. If the New Democrats went from one MHA to zero, that would be even worse.

The only real downside to having a big legislature is that it costs money. That's always an important consideration for governments, but I honestly can't think of anything more important to spend money on than the core democratic structure upon which government is built. Davis said that cutting 10 MHAs would save the government $2.5 million per year. Assuming his numbers are right, that means all in all, each MHA costs the taxpayer $250,000. In the world of government budgets, that's a rounding error. If the increased democratic accountability from those 10 MHAs prevents the government from making a $5-million mistake, then they've paid for themselves twice over.

That is why cutting the number of politicians in the legislature is bad policy.

• • •

Of course, bad policy doesn't mean it's bad politics, and since people dislike politicians and would like to see fewer of them, all three political parties have mused at one time or another about reducing the number of MHAs in the legislature.

And with the Tories far behind in public opinion polls, and the price of oil landing with a sickening thud at around $45 a barrel, saving a bit of money and doing something populist must have seemed like a no-brainer for Paul Davis. And for the Tories, it didn't hurt that the Liberals had candidates nominated in more than half of the province's electoral districts. Redrawing the political map would put them back to square one and lead to a game of musical chairs as political hopefuls fought it out for the remaining seats.

So there was Davis, saying he'd cut the number of seats. And there was Ball, struggling to come up with a coherent response. He was vaguely supportive of the government's move. At one point, he literally said, "I'm not opposing this, but…" and at another point, he said, "We'll support whatever the number is, of course, because I'm committed to less MHAs."

Ball knew he was on record calling for the number of MHAs to be reduced, and the Liberals were desperately terrified of looking like they were flip-flopping. So he said that cutting the number of politicians in the legislature was cool, so long as the process was transparent and consultative. He said that it would be fine to delay the election a month or two if was necessary to get the thing done.

But then hours later, the Liberals issued a news release with a quote from Ball which said, "(Davis) has absolutely no mandate from the public to arbitrarily decide to rush the electoral reform process and redraw the boundaries of provincial districts before the next election."

By the following week, the Liberals were leading filibuster tactics in the House of Assembly, and negotiating behind the scenes for a truce where the Liberals would get the Tories to reduce the seats in the House by eight instead of ten. By May, the Ball was demanding that the government nail down an election date, and demanding that the election should not be delayed past September — the deadline imposed by law one year from when Davis took over as premier. That new stance in May ran totally contrary to what Ball said in January: "I believe there is a window in November 2015 that we could actually move and still have an election within 2015. I really don't have an issue with that."

A lot of Liberals I talked to were frustrated by all of this. Ball was slow, and during that critical first media scrum in January, he tripped all over himself. In an effort to avoid looking like he was flip-flopping, he said a bunch of things he'd eventually have to go back on. In hindsight, it would have been more straightforward for Ball to have simply said something like, "I support cutting the number of seats in the legislature, but redrawing the electoral map just a few months before an election is a recipe for disaster. Paul Davis is deluded if he thinks that mistakes won't be made, and this is clearly just a desperate attempt to hold onto power."

• • •

By the summer of 2015, I was hearing rumblings of deep discontent coming from inside the Liberal party.

There were other incidents, like on budget day, where Ball was doing an interview with the CBC during their live broadcast from the lobby of the Confederation Building. At the same moment, Liberal finance critic Cathy Bennett was delivering a contradictory message in an interview with VOCM's live broadcast happening on the opposite side of the lobby.

Not long after that, a Liberal told me, "Dwight scrums are militantly planned." I also heard that some Liberal caucus members were beginning to grumble. A small circle of MHAs and senior staff around Ball were running the show, and some Liberal MHAs felt like they were cut out of the decision-making loop. That sort of thing is a lot easier to accept if you believe that the inner circle has everything under control, and they'll lead you to victory.

At the same time, nearly everybody in the political world was patiently waiting to see whether the Liberals would have a full-blown leadership crisis after winning the election. Leadership hopeful Paul Antle was also running for a seat in the upcoming election, and nobody thought he'd entirely retired his leadership ambitions.[7] Longtime federal MP Gerry Byrne was also running for the Liberals provincially, and there was plenty of speculation about whether he'd end up making a play for the leadership at some point. Cathy Bennett was still in the picture too.

None of these people are so politically foolish to tinker with the party's leadership less than a year ahead of an election, especially when the party was sitting first in the polls by a comfortable margin. But if Ball continues to struggle once he becomes premier, some sort of caucus revolt or leadership weirdness would not shock me at all.

• • •

I really don't know what to expect from Premier Dwight Ball. With the ability to control the agenda more, maybe he'll be well served by his slow-moving ways. Or maybe he'll spend one term in office, constantly on his heels, reacting too slowly and in half-mea-

[7] He lost to Lorraine Michael on election day, so he probably won't be a leadership threat. But that was certainly the thinking in mid-2015.

sures to whatever problems crop up. I certainly haven't seen any hints of vision, or grand policy priorities from him. But, as I'll explain in the next chapter, that sort of thing is hardly what Newfoundland and Labrador politics is really about.

NEW HEAD OF PUBLIC SAFETY WITH THE NEW DEPUTY HEAD OF NL...

MANNING

KENT

CHAPTER 18
THE BALLOT QUESTION

Here's a theory on how to understand Newfoundland and Labrador politics that's served me pretty well: the two main political parties have basically no ideology, and their entire raison d'être is about the pursuit of power. New Democrats, meanwhile, have a clear and deeply held ideology, and because they cannot compromise that, they're incapable of becoming an outfit that could credibly win government and wield real power.

I'll get to the NDP in a subsequent chapter, but for right now, let's talk about the ballot question, the Liberals and the Tories.

Here's the ballot question: which party is best able to get things done?

From what I can tell, this has always been the ballot question. The exact definition of "get things done" might have shifted over the years, but fundamentally, Newfoundland and Labrador provincial politics is always about competence. Which party can keep the roads paved? Which party can improve cellphone service? How about jobs, can they keep people employed? And can they keep the federal government from screwing us over? And along the way, can they keep the budget close to balanced? If your party can convince the voters that you're the best answer to these questions, it doesn't matter whether you're ostensibly Liberal or PC. Neither party really has a meaningful claim to one end of the political spectrum or the other — relax! I'll get to the NDP in a bit, I promise — so debates are never really about "big government" versus "personal liberty," or "progressive values" versus "traditional social attitudes."

This creates a cycle where one party ascends to government, often on the momentum of a new, magnetic leader. Once a party is able to get off the ground and gain some traction with the public, the momentum builds off itself. Sensible, professional candidates, staffers and volunteers gravitate towards the party, because they want to be on the winning team. They are pragmatic people with good ideas for what government should be doing, and they want to be part of the crowd that will get a chance to implement those ideas. A party on the rise benefits from favourable media coverage, and then eventually they pick up enough support that voters just start backing them because they want to get behind who's most likely to score a victory. Historically, getting your road paved was always easier if you had an MHA on the government side of the House, and old habits die hard.

So our party wins an election and charges into government full of heavy-hitters with populist ideas about how the old crowd was doing it all wrong. The other guys, now consigned to opposition, are disorganized and decimated. Now, our governing party has their hands on the levers of power and the business community is eager to ingratiate themselves to the people who are awarding contracts. The political donations flow freely, and the key constituencies are placated. When things go wrong, the new government blames it on the crowd who just got tossed out.

Eventually, too many things go wrong. The government becomes tired, and too comfortable in the seat of power. At the beginning, the ministers listened to the people and told their bureaucrats to make things happen. After a while, though, the balance shifts and the politicians start listening to the bureaucracy explain why people are wrong about what they want, or why it just simply can't be done. There are screw-ups, and they can't be blamed on the last government anymore. The folks who cut their teeth in opposition retire, and the heavy-hitters get replaced with party apparatchiks who aren't as strong. They get tired, complacent, dismissive and sloppy.

Around this point in time, some new charismatic leader emerges to lead the crowd in opposition and whip them into shape.

Through it all, the specific issues change, but the ballot question remains the same: which party is best able to run the government and get things done? When the folks on top no longer seem like the best bet, the cycle repeats itself.

• • •

You could make the argument — and it's one I've heard frequently from smart political observers — that Dwight Ball is the weakest leader ever to benefit from this political cycle. Newfoundland and Labrador politics is littered with messianic leaders like Joey Smallwood and Danny Williams — men who had the aura of being the smartest guy in the room, with a vision of how to lead the province into the promised land of prosperity and pride.

Dwight Ball is not one of those guys. In fact, he can be downright underwhelming.

Take, for example, an episode that happened in May 2015, when the Liberals issued a news release to announce that they had officially retired the party debt. As I've mentioned before, the debt was a albatross around the neck of the party for more than a decade, and by all rights, leading the party to debt-free status should have been a minor coup for Ball. Instead, it became a communications train wreck.

A few hours after the news release was issued, Ball spoke to journalists at the Confederation Building. He had a big grin on his face as he walked towards the cameras. He kept grinning long after it should've become clear that he'd screwed up pretty badly. Ball started by saying this was a "good news story" for the party, and there had been a "friendly negotiation" with the banks to retire the debt. But when it came to specifics, Ball was ducking and dodging. He refused to give any details, and just kept saying how happy the banks were with the deal. For example:

Q: "How much was written off in interest?"
A: "The exact number? I couldn't tell you the amount, the exact number that was written off in interest. There were three components, being the principle, the interest and some penalties that were incurred there. But as I said, the good news, as I said today, is that everybody is very happy with the outcome here, very pleased, it was a good negotiation, good news for the Liberal Party of Newfoundland and Labrador."

The assembled journalists pressed for specifics — how much debt did the banks write off? How much money was repaid? Which banks were involved in the deal? Ball refused to answer. What's more, Ball said he couldn't get into detail about the structure of the deal without first making sure the banks were OK with him talking about it.

Really? All of a sudden, this was a different story. The Liberals received an undisclosed financial benefit from three large Canadian banks based on a secret deal. Worse, the leader of the party — a guy who was always talking about transparency and accountability — was now saying that he could only disclose details if the faceless suits from the banks gave their OK. This is not the sort of thing that inspires confidence, to put it mildly.

What makes all of this even more galling is the fact that the names of the three banks were already a matter of public record, even as Ball stubbornly refused to reveal them. The information wasn't posted online, but the three banks — CIBC, Scotiabank and Royal Bank — were all listed in Liberal Party financial statements, which could be viewed by anybody who visited the Elections NL offices in St. John's. More maddening still is that Ball had already found himself in this exact situation before, when he ran into trouble over his leadership campaign donations. In that situation, too, he took a financial benefit and then awkwardly tried to avoid public disclosure because he was worried that his benefactors wouldn't want their names disclosed. Surely you would have expected him to learn from that situation and not take a financial benefit from somebody unless it was crystal clear that he could fully and immediately disclose it to the public.

It's one thing to accept a political leader who makes mistakes; it's quite a bit harder to get behind a politician who's a slow learner.

• • •

If Ball was weak, though, Paul Davis was doing a bang-up job of proving that his government was even weaker. It started within days of Davis being sworn in, when he announced his cabinet.

Davis appointed a young lawyer nobody had heard of named Judy Manning to serve as a minister in his cabinet. This was clearly supposed to be the centrepiece of the nascent Davis government. Davis was the new leader of a province in transition — especially the vote-rich capital city. Demographics were changing. There was more money than ever before in the province's history, but oil money has a darker side, and it was leading to increasingly high-profile crime. A house in St. John's was shot up with an AK-47. A spate of home invasions had people on edge. An 11-year-old boy was randomly stabbed in the neck at a soccer field in Conception Bay South, just next door to Davis's home electoral district.

Manning would be heading up the Department of Public Safety (formerly the Department of Justice) and serving as attorney general. Clearly she was supposed to be the embodiment of the new PC Party under Paul Davis. Manning could be the answer to everyone who said that the Tories could no longer attract smart, talented new candidates to run for them. She could demonstrate that the Progressive Conservatives were more than just tired warhorses and sycophants left over from the Danny Williams era.

It might have even worked, except that Manning refused to run in any of the byelections which were slated to happen later that fall. That proved to be an astute political move — the Tories lost all three byelections to the Liberals — but it focused all the wrong sort of attention on Manning. Instead of embodying a new tough-on-crime face, and a fresh burst of energy from the Progressive Conservatives, Manning came to represent an attitude among Tories that the voters don't really matter. In the same way that Dunderdale became known for dismissing the public's concern — No, it's not a crisis, I don't care how cold you are! — Manning was effectively saying that elections are a mere inconvenience, and the PC Party didn't care to ask for voters' input about who belongs in cabinet and who doesn't.

Worse, Manning symbolized an air of entitlement and cronyism. Her resumé was thin, but her connections were solid. She was the niece of Senator Fabian Manning, so patronage appointments clearly run in the family. Probably more to the point, though, Manning was in a relationship with businessman and longtime Tory insider Leo Power, who was a fundraiser for Davis's leadership campaign.

There were controversies about her past. As a commissioner for the Workplace Health Safety and Compensation Review Division, the decisions she adjudicated weren't delivered within the legislated timeframe and an injured worker contacted the media to complain about getting left in the lurch. Her official government bio claimed that she moved out west to, "pursue studies in Natural Resources, Energy & Environmental Law at the University of Calgary." What she neglected to mention is that she studied at the University of Calgary, but she hadn't actually graduated.

There was an entirely separate controversy from the legal community about changing the name of the Department of Justice to the Department of Public Safety, on philosophical grounds. One lawyer told me that it represented a "police state" mentality from Davis.

Within two weeks, Davis backed down on the whole "Public Safety" thing, opting to compromise and rename it the "Department of Justice and Public Safety." Ultimately, months later, he backed down on Judy Manning altogether, turfing her out in a cabinet shuffle early in 2015.[1]

By that time, though, the damage had already been done.

Less than a week after Davis became premier and promised to "lead by listening," his unelected minister of public safety told me

---

[1] Much to my surprise, after getting tossed from cabinet, Manning still ended up pursuing the PC party nomination in the district of Placentia-St. Mary's where she grew up. On election day, she was handily beaten by Liberal candidate Sherry Gambin-Walsh by a margin of more than 2,000 votes.

that she wasn't too concerned about the firestorm of public criticism that her appointment created.

"I guess I'm surprised by the political fodder that seems to have been made of this. At the same time, I'm encouraged by the fact that the opposition parties are obviously threatened by the change that Premier Davis is introducing overall, and they need to make, quite frankly, much ado about nothing," she said.

Seriously? You think the backlash is just opposition parties scoring political points?

"I would say it's the opposition parties feeling threatened."

• • •

If I haven't convinced you yet that the Tories' were losing decisively on the "Which party is best able to get things done?" ballot question, let me offer another example from the early days of the Davis administration, when he picked a fight with Prime Minister Stephen Harper.

Well, I'm not sure if "fight" is exactly the right word if one participant just stands there, and the other guy relentlessly punches himself in the face. The fracas was over the Canada-Europe free trade deal, and specifically dealing with minimum processing requirements on seafood. I know your eyes are probably glazing over right now, but this is important, so try to stay with me.

The CETA deal was supposed to be a godsend to the Newfoundland and Labrador fishery, because it would allow free-trade access into the world's largest, richest seafood market. Europe has a whole bunch of trade barriers and tariffs which prevent Canadian fish from being competitive across the pond, and CETA promised to eliminate all of that. Minimum processing requirements (MPRs) were a Newfoundland and Labrador policy which required fish landed in the province to be processed before it's shipped elsewhere, to ensure that Newfoundlanders and Labradorians get jobs from the resource. Europe wanted MPRs dropped as part of the overall CETA deal, and because MPRs are an area of provincial responsibility, the federal government had to get the province onboard.

After furious negotiating in 2013, the province and the federal government agreed to … something.

This is where things start to get fuzzy. In late October 2013, Premier Kathy Dunderdale held a big announcement at The Rooms in St. John's to declare that there would be a $400-million fisheries innovation fund tied to the CETA deal. The provincial government said that the money would start flowing as soon as CETA was ratified and came into force. The fund would be cost-shared 70/30, so Ottawa would kick in $280 million, and the province would put up the other $120 million. All of this was revealed by provincial government politicians. Weirdly though, no federal representative showed up to the big announcement. In subsequent public comments, and in all publicly released correspondence, federal politicians used the phrase "up to $400 million" to describe the fund. The feds never specifically came out and contradicted what the province was saying; they just mostly kept quiet.

Fast forward about a year, to the fall of 2014, and there were signs that something was amiss. In November, Davis vaguely hinted that things weren't going well — "I wouldn't say it's falling apart, but having not been able to reach a finalized agreement yet is troubling." Two days later, after a phone call from the prime minister, Davis did a total about-face, telling the House of Assembly that things were going OK and the deal was still on track. The issue simmered on the back burner for another couple of weeks until it finally boiled over in December.

On Monday, December 12th, Dwight Ball led question period by asking about the issue again.

Ball danced around it a little before getting to the central thrust of his attack: "Just over two weeks ago, the premier spoke to the prime minister on the CETA fisheries fund and told the House that they had a very good discussion. Now we hear that the federal government wants to split the $280 million with other Atlantic provinces," Ball said. "I ask the premier: During your good discussion with the prime minister, did he then say that the fund would be split with other Atlantic provinces?"

This was a new notion — that the full $280 million wouldn't be spent in Newfoundland and Labrador — and Davis quickly poured cold water on it: "Mr. Speaker, I can tell you, what the member opposite has in his preamble today is certainly not reflective of discussions I have had with the prime minister or Minister Moore, who I had the pleasure of meeting with this morning and had a discussion about the Comprehensive Economic Trade Agreement, and also about the $400-million fund. We worked very hard with the federal government to reach an agreement on that. We are working through the process now of crossing the t's and dotting the i's of the administration of the fund."

Who knows what happened between 2 p.m. Monday and 1 p.m. Tuesday, but a day after Davis said everything was cool, he called reporters to a hastily arranged news conference in the basement of the Confederation Building. Davis walked in looking grim, followed by a trio of similarly serious cabinet ministers. It had the feeling of being a defining moment for Davis, and it was, sort of, just maybe not in the way he wanted it to be.

"We made a deal with Stephen Harper's government that secured our support for CETA, and they made a commitment to us. Now they're trying to introduce stipulations that were never considered before," Davis said at the Tuesday Grim Faces News Conference.

"To this end, I'll be meeting with Prime Minister Harper tomorrow, and we will finalize the details of this agreement or the province will have to reconsider its support for CETA."

Wait, what? New conditions? Yesterday you said it was just "crossing the t's and dotting the i's." What new conditions?

"What's changed is the federal government wants to put a monetary value on MPRs so they want to be able to monetize the impact of MPRs," Davis said.

"We've been very clear since the start that MPRs were not going to have a financial impact on the processors and on rural parts of the province. They want to introduce that new condition. And as well, if the new condition doesn't bring successful utilization of the fund based on the pillars that we've agreed to, then they want to consider moving it beyond Newfoundland and Labrador."

"So what the Liberals were talking about in question period yesterday is true?" I asked.

"Um … It would depend on how they worded it," Davis replied.

OK, so a little hiccup there, but generally a good showing. A meeting with the prime minister is good. Draping yourself in the Newfoundland and Labrador flag and fighting against those bastards in Ottawa is good, too. Ultimatums make you sound like you're in charge. That's what leadership is all about, right?

Dwight Ball was unimpressed, of course, but that's his job. He said he figured Davis was just scoring a few political points, and the meeting with Harper was just a formality to firm up a deal that officials had already hammered out behind the scenes.

"If there's a deal done tomorrow, the deal is done today. There's no way this premier is going to Ottawa tomorrow and leaving Ottawa with a deal that's going to be structured by just one day," Ball said. "My guess is the deal is already done and we're just seeing a bit of grandstanding."

That would have been pretty smart, but it turns out that Ball was giving Davis far too much credit. A brief email from the Prime Minister's Office said that there was no plan to meet with Davis in Ottawa Wednesday. In fact, the prime minister wouldn't even be in Ottawa on Wednesday. Harper would be in Montreal, attending the funeral of hockey legend Jean Béliveau. Apparently a junior staffer in the PMO talked to a staffer in the premier's office, there was some sort of miscommunication, and Davis charged out and announced it before anything was confirmed.

By Friday, Davis did manage to get a meeting with Harper, but it amounted to absolutely nothing. The two men sat in a room in Langevin Block and had the same back-and-forth that had been playing out in the media all week. There was no fait accompli worked out in advance. Davis emerged from the meeting to tell any journalist who would listen that Harper is not to be trusted. The collective response of the people of Newfoundland and Labrador was, "Well, d'uh — Harper can't be trusted. Have you been living in a cave for the past eight years, Premier Davis?"

The "fight" continued for another few months, with more grandstanding, and more backtracking.

The most charitable possible explanation for the whole thing is that the federal Conservatives juked the province. With a wink and a nod, they convinced Dunderdale and her crowd that the $400 million was a done deal as a way of getting the province onside with CETA when Ottawa announced the agreement in principle in 2013. Then, a year later, they hauled the rug out from under Davis. If this is what happened, then the provincial government crowd are still idiots.

How many times do you have to be screwed by Harper before you insist on getting everything in writing? Get it all printed up in a memorandum of understanding, have two lawyers go over it, and don't agree to anything until a federal minister signs on the dotted line.

And if Dunderdale ran off half-cocked and announced a deal that wasn't done? If she got an ambiguous letter from the federal government, read it one way and didn't understand that Ottawa meant something different? Isn't that worse?

Remember, the ballot question here is: which party is best able to get things done? Can anybody reasonably say that the Tory crowd is able to get things done?

• • •

Not completely convinced? Let me give you one more example from the Davis-era shambles: the budget.

Viewed in the proper context, the 2015 budget delivered by Finance Minister Ross Wiseman was a stunning document — a damning indictment of more than a decade of Progressive Conservative fiscal management. A whole book (albeit a boring one) could be written on the fiscal trajectory of Newfoundland and Labrador between 2003 and 2015, but I'll boil it down to just one number.

$1.1 billion.

The forecast deficit in 2015 was $1.1 billion.

Eleven years earlier, newly elected as premier, Danny Williams held a news conference that was carried live on the supper-hour news, in an effort to talk directly to the people of the province about the government's fiscal situation. It was the sort of grim, defining moment for a newly elected premier that Davis was probably trying to emulate with the CETA thing. Here's a chunk of Williams' State of the Province address:

"When our government was formed two months ago, we felt that the first priority was to determine the financial condition of our province. We hired an independent external firm, Pricewaterhouse-Coopers, to conduct a thorough review of the province's finances and to assess the financial challenges for this year and the years ahead.

"Earlier today, the minister of Finance released the results of this review and the news is not good. The report, entitled Directions, Choices and Tough Choices, indicates that we have an evolving financial crisis — a situation that if ignored or unresolved will threaten the future sustainability of the province and seriously compromise our social programs and way of life.

"The consultants reported that the total deficit is $827.5 million — $161 million over budget. A component of the total deficit is the cash deficit and that deficit for this fiscal year is $507 million, some $220 million over what was budgeted. Clearly, targets outlined in the 2003-04 budget are not realistic or attainable.

"The predictions for future budgets are even more disturbing. Unless we significantly adjust our course, we are facing total deficits of $1 billion or greater for the next four years at least. This would increase our current debt, the money we owe our lenders, by approximately $4 billion to $15.8 billion. That will be nearly three times what our debt was in 1992-1993.

"Over the last number of years the maintenance of our schools, hospitals and roads has been largely deferred and the cost of these capital works is in the hundreds of millions of dollars.

"We are also facing a number of legal matters before the courts that may or may not have significant cost implications for government. These potential costs have not been factored into government's financial planning but may very well have to be addressed at some point down the road.

"The numbers are staggering to the point where it is difficult for many of us to fully appreciate just how serious the situation really is. Out of our annual $4.2 billion budget, we now spend more than a billion dollars a year — that's 25 cents of every dollar — to pay for the interest on our debt.

"This province should be no different than all of us in running our own households. But the province's situation is comparable to any of us taking out a second mortgage just to buy groceries and running up our credit card to pay for electricity and telephone bills.

"If this continues, we are in very real danger of drowning in our own debt."

On the night that Williams talked about the grim possibility of a $1-billion deficit, trading on Brent crude oil closed at $32.30 a barrel. Lucky for Danny, oil prices were already starting to climb, and they kept increasing for the next four years. At its high water mark, oil would peak at more than $140 a barrel, and the province would reap billions of dollars in royalties from the offshore production fields. From 2005-2014, the provincial government raked in $17 billion from offshore oil revenues.

The money wasn't wasted, exactly. The deferred maintenance in schools, hospitals and roads that Williams talked about in his 2004 address was no longer deferred. Services improved. The size of the civil service ballooned. The government pumped millions of dollars into economic diversification with some success stories[2] and a few boondoggles.[3][4]

What matters, though, is that only a relatively small amount of the money was spent on paying down the debt that Williams worried about drowning in. As fast as the money came in, the oil royalty cheques were cashed, and the windfall revenues were spent on government infrastructure and services.

Then the arse fell out of 'er.

• • •

On the day that Paul Davis announced his bid to lead the PC party, Brent crude closed at $108.98, nearly four dollars above the $105 that the provincial government was forecasting for the 2014 budget year. On the day he was sworn in as premier, oil closed at $95.08. In March, exactly six months after Davis took office — and

[2] Aquaculture is now a huge industry on the south coast, in no small part due to government assistance.
[3] The government poured more than $10 million into a wood pellet plant in Roddickton, which never commercially produced a single pellet.
[4] There was also the Parson's Pond oil exploration project. Nalcor Energy planned to spend $14 million on drilling three wells looking for oil in western Newfoundland. In the end, they went wildly over budget. Nalcor drilled two holes, which cost $23 million, and they gave up before they drilled the third one.

a little bit more than a month before the 2015 budget was delivered — oil closed at $60.33. A decade of high oil prices fuelling huge provincial government budget surpluses came crashing down on Davis's watch, and he was stuck picking up the pieces. Finance Minister Ross Wiseman announced that the provincial government was projecting five consecutive years of deficits, out to 2020.

Back when oil was high, it was easy to think the ride would keep going on forever. I mean, it's a finite resource, and we keep pumping it out of the ground and burning it; basic supply and demand dictates that the price has to keep going up, right? As soon as the price dropped, though, people started sagely talking about how commodity markets are "cyclical" and that this sort of thing was bound to happen. The Tories were foolish to believe that the windfall revenues would never stop flowing.

The 2015 budget was arguably the best possible answer to an awful set of circumstances. The sales tax was going to be increased by a couple of percentage points, and the government increased taxes for high income earners. Program spending was essentially frozen, but it wasn't really cut. Instead, Davis and Wiseman ran the largest deficit in provincial history and used the tax hikes to soften the blow a little bit.

So there we were on budget day, staring at the wreckage of a decade of Tory fiscal management. When Williams offered his grim warning back in 2003, oil was around $30, and he was darkly predicting a $1-billion deficit. After the richest decade in Newfoundland and Labrador history, oil had doubled in price to around $60 per barrel, and yet somehow the government was running a $1.1-billion deficit.[5]

At the end of it all, how do you look a voter in the eye and claim that you're capable of delivering sound fiscal management? If the fundamental ballot box question is about competence, about being able to run the government responsibly, how do you look back at the Progressive Conservative legacy as anything other than a dismal failure?

---

[5] And it's gotten even worse since then.

• • •

Lots of other things happened in the months after Davis was sworn in as premier.

He had to sack Transportation Minister Nick McGrath after the auditor general reported that some dodgy stuff did indeed happen around the Frank Coleman Humber Valley Paving controversy. A man named Don Dunphy was shot in his home by a Royal Newfoundland Constabulary officer tasked with protecting Davis after Dunphy posted a comment on Twitter that was incorrectly interpreted as threatening the premier. Davis pared the size of the legislature from 48 to 40, and had the electoral map redrawn in a matter of months. There was a brouhaha about privatized health-care services.

It all basically played into the same political dynamic, though. The Liberals were weak, but the Tories were defeating themselves.

CHAPTER 19
BEAUTIFUL LOSERS
2015

If the Liberals and the Tories battle back and forth on the question of competence, then the Newfoundland and Labrador NDP tends to its own garden, neither trying particularly hard to look competent, nor fretting too much that most voters wouldn't trust them to run a lemonade stand.

What people trust the New Democrats to do is talk. And talk, and talk, and talk some more.

The New Democrats aren't actually a political party in the same sense as the Progressive Conservative Party or the Liberal Party. Instead, the NDP in Newfoundland and Labrador is best understood as a lobby group akin to the St. John's Board of Trade, or their more ideologically intense cousins, the Newfoundland and Labrador Employers' Council. The tactics are different, but the strategy is basically the same for the Board of Trade or the NDP: cultivate enough of a constituency to give yourself political leverage, and then press the government to lower taxes or improve daycare or whatever aligns with your agenda.

The Board of Trade holds regular networking luncheons, and behind the scenes, they arrange meetings with cabinet ministers to press for their policy priorities. The New Democrats run candidates and pound away at their issues in the House of Assembly. In both cases, it's advocacy work, pure and simple.

There are other parallels, too. Whether it's the business crowd or the lefties, both groups have this grating attitude of moral superiority. They act like they're the only ones who really get it.

In its most extreme iterations, members of the business community act like the entire arena of political debate is childishness beneath them. They're the only ones who really understand economics, and so they debase themselves by occasionally wading into the political fray to impart some wisdom to the folks up in the Confederation Building.

The other end of the spectrum can be even worse. There's an imploring, guilt-trippy tone the New Democrats and their social justice allies adopt: "You either agree with us and do what we say, or you're heartless, and you don't care as much about vulnerable people as we do."

Worse, they frequently claim that their ideology is what New-foundlanders and Labradorians truly believe, and they're the only ones speaking for the so-called "real" people.

Lorraine Michael gave voice to this idea, even on the cold Tuesday morning when she finally conceded defeat as party leader.

Just after New Year's, she called reporters to the media centre in the bowels of the Confederation Building to announce that she was stepping down. Michael admitted what had been abundantly clear to everybody else for more than a year: since the 2013 caucus revolt, her leadership had become untenable, and the only way for the party to truly move on was for her to step aside.

"It has become clear to me throughout the four byelections held since our convention that the message of the party — which I know people believe in — is becoming secondary to public perception of the party," she said, once again repeating the myth that Newfound-landers' and Labradorians' ideology is the same as the NDP's.

"We had great candidates in all four of those byelections. We talked about important concerns of people in the province: student debt and minimum wage and municipal funding and fracking. But the story in the public eye continues to be not what we stand for, but how far we've fallen and whether we're relevant. I know the New Democratic Party is more necessary than ever, with a stumbling government and an opposition that seems more interested in scoring points than getting anything accomplished, and an ever-growing gap between those who have and those who have not in this province."

I might quibble with Michael a bit about the calibre of New Democrat candidates they fielded in those 2014 byelections, but never mind that. Just stop and think about her main point — that the NDP is giving voice to the true beliefs of the people of the province.

It's astoundingly conceited.

If the New Democrats represent the true ideology of the people of the province, why have they never won even half a dozen seats in the legislature? They've been around for decades; are we really to believe that Newfoundlanders and Labradorians won't vote for them out of political inertia? Ontario, Nova Scotia, Manitoba, Saskatchewan and British Columbia have all elected New Democrat governments. Heck, even Alberta gave 'em a go. But apparently, despite the fact that New Democrats are "speaking the voice of the people," according to Michael, those same people have never seen fit to elect enough New Democrats to serve as pallbearers at a funeral.

Michael repeated the same sentiment again a few months later at the convention to pick her replacement.

"We're speaking the voice of the people, and it eventually gets through to the numbskulls that we're trying to speak to," she thundered from the podium, in her last real speech as leader.

I guess when you're consistently pummelled in elections and ridiculed by the winners, you've got to tell yourself something to keep on going.

But if claiming to speak on behalf of the people of the province is conceited, on the day of her resignation in January, Michael saved the most galling claim for her assessment of her own leadership.

"If there is any chance that the politics that swirled around my leadership are standing in the way of the party rebuilding and doing its good and necessary work, then I cannot in all conscience remain as leader. A good leader knows when it's time to go."

In October of 2013, Michael engaged in a divide-and-conquer strategy that directly led to 40 per cent of the MHAs in her caucus leaving to join another party. She then led her party through a series of byelections where the results, by her own admission, were dismal. She had led her party to first place in some public opinion polls, and the strongest showing in any general election in provincial history. Then she led her party right back to the political wilderness.

That's what made her self-assessment during the resignation so tin-eared. If she felt she was unfairly maligned and mistreated in the caucus revolt, that's sad. But politics isn't fair, and 2013 was undeniably the time for her to go if she wanted to give the party any reasonable shot at rebuilding. A good leader knows that when four of her caucus members sign a letter asking her to step aside and then the letter gets leaked publicly, and then one of your MHAs goes on the radio and cries and another one of your MHAs goes on the radio and accuses him of being a liar, it's time to go. For Michael, it took more than a year for it to become abundantly clear to her that the party had been erased as a credible option in the minds of voters.

So was Michael a bad leader? Well, that depends on how you define a "good" New Democrat leader.

If the objective of a political party is to win elections and wield power, then Michael was a bad leader indeed. There was an opportunity after the 2011 general election to consolidate the significant gains made, and start to move the party away from its role as a left-wing advocacy group. Michael did not do that. This was a significant source of tension inside the NDP. In fact, by some accounts that's exactly what the 2013 caucus revolt was about.

But instead of building on the party's successes, and in the way the whole caucus revolt went down, Michael torched any chance of mainstream success in the 2015 election. Instead, she stuck around long enough to entrench the party's status as a bunch of disorganized ideologues advocating from the political hinterland. Then, 14 months after the caucus revolt, and less than a year before the general election, Michael quit as leader, but simultaneously announced that she would run for re-election as an MHA — a move bound to cause friction if the new leader tried to steer the party in a different direction.

All of this, you could argue, makes Michael a godawful political leader.

On the other hand, though, judged purely through the lens of an advocacy organization, Michael's time at the helm of the NDP produced a lot of success. In her political swan song, speaking at the convention where she would hand off the party leadership to a successor, she rattled off a long list of policies that the New Democrats championed before they were eventually enacted by the government.

The government adopted all-day kindergarten, cut small business taxes, added transgender to the human rights code, enacted whistleblower legislation, backed down on Bill 29, removed the tax on home heating[1] and more. Some of that stuff would've happened anyway. And, it all happened between 2006 and 2015, when the oil money was rolling in. It's a lot easier for the governing party to say yes to left-wing demands when the treasury is flush with cash. But the NDP advocated for it, and then it happened. That's got to count for something.

"We may be small in number, but we have achieved much. I can tell you, none of those things would have happened without a strong, consistent NDP voice bringing them up," Michael declared, in between cheers from the crowd. "We're speaking the voice of the people, and it eventually gets through to the numbskulls that we're trying to speak to."

● ● ●

I'm not going to spill much ink on the actual NDP leadership "race." That may seem unfair, given the breadth of the Liberal and Tory leadership chapters. But the NDP leadership was neither a competitive race nor a farce, so there's not much to say about it. And frankly, if politics is primarily about the pursuit of power, then the NDP has been largely irrelevant since Chapter 2.

Earle McCurdy won. It wasn't close.

An idealistic 20-something named Christopher Bruce ran, but he seemed to be mostly in the race to stir up debate and get people talking about ideas. A union guy from Labrador City named Mike Goosney also ran, but I'd never heard his name before he announced that he was jumping into the fray, and he basically disappeared from the public eye as soon as he lost.

McCurdy was just a few months' retired as the longtime head of the Fish, Food and Allied Workers union, and while he insisted there was no orchestrated handoff from Michael to him, the timing seemed a little bit suspect.

McCurdy won, because he was a heavyweight up against two featherweights.

---

[1] Temporarily, anyway. The tax was added back in the 2015 budget, as the government grappled with its $1.1-billion deficit.

And for what it's worth, McCurdy really is a heavyweight. At the time, it seemed entirely possible that he would turn out to be a political force of nature for the NDP. As the president of the fishermen's union for a couple of decades, McCurdy had a whole lot of experience in the rough-and-tumblest part of the rough-and-tumble world of NL politics. His union background also meant his lefty labour bona fides were rock solid. His connections to the fishery also gave him a level of familiarity with rural Newfoundland and Labrador that's usually sorely missing in the NDP. Historically, they've been more of a downtown St. John's arts and university crowd.

McCurdy is quick on his feet and has a face recognizable to anybody with even a passing familiarity with provincial politics. He knows how to run an organization with a provincial scope, and he could be the guy to whip the NDP into shape.

On the other hand, he is also firmly rooted in the advocacy tradition of the NDP. The Fish, Food and Allied Workers union's raison d'être is lobbying governments and pushing pet issues.

When I sat down with McCurdy for an expansive interview for this book in September of 2015, he acknowledged the gap between how the NDP sees itself, and how voters cast their ballots.

"Perhaps it's been fuelled by the way our party has conducted itself," he said.

"We've sort of had this optic of being a kind of protest party. Almost like beautiful losers, you know, standing for a lot, but at the end of the day, we can't put it together. But, the world's changed now. I mean, the obvious change being a huge one in Alberta, but also federally where our party federally is being taken more seriously at this stage in an election campaign than it ever has before."

At the time, in the summer and early fall of 2015, so many things seemed possible for the NDP. This was before Tom Mulcair stumbled in the federal election, before the realities of the provincial campaign sunk in. For a moment, it was almost possible to imagine McCurdy catching fire and turning the whole party around based on his characteristic brand of folksy quips and hard-nosed politicking.

It was McCurdy's party now, albeit with Michael still running as a candidate, standing just over his left shoulder.

A good leader knows when it's time to go.

CHAPTER 20
THE BUBBLE
NOVEMBER 2015

You'll sometimes hear people talk about "the bubble" in politics, as though politicians are able to surround themselves with some impermeable barrier that keeps reality out.

On the mainland, I guess, political leaders are able to shield themselves with staffers and supporters and well-vetted campaign events. As prime minister, Stephen Harper certainly seemed to do that.

But in Newfoundland and Labrador, there's no real bubble like that; there's little chance of escaping the people. If you do, you can be sure it won't last long.

On the first regular day of the 2015 election campaign, Premier Paul Davis visited a long-term care home where he had his ass grabbed three times by octogenarians.

Later on, when he went to the bathroom after dinner, he was greeted by a guy as he walked away from the urinal.

"How's the campaign going?" the guy asked cheerfully, while Davis washed his hands.

"It's going good! But *The Telegram* is getting a little bit close for comfort," Davis joked, given that I was standing at the urinal just a couple of metres away.

The bubble manifests itself in a more insidious way when you're campaigning in Newfoundland and Labrador.

"The problem is," a seasoned politician told me once, "nobody calls you an arsehole to your face."

• • •

Davis called the election on the first Thursday of November, and held a high-energy campaign kickoff rally in his home district of Topsail-Paradise, at the same community centre where he had launched his leadership.

Exactly as with his leadership, he timed his kickoff to coincide with the 6 p.m. news. Right on cue, with "Uptown Funk" by Mark Ronson ft. Bruno Mars playing, Davis burst into the room and wove his way through the crowd, arriving at the podium just in time to get nearly 10 minutes of free airtime on the CBC supper-hour television newscast.

He talked about the four pillars of his campaign platform: health, opportunity, people and economy — HOPE, get it? — about how the Tories had made the province better, and would make the province better still.

It was a serviceable speech, and it earned him plenty of cheers from the crowd of Tories in the room, but for anybody listening with a critical ear, it foreshadowed all the internal contradictions and flaws that would plague Davis for the next month.

For now, though, let's just say it was an energetic and defiant speech — both a full-throated defence of Tory government, and a fierce attack on the Liberals.

"The campaign is on. The Opposition's free ride on accountability comes to an end today," Davis declared. "Their lack of ideas; their arrogance; their taking you, the voters, for granted, comes to an end right here, right now. I don't have to tell you, they've been hiding, and now is the time to demand openness. Ask them who, and what, is hiding behind that red door."

● ● ●

About nine minutes into the speech, Ryan Cleary bounded onto the stage and patted Davis on the arm before taking his place behind the premier. It was a strange moment, and a bit of a distraction for people watching the live TV broadcast.

Cleary was a distraction, period.

Just a few weeks earlier he was running for re-election as the New Democrat MP for St. John's South-Mount Pearl, before he was handily defeated by Liberal Seamus O'Regan. Less than two weeks after the federal election, rumours started to bubble up that Cleary was thinking about running for the Tories in the provincial election. And then, just as I was confidently telling everybody that those rumours were total bunk, there was Ryan Cleary, striding into a news conference alongside Paul Davis, announcing that he would run for the Progressive Conservatives in the new district of Windsor Lake against Liberal Cathy Bennett.

In the following weeks, I talked to a lot of Tories about Cleary and asked them why he would want to run for the party. Nobody had an answer. Nearly all of the MHAs and campaign staffers I spoke to said he was a goner. A couple of MHAs shrugged and said that he'd at least keep Cathy Bennett focused on her home district instead of striking out to help Liberals in other parts of the capital city. Some other folks just said, basically, anything is possible.

"It's crazy, but if you look back at the past 24 months, there's been a whole lot of crazy," one MHA told me, laughing, at Davis's campaign launch.

From Cleary's perspective, it didn't make any sense.

A year earlier, city councillor Danny Breen had gone up against Bennett in a byelection in Virginia Waters, and barely lost by 40 votes. In that byelection, the Tories were able to pour all their resources into the district, with a gang of cabinet ministers going door to door, with Danny Williams in the mix.

Cleary would have none of those advantages. Instead, he'd be an NDP apostate and a Tory carpetbagger.

For the PC Party, the move made sense. He was a recognizable name, and he plugged a hole in Windsor Lake at a time when the Tories were struggling to find candidates to run. It also fed the idea the NDP was in shambles, and that high-profile members were jumping ship. Cleary's stated reason for joining the Tories — in part because NL needed a strong voice to stand up to the newly elected Trudeau federal government, and only the Tories could do that — was a central theme of Davis's campaign message.

But it still didn't make sense, and that made it a distraction.

And those distractions kept piling up.

Steve Kent repurposed his leadership campaign materials for the provincial election, and the colour scheme was slightly different than that of the typical PC Party kit. A few people remarked to me that it looked like Kent was trying to run for a different PC Party, distancing himself from Davis.

Eleven days after the campaign was called, the Tories still had six districts out of 40 without candidates, including Burin-Grand Bank and Gander, two seats that were previously held by high-profile cabinet ministers Darin King and Kevin O'Brien.

And then in downtown St. John's, there was a trio of candidates — Kathie Hicks, Alison Stoodley and Tina Olivero — who were running some sort of bizarre joint campaign. It was like they were running as a sub-party within the PC Party; on campaign literature their three smiling faces appeared side by side, and they had their own "We can, we will" slogan.

I was planning on doing a story on the whole thing for *The Telegram* until Olivero had a social media meltdown and changed the story entirely. She loudly declared on Twitter, "I will NEVER accept criticism in politics. I give a damn and care about the future. Not tolerating abuse for that!"

Later she announced, "Twitter 'haters & bashers' are not tolerated here. Honour people who step up for others and your province!"

Declaring that you will never accept criticism in politics is a weird thing to do, and it's especially weird coming from a Tory candidate after the party had been perceived for years as out of touch and dismissive of public criticism.

The more I dug into Olivero, the weirder it got.

She had a GoFundMe crowdfunding page set up, where she was seeking to raise $10,000 for her campaign. In the end she raised $60.

The language of the crowdfunding campaign was nonsensical: "We are global citizens of the world and we have the determination and endurance muscle to make Newfoundland and Labrador a world leader. With our unprecedented kindness, our passion, our art, music, technology, our resources and of course our inviting people to this magnificent province — a place we call home, this is our time to be strong and work together.

"Beyond the gates of right or wrong, beyond the gates of good and bad, you will find us there, getting on with the business of making a future that truly inspires us to jump out of bed in the morning and work on something meaningful and sustainable for our province and our people."

Her personal website, "Transform With Tina," was just as strange. She described herself as a "global visionary" and offered "transformational training" courses; her expertise included "Coaching for Personal & Professional Mastery (Ontology)." I don't have a damn clue what any of that means.

Eventually, when she started making claims about self-awareness being capable of curing cancer, media outlets started writing stories about her, and the whole thing turned into a brief political feeding frenzy. Then she abruptly dropped out of the race just before the CBC reported on her having lost a judgement by the Labour Relations Agency for underpaying her nanny by more than $23,000. According to the CBC story, Olivero obtained a work visa for a live-in Filipino nanny under dubious circumstances. She was supposed to pay the caregiver $10.50 per hour, for a 40-hour work week — a salary of about $1,700 per month. Instead, Olivero deducted living expenses and paid the woman $400 per month cash, which was bumped up to $500 per month shortly before the nanny quit and filed a labour relations complaint.

Each one of these little distractions was just a sideshow, but they derailed the Tories' message. If journalists are asking you questions about how your candidate-vetting process could allow somebody like Olivero to run for the party, then journalists aren't writing about the Tory record. If you're being asked whether Ryan Cleary was promised some sort of post-election job in exchange for running, then you don't have the opportunity to talk about why voting Liberal would be a mistake.

● ● ●

On the night that Davis launched his campaign, after the rally was over, I was sitting at the back of the room writing my story for the next morning's paper, while workers packed up the campaign backdrop and stacked the discarded election signs that supporters had been waving. Just a few metres away, I could see Davis and his wife, Cheryl, posing for a photo with Hicks, Olivero and Stoodley.

Almost at the exact moment that they were smiling for the camera, still riding high from the energy of the crowd and Davis's speech, an email hit my inbox. Abacus Data had done a poll in the days immediately before the writ dropped, and they were providing it to reporters under embargo ahead of a Friday morning release.

The results were grim.

The Tories were a whopping 47 percentage points behind the Liberals, according to Abacus. Worse, a crushing 75 per cent of the people Abacus polled said that they wanted to see a change in government. Seventy-six per cent of voters said they believed the Liberals would win the next election; even a majority of Tory supporters said they thought the Liberals would win.

Davis smiled, posed for pictures and chatted with his candidates, happily ensconced in the bubble.

● ● ●

The Tories ran a bad campaign.

The message was at odds with itself.

Davis would claim that he was a "new premier" and then moments later expound on the wonderful things the Tories had done since they were first elected in 2003.

He would castigate the Liberals for being entitled and trying to coast to victory without putting forward any substantial policies or vision. At the same time, the Tories' policy promises were opaque and underwhelming. The party was promising a hodgepodge of vague, aspirational goals, mixed with little concrete tweaks to government that seemed to provoke the question, "Really? After 12 years in power you haven't gotten around to this yet?"

The Tories fatally misjudged the mood of the province. The overwhelming feeling I got from people I talked to wasn't anger or fear or excitement or contentment. The main feeling in the air was pure, full-body exhaustion. Canada had just come through the longest federal election in modern times — a bruising, polarized campaign that dealt with real issues, and felt like it ultimately cut to the heart of what Canadians want their country to be. And then it was over, and Stephen Harper was gone, and Justin Trudeau was prime minister, and anybody who followed politics just wanted to switch off for a while.

Instead of a break, Newfoundland and Labrador got a provincial election about … well … that's precisely the point, isn't it? It was an election about nothing. No vision, no energy, no drive to present any big ideas from the Tories.

The Liberals were almost as bad — worse, in some ways — but they hadn't been at the helm for the past decade and more. People were exhausted, and presented with a non-choice over non-issues, people were tired of looking at the Tories.

The arrogance and entitlement didn't help. After the years of Kathy Dunderdale's dismissiveness, then Frank Coleman's presumptuousness and Judy Manning's patronage, Davis was elevated to the premier's office by fewer than 500 Tories at a convention in St. John's, and he felt entitled to a year at the helm, with his hands on the levers of power. After years of Progressive Conservative conceit, there was nothing humble or modest about Davis making himself comfy in the premier's office for so long before finally submitting himself to the electorate.

On top of everything else, for the life of me I don't know why Davis decided to pick a fight with Justin Trudeau over literally nothing, at the apex of the new prime minister's popularity. In one breath, Davis would say that he was happy Harper was gone and he looked forward to working with Trudeau, who had publicly and repeatedly committed to a more collaborative relationship with the provinces. And then in the next breath, Davis was saying that inevitably the new Liberal government would somehow slight Newfoundland and Labrador, and then we'd have to start scrapping.

Davis said he'd be better situated than Dwight Ball to fight the Trudeau Liberals in Ottawa.

Maybe the line worked on a few people. But it seemed to me like Davis was just reminding people that Canada had a charismatic, energetic new prime minister, and Newfoundland and Labrador had the same old crowd who went around picking fights with people and coming away from it bruised and sore.

"I can tell you, Dwight Ball is not Justin Trudeau, and I'm not Stephen Harper," Davis would say, trying to beat back against the swell of support the NL Liberals were enjoying in the post-election Trudeau honeymoon.

There's a story from U.S. President Lyndon B. Johnson's early days in Texas politics that Hunter S. Thompson recounts in his seminal political work, Fear and Loathing: On the Campaign Trail '72.

Johnson, so the story goes, asked aides to spread rumours that his opponent engaged in bestiality.

"Christ, we can't get away with calling him a pig-fucker," the campaign manager protested.

"Nobody's going to believe a thing like that."

Johnson responded, "But let's make the sonofabitch deny it!"

Every time Paul Davis said "I am not Stephen Harper" during the election campaign, all I could hear was the pig-fucker story.

• • •

Some of the staffers around Davis looked like they had given up. I heard a lot of people saying things like, "We're doing our best; on election day, whatever happens, happens."

The days on the Tory campaign tour were slower than on the Liberal bus, with fewer events. Both parties went through the same motions, but whereas Dwight Ball looked hungry, like he was hunting something, Paul Davis looked like he was just doing what he'd been told he was supposed to do.

At other times, Tory staffers seemed like they were out of touch with reality. On one campaign flight, I overheard Davis's director of communications talking with another reporter, claiming that the PC Party internal numbers had the local candidate close to winning in Humber-Gros Morne — where he was up against Ball.

"We have a shot," she said. "Our polling is kind of not bad in his district. It's on our radar."

On election day, Ball won his seat with 76 per cent of the vote.

• • •

The bubble briefly seemed to burst on November 19th, two weeks after the election formally began.

Davis was in Corner Brook at the university campus, where he'd be speaking as part of the ACAP Forum. The western Newfoundland environmental advocacy group had invited each party to send a representative to give a speech about environmental issues, and then take questions. Both the Liberals and the NDP sent local candidates when it was their turn. The Tories sent Davis.

Before the speech, Davis held a media availability where he re-announced some of the forestry and science policy proposals the Progressive Conservatives had put forward, flanked by a gaggle of local candidates. Then it was media questions, and nobody bothered to ask even a single perfunctory question about forestry and science policy.

Right off the bat, Davis was asked about the awkward fact that his party was still six candidates short of a full slate with only about 24 hours until the Elections NL cutoff for nominations.

"Yeah, I was quite confident that we were going to have a full slate. I can tell you, I'm not as confident today," Davis said bluntly.

This was suddenly a big deal; not since 1972 had an incumbent governing party failed to run candidates to contest every seat in the legislature. If the Progressive Conservative party couldn't pull together 40 half-sensible people to put their names on a ballot, it would suggest an astounding level of disorganization and incompetence within the party.

One of Davis's core campaign motifs was "Leadership." What does it say about your leadership if you can't convince 39 other candidates to follow you?

"You know, it's a hard go for us," Davis said. "When I put my hand up last year, we're facing some very significant challenges. We're struck with the falling oil prices, significant drop in revenues, that impacts how we can operate as a government and how we can develop and offer new programs and services. That was a challenge for us from the start."

As the journalists kept pushing, for the first time in the campaign it looked to me like Davis knew he was losing. He was defiant and righteous, but he also seemed to know that this wasn't simply an uphill battle — it was a slaughter.

"I talked to a ship's captain a few months ago, and he said to me, he said, 'Paul, you know, when you're a mariner, until you've weathered a storm, you're not considered to be captain of a ship.' And we are weathering a storm," Davis said. "We had a storm hit us a couple years back; we had a tough couple of years. I put my hand up and I said, 'I'm going to turn this ship around.' And while everything that Mother Nature has is being thrown at us — we have really good days, and then we get the left curveballs coming at us. They've thrown everything they can at us, and we're not giving up. And I'm not giving up. I'm not done. I believe I'm the best choice to lead this province."

After the scrum wound up, Davis headed into a small lecture hall, where he was giving his ACAP Forum speech. I counted fewer than 20 people in the room, including staffers, local Tory candidates and media.

A little while later I got a message from Western Star reporter Cory Hurley, who was in the audience to cover the speech. He said if you subtracted ACAP people and university senior staff, Tory candidates and Davis's own political staff, there were only two or three "real people" in the audience.

The rest of the day, Davis didn't do much. He sat in the back of his campaign bus and spent a lot of time on the phone. He was stone-faced, like he was receiving bad news.

The bus drove around aimlessly along the north side of the Bay of Islands. He was supposed to visit another seniors' home, but Elections NL was doing special balloting in the afternoon, and Davis couldn't be campaigning in there while voting was happening.

In the evening, the bus ended up in Deer Lake where Graydon Pelley was holding a campaign rally. A hundred people, or thereabouts, attended. It was the biggest Tory crowd I'd seen since the campaign launch, and the politicians drew energy from it. Pelley gave a lengthy introduction, and then Davis gave an even longer speech. Together, the two men spent more than 45 minutes talking, but the audience was into it. There were cheers and spontaneous shouts of encouragement.

I think Davis kept talking just because it felt good. After weeks of getting torn to pieces, here, finally, there was a pocket of people who wanted him.

And just like that, he was back in the bubble.

I left the Tories not long after that, and moved over to covering the Liberals. But by the end, there wasn't much of a Tory campaign left to cover. For the final week of the election, amid awful poll numbers, Davis campaigned almost exclusively in his home district of Topsail-Paradise. He'd pop up briefly to berate the Liberals, but for the most part, he had given up on winning the provincial election. He was just fighting to save his job as an MHA.

• • •

On election night the Tories lost, of course, but not as badly as expected.

The Liberals secured a commanding majority with 31 seats, but the Tories held onto seven, and the two NDP incumbents managed to prevail.

By all accounts, the mood among Tories on election night was upbeat, gathered at that same Paradise community centre where Davis had launched his campaign, and his leadership bid before that.

Davis won his own seat, and Deputy Premier Steve Kent managed to hang on, along with a good mix of Tories. It wasn't a win, but it wasn't an absolute disaster either. Tory candidate Barry Petten even managed to steal a seat away from the Liberals in Conception Bay South, after being narrowly defeated a year earlier in a byelection there.

In his concession speech, Davis was already looking ahead to the next election.

"I commit to you tonight that the Progressive Conservative Party of Newfoundland and Labrador will be ready in 2019," he said, before he was drowned out by a huge cheer from the audience.

"We will be ready to fight another day. We'll be ready to fight another election, and we'll fight to ensure that Newfoundlanders and Labradorians in the next election have a choice to make."

He thanked his family, the candidates who stepped forward and the volunteers.

I wasn't there to watch it, but based on the tape, the concession speech might have been Davis's best speech of the entire election campaign.

"Our party has some great traditions. We have a great past, and we have a great history. We can hold our heads high tonight. We can be proud of the efforts and the work that we've done. We can be proud of the province that we've created," he told the Tories.

"This is what we do, and this is who we are, and we will do it again another day."

It's worth noting that even as voters were handing Davis a decisive defeat, I never really got a sense there was widespread animosity for him, personally. People wanted the Tory crowd gone, but as the guy at the helm, Davis never really engendered the sort of vitriol that Stephen Harper, or even somebody like Kathy Dunderdale, did.

He was seen as a nice guy doing his best in an untenable situation. Even in the dying days of the campaign, when the Tories' defeat was imminent, polling from Abacus Data showed that 39 per cent of voters said they had a positive impression of Davis, compared to just 20 per cent who had a negative impression. Even as voters were saying they wanted a change of government, 53 per cent said that Newfoundland and Labrador was headed in the right direction; only 20 per cent of people thought that the province was on the wrong track.

Privately he could sometimes be nasty[1] and entitled, but for people who didn't know him personally, the consensus was that he was a good guy, a cop, a decent politician maybe in a little bit over

---

[1] There was one media availability at a campaign event in Placentia when I was pursuing an aggressive line of questioning. Afterwards, Paul Davis found me alone, sat down beside me, and spent the better part of 10 minutes berating me for a lack of professionalism, and accusing me of being biased in favour of the Liberals. This was not an isolated incident.

his head, but doing his best. And if it got negative and desperate and weird at the end, well, that's just the sort of thing that happens when you're put into that kind of position.

Inasmuch as history remembers him at all, I think he'll land in the same club as Tom Rideout and Roger Grimes — the bookends. Davis wasn't the one who steered into the iceberg; he was just the captain who went down with the ship.

CHAPTER 21
GONE TO THE DOGS
NOVEMBER 18, 2015

In mid-September, coming away from a New Democrat pre-election event with Earle McCurdy, I wrote a piece for the paper headlined "The NDP could win. No. Seriously."

What an idiot I was.

At the time, it looked like McCurdy had the most energy and the most political smarts compared to Dwight Ball and Paul Davis. Moreover, this was in the midst of the federal election campaign, when an NDP win still looked like a very plausible outcome. And at the time, McCurdy was rolling out a series of impressive candidates like lawyers Bob Buckingham and Mark Gruchy, along with economist Alison Coffin and actor Sean Panting.

But then Justin Trudeau swept to victory in the federal election by encouraging the country's progressives to flock to his banner.

The New Democrat campaign provincially was focused almost entirely on St. John's and the surrounding area. Fellow journalists told me that the few trips McCurdy took to other parts of the province were furtive and highly disorganized.

And though McCurdy can be extremely quick-witted, he didn't always come across well during the campaign. Even if he did land a witty retort once in a while, mostly he seemed to get lost in tangents and bogged down in details during the debates.

Despite his decades of work with the fisheries union, he made no significant inroads in rural parts of the province.

"Just a few years ago, there were fish plants here. Now there are none," one Liberal MHA told me. "I heard from someone today that got contacted by the NDP in my district to run for them. And they said, 'Oh, thank you for calling, but I don't think I'll get along with your leader.'"

McCurdy actually got less and less popular, the more people saw of him. By the end of the election, he was the only leader in the Abacus Data polling where more people said they had a negative impression of him than positive.

On election day, only incumbent NDP candidates Gerry Rogers and Lorraine Michael would win their seats back.

By the time I caught up with him for a day, about halfway through the election, McCurdy was already focusing heavily on just campaigning in his own district of St. John's West. And despite whatever foolishness he might've read in *The Telegram*, he'd given up any pretence that the NDP could win.

Mostly, as he knocked on doors, he told voters, "I think it's important to get some opposition."

It was a grey November day, with flurries getting whipped around in the wind. McCurdy wore a floppy black tuque that said "FAIRNESS WORKS" on the front. It was the middle of the afternoon, and over the hour or so that I followed him, there was nobody home at most of the houses.

In one house, after knocking, a medium-sized dog greeted him at the front window, barking his lungs out. The dog was so close to the glass that he'd fog up the window a little bit every time he barked.

McCurdy looked down to consider the animal for a moment, before turning to leave.

As he walked away from the house, he said to me, "You know, dogs are keen political observers and commentators."

CHAPTER 22
EMPTY CALORIES
NOVEMBER 30, 2015

I had an interesting conversation with longtime Liberal MP Gerry Byrne in the ballroom of the Greenwood Hotel in Corner Brook on election night, as the early results were coming in.

All night I'd been hearing Liberals say the same word, as though it was an answer to my questions: "Change."

This was a change election, I was told. Voters wanted change. And when change happens, hoo boy, watch out buddy. Change is a Liberal avalanche, and you don't stop an avalanche. The best the Tories could do was brace for impact and try to avoid being completely buried by all that tumbling change.

But on its own, is there anything more vacuous than change? Most Liberals couldn't even really tell me what exactly change would look like with Dwight Ball as premier.

Byrne looked at it differently, though. He said change is an avalanche made up of snowflakes and boulders. The little things and the big things — Kathy Dunderdale's dismissive tone, Bill 29, Gerry Rogers getting kicked out of the legislature for being a member of a Facebook group, the Tories laying off 1,000 civil servants in 2013, Kevin O'Brien blocking New Democrats from attending a pancake breakfast, and Judy Manning getting appointed to cabinet. It all piles up, until the individual complaints are indistinguishable and cannot be articulated. It all becomes part of an avalanche of frustration, and a bone-deep desire to hurl the bastards out of office, and when voters are asked, they just say they want "change."

So the Liberals were "change" and it didn't matter what form that change took; they weren't the Tories, and that was good enough to win the 2015 provincial election.

In fact, in a change election, it actually helps if you're not too specific about yourself. It's better to be just a blank canvas and let the voters project onto you whatever they want you to be.

Dwight Ball did that.

Throughout the campaign, I kept coming back to the same metaphor for Ball's political style: empty calories.

His standard campaign speech was full of rhetorical empty phrases that sounded good and filled you up, but didn't really mean anything.

"The province is at a critical juncture," Ball said at his campaign launch. "At no other time has it been more important for us to get our province back on track, because a stronger tomorrow starts with making the right decisions today. Paul Davis and his Conservatives will talk about tough decisions. But I think we all agree, we've had enough of their tough decisions; it's time to start making the right decisions."

It didn't really matter what he said. Ball won anyway.

This book was never about the stunning rise of Premier Dwight Ball, and neither was the election campaign.

Sure, the Liberals were well-organized, and they ran a respectable slate of candidates. There were no major hiccups in the lead-up to the campaign, and obvious liabilities were minimized and addressed. There was a little controversy when Ball declined to participate in the VOCM radio debate, but the Liberals stuck to their message and rode it out. There were some raised eyebrows when Liberal gadfly Danny Dumaresque won the party's nomination in Conception Bay East-Bell Island. But somehow, the party managed to put a muzzle on him, and Ball pointedly failed to show up in that district at any point during the campaign.

Apart from those little bumps in the road, the Liberals appeared to have a clear roadmap for the campaign, and they stuck to their plan without difficulty.

If Paul Davis had managed to somehow knock the Liberals out of their groove and forced Ball to react quickly, perhaps things would have gone differently. But the fact is, the Tories' campaign started placidly, ramped up, and ended as an unhinged, paranoid, deluded mess. During the final days of the election, Ryan Cleary posted a video online which showed him yelling at a poster of Dwight Ball in a darkened bus stop. This was supposed to be one of the Tories' star candidates; did he imagine that lo-fi theatre of the absurd would somehow blow the election wide open?

Around the same time, you had Paul Davis holding a news conference in front of a NL Hydro terminal station claiming that the Liberals would privatize the government-owned utility if elected —

despite the fact that Ball had specifically said he wouldn't privatize Hydro earlier in the week. And then the following day, Davis acknowledged that he had entertained a proposal to sell off NL Hydro.

The same thing happened when the Tories complained that the Liberals weren't putting forward much substantial policy. Really? You're not putting forward anything substantive either. Oh, so you're running on your record? Bill 29? The 2013 public sector layoffs? Oh, not that record? Then what are we really talking about? (Hey look! We're no longer talking about the Liberals.)

The bottom line is that the 2015 election was a referendum on the Tories, and that referendum was decided months — maybe even years — before anybody cast a ballot.

Ball won by being organized, and by being inoffensive.

And by offering empty calories instead of anything substantive that might get him into trouble.

• • •

As the campaign bore down on election day, Ball's obvious victory started to feel like failure.

According to multiple public opinion polls, he was liked by more people than either of his opponents, and people believed his party was better positioned to deliver the sorts of things that they cared about.

The Liberal party also had a solid slate of candidates, recognizable local leaders drawn from communities across the province.[1]

The Liberals were much better organized than their opponents. Whereas the Tories and the NDP went door to door with clipboards and sheafs of paper, the Liberals in St. John's West had iPads.[2]

---

[1] This was more than either the Tories or the NDP can say; both the other two parties had to run staffers because they were unable to drum up 40 respectable local candidates to run in seats across the island. In the northern Labrador district of Torngat Mountains, there was effectively no campaign, because both the PC and the NDP ran staffers from St. John's on the ballot, and they never actually stepped foot in the district during the election. The logic goes that it's better to have someone — anyone! — representing the party on the ballot rather than suffer the embarrassment of failing to run a full slate. I'm not so sure.

[2] Going door to door isn't actually about convincing people to vote for you; it's about identifying your vote, so you can hector them and ensure they make it out to the polls on election day. If you're hooked into a web-based database for your voter identification system, you're a generation ahead of the folks going around with clipboards and pencils.

In short, in every measurable way, the Liberals were the better bunch. And that's why they were winning.

But better isn't the same as good, and the fact of the matter is, the Liberals were winning mostly because the NDP and the Tories were losing — spectacularly.

Like I say, all of this felt like failure. Democracy is an adversarial system, and it depends on political opponents challenging each other. There should be healthy, fierce debate about policy and vision, and from the crucible of that adversarial system, we should receive the best government possible.

Instead, for at least the third election in a row, Newfoundland and Labrador had a non-election. In 2007, Danny Williams was utterly dominant. In 2011, the only party that could credibly win power was the Progressive Conservatives led by Kathy Dunderdale. At the time, the Liberal Party leadership was in shambles, and the pro forma campaign they ran never had a serious chance of forming government.

In 2015, the tables turned. The incumbent Tories were a mess and the Liberals were coasting to a huge victory only because they were the only party really actively contesting the election.

I have deep misgivings about what Premier Dwight Ball holds for Newfoundland and Labrador. I've seen him play fast and loose with the line between partisan politics and government.

During the campaign, the one of the Liberals responsible for organizing media logistics emailed me flight itineraries from her provincial government @gov.nl.ca address. I've also seen hints that under Ball, the Liberals were willing to use taxpayer-funded Official Opposition resources for party organizing and electioneering. It's a fine line between the partisan legislative work of the Official Opposition and the partisan work of election campaigning, but there should be a line of separation. These may seem like minor infractions, but if this is the sort of line Ball is willing to muddy in opposition, I worry what he'll let slide once he's in government, with a multi-billion-dollar budget at his disposal.

It doesn't help that the cast of Liberal candidates includes a few people with the whiff of political entitlement and cronyism. The Liberal Party has a historical reputation for being a home to that sort of cosy corruption, and I see hints of it in the current makeup of the Liberal Party. They're only little shoots now, and maybe Ball will be big enough to nip them in the bud, but I worry they'll be allowed to flourish and grow in the coming years.

Even setting aside those misgivings, a look at the Liberal party platform fills me with dread. At a time when the province is grappling with an enormous structural budget deficit, Dwight Ball was running on promises of tax cuts and massive new government spending. His commitment to balance the budget in four years relied on a very murky promise to shrink the size of the public service, and find hundreds of millions of dollars-worth of spending reductions. He said there would be new revenue realized from the sale of government assets, and a suspiciously vague $359 million line item called "improved revenue from economic diversification."

Even a cursory read of the Liberals' financial plan left you scratching your head. They promised, in the first year of their mandate, to spend around $8.1 million in economic development, and then by the second year, the party was counting on almost $79 million worth of improved tax revenue from economic diversification. This is pure fantasy.

By cutting the province's sales tax by two percentage points (well, actually, reversing a two point increase the Tories enacted) they were effectively promising to rob the government of $180 million in revenue in the first year of their mandate, and slightly more money every subsequent year. They were promising to replace the Waterford Hospital as the centrepiece of a new focus on mental health issues, which was laudable. But I'm guessing that project will cost somewhere in the neighbourhood of half a billion dollars, and guessing is all I have to go on, because the Liberals didn't budget any money to pay for that signature infrastructure promise. The party was promising to strike an all-party committee to do a review of the province's electoral system, at a cost of $100,000 over two years. If it's done right, it will cost much more than that. The Liberals planned on drumming up $50 million per year by selling off Crown land and unused government buildings; that's one of those things that doesn't sound as bad in the abstract, but when it comes to selling off specific bits of real estate, it'll churn up a lot more controversy.

In large ways or small, the Liberal numbers were creative, dubious, opaque and they didn't add up. But they were numbers on a page, and taken together, they were a reasonable facsimile of a four-year fiscal plan, and that put them head and shoulders above either the NDP or the Progressive Conservatives.

When the PC Party released their platform, the back pages just contained a point-form listing of policy promises, and the vast majority were simply marked "EBE" — short for "existing budget envelope" — meaning that to fund the new thing, they'd have to cut some other thing somewhere else.

And the fact of the matter is, only the Liberals were really talking about anything interesting or new or substantial. The Tories promised a bunch of money for a mental health strategy, which might have been interesting, but the components of the "strategy" were vague statements like "expand access to addictions treatment services" and "develop mental health services for residents of foster homes."

In fact, when Davis was asked about his platform commitments, mostly he just pivoted to attack the Liberals. When I started asking him about specific policies the Tories were putting forward, he said, "I didn't realize we were going to go through this line by line."

In the year leading up to the election, as the Liberals led in the polls, they were relentlessly hammered for flip-flopping and simply criticizing the government without putting forward any substantive ideas of their own.

Many months before the formal campaign started, I found myself chatting with a senior Liberal strategist about it.

He shrugged the whole thing off.

"The thing about the light-on-policy thing is," he said casually, "if that's all they've got, when you release your full platform with a lot of policy during the election campaign, then they've got nothing."

And then in November, that's exactly what happened.

While Paul Davis was trying to smear Dwight Ball for being opaque and shifty, Ball was marching out his "Five Point Plan" with each successive plank containing more detail, and more interesting ideas than anything the Tories were putting forward.

While Ball was talking about concrete steps to improve government accountability or diversifying the economy, Davis was mostly talking about ... well ... Davis was mostly talking about Dwight Ball.

•••

Now seems like the point when I should draw some conclusions and observations about what people should expect from Premier Dwight Ball and his Liberal government.

Sorry to disappoint you, but I've got nothing.

For years, I've tried to understand Dwight Ball. For a little while, I thought he was a political genius. For a much longer while, I thought he was a bumbling, risk-averse pharmacist who wandered into politics and got lucky. Now he's premier of Newfoundland and Labrador, and frankly, I just don't know.

I don't think he's in politics for personal enrichment; if that was his game, there are easier, less stressful, more productive ways to go about it. He might be in it for ego, but I haven't seen much braggadocio from him. If he's an ideologue, he's hidden it very, very well over the four years since he became leader of the Official Opposition.

I've given up trying to find out what he stands for by asking him questions.

A couple of months before the election, I sat down for an interview with Ball for this book, and I asked him what he stands for.

What is the Liberal party of Dwight Ball? What does it mean to be a Newfoundland and Labrador Liberal in 2015?

Ball said for him, one of the core things he believes in is transparency and accountability in government.

"I think there's a time for us, as elected officials, to actually kind of raise the bar a bit again," he said. "The only way we can do that is by clearly being open and transparent about the decisions that we make. Like, I want to make some fundamental changes in politics. I really believe the House of Assembly can work better; I really believe we can put a committee structure in place where we can work together better."

Despite his own dubious record when it comes to disclosing political contributions, again and again over the years, Ball goes back to talking about transparency.

And yet, on the day after he was elected premier, CBC reporter David Cochrane reported that updated budget projections from the Department of Finance pegged the provincial deficit at $1.8 billion — a huge increase from the already-sickening $1.1-billion deficit the Tories tabled in their budget seven months earlier.[3]

This news was leaked out literally the day after people cast their ballots.

Well, "leaked" isn't quite the right word. The exact number was a bit of a shock, but it shouldn't have been a surprise to anybody that the deficit was huge. The price of a barrel of oil is not a state secret. It's common knowledge, too, that the Newfoundland and Labrador government relies on oil royalties for a big chunk of overall operating revenues.

For months leading up to the election, crude had been trading far below the forecast prices in the 2015 budget, so of course the deficit was going to be bigger.

But pretending that the deficit was still $1.1 billion or thereabouts was a convenient fiction for all three parties to maintain. The New Democrats were promising big new spending on government programs, so they didn't want to talk about how broke we were. The Tories didn't want to talk about how they'd shagged things up so badly.

To be fair, Ball made halfhearted attempts to talk about the government's finances. He said he sent a letter to Premier Paul Davis a couple of months before the election, asking for a fiscal update. Davis didn't bother to reply. During the campaign, Ball used that to sort of shrug and say he'd tried his best, and shift the blame.

Ball could've done more. He could've come out and said something like, "We know the situation is much worse than the government says. We don't know how much worse it will be, because they

[3] In fact, when Premier Dwight Ball held a news conference a few weeks later, the official number was even bigger. The deficit was forecast at a hair's breadth below $2 billion.

won't tell us. But if the numbers are as bad as oil prices seem to indicate, here's my plan for dealing with the most serious crisis facing Newfoundland and Labrador today …"

That would have been … I don't know … Transparent? Accountable? Leadership? Instead we got a convenient fiction and partisan sniping until somebody leaked out the real number one day after voters were allowed to have their say.

If this is Dwight Ball transparency, I don't know what to expect from Dwight Ball governance.

But I've given up on finding out what he stands for by asking him questions.

Let me give you another example.

In late October, just before the formal campaign started, Ball gave a speech to the biennial convention of NAPE, the province's largest public sector union. In his speech, he promised hope and transparency and doing things differently, but he also sought to reassure the union leaders.

"While other parties talk about job cuts and job losses, I'll tell you one thing: that is not my idea of doing things differently," Ball declared.

During the campaign, the Liberals repeated that message again and again: no job losses, no job cuts.

But then their platform was released, and the entire fiscal framework was built off the Tory budget, which included a five-year attrition plan that would shrink the civil service by 1,420 people to save around $300 million. If Ball wasn't going to cut any civil service jobs, then there was a $300-million hole in his fiscal plan. If he was sticking with the attrition plan, there would clearly be job losses.

When I sat down to confront him with this contradiction, Ball said he would be jettisoning the Tories' attrition plan, insofar as he thought that the broad principle of only hiring eight people for every 10 retirements was reckless. However, he was counting on that $300 million in savings from shrinking the public sector workforce. In some areas, the job reductions could be deeper, and in other areas, the government simply needed to replace every worker who retired, because they were all necessary.

He said really, he was only promising that there would be no layoffs. In his mind, reducing the number of civil servants through attrition did not count as job cuts.

But, I asked, if there are fewer people doing the work in government, clearly that's a job loss, no?

"You can call it what you want. I don't see it. What I see there is the person is retired, the position will just not be filled," he said. "So that person does not lose their job. So it's not a job loss for the individual."

I reported all of this: that the Liberals would cut the civil service through attrition, that Ball wouldn't say how deep the cuts will be, that he was firmly committed to no layoffs, etc. The headline was, "Ball says he would cut public-service jobs through attrition."

The next morning, after the story was in print, the Liberals bombarded social media with an image of the sun rising over the sea, along with text that said, "Cutting jobs is not part of our plan. Under a new Liberal government, public service jobs are safe."

Later in the day, Ball again confirmed that he would cut public sector jobs through attrition.

And behind the scenes, the Liberals were getting in touch with my boss to complain that I was putting words in Dwight Ball's mouth, and that I had gone into the interview with a foregone conclusion.

That's half-true. I went into the interview with two contradictory sets of words, both coming from Dwight Ball's mouth. Apparently giving clear, consistent answers isn't part of the Liberals' version of transparency and accountability.

So I've given up on finding out what Dwight Ball stands for by asking him questions.

Watching him in action is the only way to tell what he is.

And for now, mostly he's just … bland.

The most notable thing about Ball's victory speech on election night was that he had to spend about five minutes standing awkwardly in the hallway outside the election night party because former Liberal leader Yvonne Jones gave an interminable introduction.[4]

[4] Ball had enough time to take a photo with Ivan Winsor, the Liberal campaign bus driver, and then he just sort of stood around awkwardly, peering into the room waiting for his cue to enter.

When he finally made his way to the stage, aside from a brief mention of family, and a few words about encouraging more women to get involved in politics, Ball's victory speech was an amalgam of the same empty calories he'd been delivering all campaign.

"Success just does not happen by itself. You need a strong team. And that's the dedication, that's the commitment, and that's the strength of our Liberal team," he declared, not really saying anything.

Until he does something more substantive, the fact that a bland guy was able to win election to become premier of Newfoundland and Labrador might be the most significantly interesting thing about him. That's arguably never happened before in NL history. The province's premiers have tended to be big men who push their way to the top with big talk. Ball is an enigma by comparison.

During the election campaign, Earle McCurdy was fond of quoting a biblical verse: "By their deeds, ye shall know them."

Now, the empty calories and flip-flops no longer matter. Over the next four years, we will find out what Dwight Ball is.

It has been said, "Never let a good crisis go to waste." Ball is now facing a fiscal crisis, and he will have the opportunity to dramatically reshape the Newfoundland and Labrador government. He could drastically reduce public services, and then we'll know he's an ideological conservative. He could use the brutal budget shortfall as political cover to jack up taxes, and then we'll know he favours a more expansive sort of government. Or maybe he'll just fiddle around the edges and do nothing. And then we'll know he really is nothing more than a bland guy with a big chin and nice hair and an expensive suit.

Acknowledgements

This book would not be possible without a lot of people who taught and encouraged me to become a better journalist. I owe a lot to the great instructors at Ryerson University, and the informal lessons learned at The Eyeopener. In particular, I owe a debt to Anne McNeilly who sent me to St. John's eight years ago for what was supposed to be a six-week internship.

Telegram editors like Craig Jackson, Kerry Hann, Steve Bartlett and Pam Frampton took a clueless mainlander and taught me what the difference between a townie and a bayman is, and where to find the trees in Newfoundland (between the twos and the fours.)

Pam also edited this book, so it's doubly her fault.

I should thank Donna Francis, too, who encouraged me to write this book.

Most of what is in these pages was drawn from events that I covered directly, but there were times when I just couldn't be there, or I couldn't be in more than one place at once. I owe a debt of gratitude to the other reporters and photographers at the Telegram, along with friendly compatriots at NTV, CBC and VOCM, who all filled me in on political details when I couldn't be there personally.

Without friends offering encouragement and criticism, this whole thing would've turned out very differently. Over the past couple years, many people have offered helpful suggestions large and small. I can't name everyone, but in particular, Karen Lawlor, Gerry Porter, Nicki Doyle, Adam Walsh and Laura Howells all made this book better by pointing out what I did wrong.

This book would not have been written without Rocket Bakery, Coffee Matters, the Watershed in Petty Harbour, Jumping Bean and Fixed Coffee and Baking, because my apartment is too full of distractions to get any meaningful writing done there.

I should also probably thank the politicians of Newfoundland and Labrador, who delivered an embarrassment of riches to a political journalist writing a book. For the most part, they meant well.

Born and raised in Toronto, Ont., James McLeod came to St. John's, NL for a six week unpaid internship in the spring of 2008. Eight years later he still hasn't found his way home. He covers politics full-time for the Telegram newspaper, an occupation which appears to be leading to significant hair loss.